Sex Role Identity
and Ego Development

Jeanne H. Block

Foreword by Jack Block

Sex Role Identity
and Ego Development

Jossey-Bass Publishers
San Francisco • Washington • London • 1984

SEX ROLE IDENTITY AND EGO DEVELOPMENT
by Jeanne H. Block

Copyright © 1984 by: Jossey-Bass Inc., Publishers
433 California Street
San Francisco, California 94104
&
Jossey-Bass Limited
28 Banner Street
London EC1Y 8QE

Library of Congress Cataloging in Publication Data

Block, Jeanne H. (Jeanne Humphrey), 1923–1981.
    Sex role identity and ego development.

    Bibliography: p. 283
    Includes index.
        1. Sex role—Addresses, essays, lectures.
2. Sex differences (Psychology)—Addresses, essays,
lectures. 3. Ego (Psychology)—Addresses, essays,
lectures. 4. Women—Psychology—Addresses, essays,
lectures. I. Title.
HQ1075.B56   1984   305.3   84-7918
ISBN 0-87589-607-3 (alk. paper)

Manufactured in the United States of America

The paper in this book meets the guidelines for
permanence and durability of the Committee on
Production Guidelines for Book Longevity of the
Council on Library Resources.

JACKET DESIGN BY WILLI BAUM

FIRST EDITION

Code 8421

The Jossey-Bass
Social and Behavioral Science Series

Foreword

Jeanne H. Block is recognized as one of the foremost contributors to the understanding of sex role development. In the series of papers bound together here, she brought forward a seminal perspective that continues to influence thinking and research on the psychology of males and females. Beginning with a conceptual reformulation of sex roles, Jeanne went on to rigorously analyze and reshape the way we understand the implications of data on sex differences. On her own, she produced solid and novel research on the antecedents and consequences of the psychological differences between the sexes. And, throughout, her sensibility allowed her to recognize new developmental possibilities and to elaborate their meaning for the self-realization of individuals and for society.

The works selected for inclusion in this book are Jeanne's principal contributions to understanding sex role differences. The original versions of most of these chapters have appeared in scattered publications; one was the text of a speech and one has never been published before. This volume shows the reader the coherent sequential development of a human psychology that takes into account biosocial influences on sexual development and individual self-realization.

Psychologists, educators, counselors, and sociologists will value this book for the light it sheds on social and familial forces that shape ego and gender differences and that account for value conflicts that are at the roots of many contemporary social disputes. Jeanne's work went a long way toward exposing those roots; it also shaped and elucidated the terms in which we debate such complex, passionate issues as men's and women's roles in the home and in the workplace and people's rightful expectations regarding education, employment, and personal and economic power.

Chapter One presents Jeanne's initial, far-reaching conceptualization of sex role development. It places sex role development in the larger context of ego development, takes an evolutionary and cross-cultural perspective, and adduces many kinds of evidence in support of her important recognition that for females but not for males the development of the culturally prescribed sex role orientation often fundamentally constrains the individual's development of self. This chapter, in its original form, was the basis of Jeanne's Bernard Moses Memorial Lecture and was awarded the Hofheimer Prize of the American Psychiatric Association.

Chapter Two is a closely reasoned, rigorous evaluation of the evidence for psychological differences between the sexes. It was written in response to the formidable, widely accepted work *The Psychology of Sex Differences* (Maccoby and Jacklin, 1974), which reviewed the extant literature and concluded that there were few important sex differences. Jeanne's analysis, a model of its kind, probed both evidence and conclusions to reshape the way data about sex differences are interpreted. Her sophisticated and careful scrutiny of the literature revealed important and implicative relationships not earlier discerned. I believe it is fair to say that this chapter, upon its original publication, effected fundamental changes in the ways sex differences are looked for and understood.

The next chapter extends the topic of psychological differences between the sexes but focuses pointedly on differential parental and societal socialization. The Maccoby and Jacklin review of this literature had concluded that socialization differences were slight. Jeanne's evaluation of the literature, by considering childrearing behaviors often neglected, by evaluating the role of the father in childrearing, and by observing the changes in parental attitudes as children become older, revealed socialization differences that were frequent, pervasive, and consequential.

Chapter Four goes on to trace the psychological development of female children and adolescents and to understand the personality and cognitive implications of gender differences in socialization. In particular, this chapter points out the personal costs to girls of "oversocialization": the inculcation of prudence and proprieties with the sacrifice of independence and self-confidence. To prevent or reverse these constraints on self-realization, Jeanne emphasizes the possibilities afforded by learning contexts that are less circumscribed, less closely supervised, less fully predictable while still remaining supportive.

A novel study of different sex role and socialization patterns manifested by men and women and their implications for personality structure is reported in Chapter Five. After categorizing women and men according to the conventionality of their sex role orientations and, separately, their level of acceptance of societal standards, Jeanne studied the many personality implications of these fundamental classification dimensions. The availability of longitudinal data permitted further inquiry into the environmental antecedents of these different sex role and socialization patterns. The regularities she discerned in parenting environments led to a formulation of the various ways identification and identity are sought and perhaps achieved by women and men.

Chapter Six formulates, in conceptual terms, some differences between expectations males and females develop about the world. This topic became a central area of concern for Jeanne as she came to recognize that early divergence in the kinds of situations experienced by boys and girls had deep implications for the assumptions and strategies upon which each sex tended to predicate behavior. Abundant evidence had accrued testifying to the different ways boys and girls, men and women, acted on and reacted to their environmental contexts, but these findings were not readily encompassable. In this essay, Jeanne provides a first theoretical statement regarding gender differences in the nature of the perceptual, affective, and action premises children develop about the world.

Chapter Seven, previously unpublished although known in educational circles, draws on Jeanne's general conceptual formulation and her knowledge of empirical findings about sex roles to state some implications for educational policy. Given continuing differences in socialization that shape boys' and girls' expectations and ways of learning, Jeanne believed that for many young women seeking to redefine and extend their sense of self, a single-sex college would provide an encouraging, constraint-escaping, transitional learning environment of great value.

Chapter Eight is both a summation and extension of Jeanne's views. This final, integrative essay is based on her master lecture before the American Psychological Association. It was completed in the final months of her life and brings together her last, incisive conclusions from the contemporary literature on sex differences and her final effort to provide a conceptual basis for understanding the psychology of sex roles. Her abiding values shine strongly throughout and, if the reader is restricted to the reading of but one chapter, it should be this last one.

The achievements in thinking and writing reflected in this work Jeanne accomplished over a period spanning less than a decade—while her scientific and professional life was extremely active, while she was the prime mover of a monumental longitudinal study of personality and cognitive development, while she was engaged with large family responsibilities and pleasures, and while she was buffeted by a chronic illness early understood to be ominous. My partner in life and in science for thirty-two years, Jeanne died of cancer after a long and gallant struggle. If hers was a life fatefully, unfairly, cut short, it was also a life extraordinarily full, lived with zest and wisdom. She was a woman of valor, grace, intelligence, verve, warmth, and love. I miss and our children miss her heartening presence. But for us and for all who knew her, the meaning and usefulness of her life extend beyond us through her work to a better understanding of how our society shapes its children into the women and men they become.

June 1984   Jack Block
                                              Professor of Psychology
                                   University of California, Berkeley

ACKNOWLEDGMENTS

Organizing the separate works that make up the chapters of this book into their present sequence was greatly facilitated by Harriet Reynaud's perceptive editing. The large chore of preparing a publication-ready manuscript on a word processor was lovingly accomplished by Carol Anne Block.

Contents

Jeanne H. Block
(1923-1981)

Jeanne Humphrey Block, who died on December 4, 1981, is probably known to the widest number of psychologists for her contributions to the field of sex role socialization from 1973 to 1980, when gender issues were receiving much attention. She is also known for her longitudinal research on ego development, for work on student activists, and for studies of asthmatic children and their parents. Most of this work was published after she was 45 years old. She was a valued participant on many advisory panels and professional committees, but not until her mid-50s. In this and other ways her career reflects the life story of the wife-mother-careerist of her era.

Jeanne Humphrey was born on July 17, 1923, in Tulsa, Oklahoma, but the family soon moved to Oregon. Her mother was a bright, energetic woman who was active in civic reform and who was once asked to run for the U.S. Senate against Wayne Morse. Her father was a general contractor, a man of strong convictions and high principles. There was one son, nine years younger than Jeanne.

Reprinted from *American Psychologist*, 1983, *38* (3), 338-339. Copyright 1983 by the American Psychological Association. Reprinted by permission of the publisher and author.

Jeanne began college at Oregon State as a home economics major. But these were World War II years. She dropped out to join the Coast Guard, becoming an ensign and then a recruiting officer. It was an enjoyable time except for a traumatic accident in which she suffered massive third-degree burns. For several days she was near death. The malfunctioning of her autoimmune system, later to cause much difficulty, may have begun with this injury.

After leaving the Coast Guard in 1946, she finished her undergraduate education at Reed College and went to Stanford in 1947. There she found that she had many interests in common with a young man named Jack Block. They did the research for their dissertations jointly and married in 1950.

It was an exciting idea at that time to devise empirical methods for studying constructs previously regarded as hopelessly mentalistic. Both Jack and Jeanne's doctoral theses were experimental studies of the ego, conceptualized in relation to constructs from psychoanalytic and topological theory. This subject was one in which they had a lasting interest and again studied in collaboration 20 years later in their longitudinal research. Jeanne's dissertation committee consisted of Maud Merrill James (chair), Frances Orr, and Quinn McNemar.

Between 1952 and 1959 the Blocks had four children: Susan, Judith, David, and Carol. Jeanne was a conscientious, knowledgeable, and committed homemaker. Through the years of parenting young children, she worked in a series of part-time research positions. In 1963–1964, when Jeanne was 40, the Block family spent a year in Oslo, and at this time she gathered data about cross-cultural socialization practices later to be used as a basis for her first Career Development Award. In 1967 she became associated with the Institute of Human Development at the University of California at Berkeley, where she retained an affiliation for the rest of her life. She studied student activists, published her first single-authored paper in 1968 (on asthmatic children and their parents), received a Career Development Award for 1968–1973, and was promoted to research psychologist in 1970.

The work on asthma shows a characteristic Block pattern.

Some people thought asthma was constitutionally determined, others thought it was psychosomatic. Block and her collaborators developed an index of constitutional predisposition to allergy. Children scoring above and below the mean on this index were compared on various psychological measures, and so were their parents. The findings showed that children with low constitutional predisposition scores had more psychopathology. There were different "paths to asthma."

This pattern of identifying loci of truth in areas of controversy by insightful analysis and thorough measurement may be seen again in her study of generational continuity and discontinuity among student activists. Block showed that both ideological and socialization factors contributed to rejection of social institutions by youth. Here again, she studied both the students and their parents.

In late 1971 Block developed a condition finally diagnosed as a disease of the auto-immune system. She was hospitalized four times over the next eight years. However, her professional life continued to expand. She became an APA Fellow in 1972. Her best-known paper, "Conceptions of Sex Role: Some Cross-Cultural and Longitudinal Perspectives," was published in the *American Psychologist* in 1973, when she was 50. Her Career Development Award was renewed, and in 1974 she received the Hofheimer Prize for Research from the American Psychiatric Association. She and Jack had launched a longitudinal study of ego development in children that was rich in possibilities but very time-consuming. Still she managed to contribute importantly to many conferences and to take on increasing responsibilities in professional organizations. She was in much demand as a consultant. In 1976 she published two influential critiques of *The Psychology of Sex Differences* (by Maccoby and Jacklin) that showed a new level of methodological sureness and confidence. Although not a faculty member, she was much sought out for dissertation committees, where she was invariably a strong resource. In 1979 she was made an adjunct professor in the Department of Psychology at Berkeley. That was the year she gave a Master Lecture at APA on the differential socialization of males and females. In 1980 she was president-elect of the Division of Developmental Psychology, on the advisory board of the Women's College Consortium, chair of the NIMHCD Research Review Committee, and had other commitments as well.

One of psychology's most prominent couples, the Blocks shared high standards that may sometimes have been a strain on them as well as a contribution to the field. But the partnership was a source of many strengths, because their respective talents both complemented and supplemented each other. Family, social, and professional life were merged. The Blocks entertained colleagues frequently and made a recreation of it. Jeanne was an excellent cook, and the children helped as they grew older. Their home was lovely to look at, and the atmosphere was warm and stimulating.

Block lived her values of fair-mindedness, hard work, and responsibility. Like most women of her time, she had to regain intellectual confidence after years devoted largely to motherhood, and there was the additional problem of having to develop for a while in the shadow of her husband. But she was a very capable woman, and she grew with the honors that came to her and the opportunities that the Blocks worked jointly to create. She was courageous and persevering through years of physical tribulation.

After a severe bout with the auto-immune condition in 1980, Block was eager to get on with many projects and to pursue many ideas. The longitudinal study she had seeded with so much of her intelligence, perceptivity, and energy, and for which she had so many anticipations, was reaching a time of fruition and harvest. But she developed the fatal illness that had caused the death of her father. Her spirit in the hardest times and during a few months of miraculous remission in the fall of 1981 stirred friends with awe and left us with a heightened sense of having known an exceptional human being.

March 1983   Ravenna Helson
                             Adjunct Professor of Psychology and
                                        Research Psychologist
                             University of California, Berkeley

Sex Role Identity
and Ego Development

Chapter One

Conceptions of Sex Role

In this chapter, I am concerned with some socializing influences as they impinge on the development of sexual identity. A framework is presented for examining the concept of sex role identity, a framework that attempts to integrate changes in sex role definition with the larger developmental tasks faced by individuals, the tasks of ego and cognitive development. The model I shall be describing deviates from traditional approaches to the study of sex-typed behavior in that I am assuming, with a growing number of others, that the ultimate goal in development of sexual identity is not the achievement of masculinity or femininity as popularly conceived. Rather, sexual identity means, or will mean, the earning of a sense of self that includes a recognition of gender secure enough to permit the individual to manifest human qualities that our society, until now, has labeled unmanly or unwomanly. According to this formulation, hypotheses can be derived and tested empirically that would seek to examine the relation between personal ego maturity and less traditional definitions of sex

Originally published in *American Psychologist*, 1973, *28*, 512–526, with the title "Conceptions of Sex Role: Some Cross-Cultural and Longitudinal Perspectives." Copyright 1973 by the American Psychological Association. Reprinted and adapted by permission of the publisher. This research was supported by two awards from the National Institute of Mental Health: a Research Scientist Development Award and a Special Research Fellowship.

1

role. As I move through argument and empiricism to describe the model, substantiate its utility, and examine its implications, I shall be drawing on two bodies of research: cross-national studies of self-definition and socialization values I conducted for several years in collaboration with European colleagues and data derived from the studies conducted at the Institute of Human Development over more than forty years, in which the paths of lives through time have been studied using the longitudinal method.

Having outlined my aspirations, I can begin tracing the development of sex role definition, embedding it in the larger context of ego and cognitive development, and relating it to the forces for socialization that derive from parents and culture.

Before proceeding to discuss the model, it is necessary to delineate the behavioral terrain with which I am concerned here and to make explicit several underlying assumptions.

I shall be discussing conceptions or definitions of sex role, the generality of definition of sex role across particular cultures, and the relation of sex role definition to personal maturity. By *sex role* I mean the constellation of qualities an individual understands to characterize males or females in the culture. By direct implication, an individual's conception of sex roles will influence in important ways both his or her behavior and self-evaluation. I am not concerned here with sex differences *per se,* nor shall I be considering the larger question of psychosexual development.

The development of sex role identity is influenced by both biological and historical/cultural factors complexly interacting, with changing degrees of ascendancy at different critical periods. I reject Freud's absolutist dictum that "anatomy is destiny" and am in accord with Erikson (1968) that anatomy, history, and personality combine to form one's destiny.

I regard as a fundamental task of the developing individual the mediation between internal biological impulses and external cultural forces as they coexist in a person's life space and life span. The process of mediation is a complex derivative of contemporaneous ego and cognitive development. Sex role definition, then, represents a synthesis of biological and cultural forces as they are mediated by cognitive and ego functions.

The Developmental Model

The theoretical framework underlying the conceptualization of sex role development presented here derives from the work of Loevinger (Loevinger, 1966; Loevinger, Wessler, and Redmore, 1970), whose explication of ego development is summarized in the first four columns of Table 1.1.* Loevinger's system postulates a hierarchical model of development wherein there is an invariable order of the developmental stages, each more complex than the stage earlier in the sequence, each transition from one stage to another being mediated by a dialectical process.

Let me quickly sketch these stages, then extend each to the fifth column I have added, which represents my attempt to integrate sex role development with ego development as viewed by Loevinger. It is perhaps already apparent to the reader that the ideas explicitly stated in the last column are implicit in the two columns headed "Interpersonal Style" and "Conscious Concerns."

In the earliest period, the developmental task of the infant is to distinguish self from nonself. Gender is too sophisticated a concept to be relevant at this period. Following this stage, at the impulse-ridden level, the infant begins to develop primitive notions of gender identity that are essentially denotative: "I am a girl" is understood in the same way as "It is a dog." Gender identity at this level is essentially sexless, although the characteristic behaviors of the child during this period include those that have been defined traditionally as masculine—concern with self-assertion, self-expression, and self-interest. The young child is oriented toward an un-self-conscious, and still unsocialized, expression of sexual and aggressive impulses: "I do it." The next stage, the self-protective stage, represents a dialectic between the imposition of rules by socializing agents and the child's determination to maximize his or her own advantage. The young child is still concerned primarily with the extension and enhancement of self; the other person is seen as someone to be controlled, bested, deceived, and exploited for

*Tables appear at the end of the chapter.

one's own gain: "I want it." The conflict of wills between child and other at this period encourages the invocation of parental authority and the implacable pressures of socialization.

At the next level, conformity becomes the mode, with respect to both rules and roles. It is at this period of development that a critical bifurcation in the sex role development of boys and girls occurs. Socialization patterns impinge differently on the two sexes: Boys are encouraged to control affect, while girls are encouraged to control aggression. Because this is a critical period in the acquisition of sex role definition, I will return to it later, after the description of the remaining ego levels.

At the conscientious level, introspection and self-consciousness permit self-criticism—the examination and evaluation of self with respect to certain abstract values and ideals. Notions about the "kind of person I would like to be" are developed, and behaviors are moderated in accordance with internalized values. With respect to sex role definition, it is a period of moderated masculinity/femininity; sex roles are moderated by notions of responsibility and duty.

At the next, the autonomous, level, differentiation of self, feelings, values, and roles requires the individual to engage in a series of attempts at conflict resolution. With the articulation of notions about the self, an awareness develops of values, predispositions, and behaviors that depart from traditional sex role definitions, and these more complex, sometimes conflicting aspects of self must be integrated.

At the integrated, or highest, level of ego functioning, according to Loevinger's analysis, the individual has evolved for himself/herself an identity consonant with history and aspiration. With respect to sex role identity, the definition given by the individual represents an integration of traits and values, both masculine and feminine. Such sex role definitions, integrating both aspects conventionally considered feminine and those traditionally defined as masculine, I refer to here as "androgynous" to emphasize their nonparochial nature.

With respect to her developmental model, Loevinger cautioned against the equation of personal adjustment with stages higher in the sequence, suggesting that it is more realistic to view successive ego stages as reflecting the individual's attempts to cope with increasingly deeper problems—those of self-ideal, morality, meaning, and existence—rather than the attainment of a formula for successful solutions.

Having thus delineated the terrain, it is necessary now to describe the topography and to introduce some central concepts that shape the subsequent discussion. So far I have described the tasks in sex role definition at each developmental level and have used the terms *masculine* and *feminine* to describe prototypical sex role behaviors and attitudes. However, conceptualizations of sex role according to more general and less specifically sex-linked behavioral and attitudinal orientations provide greater opportunity for the integration of sex role definitions with personality theory. Gough (1968a) has defined a bipolar dimension, "initiation/conservation," which, though integral to traditional concepts of masculinity/femininity, is not their equivalent, although it does permit both stable and differentiated assessments of individuals with respect to sex-typed behavior. Gutmann (1965) maintains that men and women do not experience the same primary coordinates of reality and describes the masculine milieu as impersonal, unpredictable, inconsistent, and allocentric and the female milieu as familiar, personal, constant, and autocentric. This formulation of sex differences in the psychosocial ecology of the male and female parallels Erikson's observation that girls are more concerned with inner space, while boys are more oriented to the external world. But it is a conception developed by Bakan (1966) that I wish to draw on most heavily here.*

In his book *The Duality of Human Existence*, Bakan (1966) conceptualized two "fundamental modalities" characteristic, he argued, of all living forms—*agency* and *communion*. Agency is concerned with the organism as an individual and manifests itself in self-protection, self-assertion, and self-expansion. Communion, according to Bakan, is descriptive of the individual organism as it exists in some larger organism of which

---

*I am grateful to Rae Carlson (1971a) for bringing Bakan's theorizing to my attention.

it is a part and manifests itself in the sense of being at one with other organisms. Bakan went beyond this descriptive model, however, and conceived a developmental approach in which the fundamental task of the organism is "to try to mitigate agency with communion" (p. 14). "Unmitigated agency," whether in metastasis, exploitation, or unrestrained technological expansion, represents evil, whereas viability—both for the individual and for society—depends on the successful integration of agency and communion.

Although Bakan's dichotomy overlaps with the initiation/conservation and impersonal/interpersonal polarities, its contribution to our thinking about sex role definitions lies in its emphasis on balance and integration, mitigated agency and communion, the tempering of masculinity and femininity via development. If we now reconsider the developmental stages in sex role definitions shown in Table 1.1, superimposing the conceptualizations of Bakan, some additional insights are gained.

It is apparent that the impulse-ridden and self-protective levels, when the child of either sex is concerned with self-assertion, self-expression, and self-extension, represent the condition that Bakan has described as "unmitigated agency." At the conformity level, children, by virtue of a complex of determinants, including their cognitive conceptualization of gender identity, identification with the same-sex parent, and the differential socialization pressures to which they have been subjected during the earlier stages, now develop a set of sex role stereotypes conforming to the cultural definitions of appropriate boy or girl roles. It is at this point in development that a critical branching occurs whereby the interests, activities, and attitudes of boys and girls diverge dramatically. Little boys are taught to control the expression of feelings and affects, while assertion and extension of self are abetted. Little girls are taught to control aggression, including assertion and extension, while being encouraged to regard the inner, familial world as the proper sphere of their interest. Communion is emphasized in the development of girls but is explicitly discouraged in boys.

For those advancing to the conscientious level, there now begins a self-conscious process of evaluating personal, internalized values and the prevailing expectations of the culture. Awareness of the deviance of one's own values from societal values appears, and both are examined critically. This, I propose, is the beginning of the process of balancing of agency and communion that will preoccupy the individual in the autonomous level during attempts to cope with the competing demands and costs of agency and communion. This process will, for some few individuals, ultimately eventuate in the integration of the two modalities in the highest developmental stage.

For men, the integration of agency and communion requires that self-assertion, self-interest, and self-extension be tempered by considerations of mutuality, interdependence, and joint welfare. For women, integration of communion with agency requires that the concern for harmonious functioning of the group, the submersion of self, and the importance of consensus characteristic of communion be amended to include aspects of agentic self-assertion and self-expression—aspects that are essential for personal integration and self-actualization.

With the model described, let us examine some empirical evidence for certain derivations.

Sex-Linked Socialization Emphases

I have asserted that sex-related socialization practices during the impulse-ridden and self-protective stages tend to emphasize agency in males and communion in females. Let us look at some of the evidence. Miller and Swanson (1958) observed that a majority of mothers interviewed in the Detroit, Michigan, area channeled the behavior of their children in ways consistent with the traditional division of labor between the sexes. In a sample of Norwegian mothers, Brun-Gulbrandsen (1958) found support for the Miller and Swanson findings and noted also that mothers exerted more pressure on girls to conform to social (or communal) norms. Hartley (1959a, 1959b) has suggested that parents impose earlier and more rigorous demands on boys for conformity to societal notions of "what is manly"—and what is "manly" is agentic.

Some of my own investigations of childrearing orientations provide further data that spell out the differences in the way boys and girls are reared. In four separate studies, mothers and fathers of boys and girls representing different ages—early childhood, middle childhood, adolescence, and youth—were asked to describe their childrearing attitudes and behaviors vis-à-vis a specific child in the family, using the Child-Rearing Practices Report (Block, 1965). This instrument contains ninety-one items in the socialization domain that were arrayed by each parent independently on a continuum of importance, or salience, with respect to parental goals, methods, and reactions to the particular child. It seems fair to expect that parents of boys are not intrinsically different from parents of girls, and so differences in the way parents socialize boys and girls can be understood to reflect the sex typing that parents are, for whatever reason, impressing on their children.

In Table 1.2, which compares the mothers and fathers of boys with the mothers and fathers of girls across the several studies, we find significant differences in socialization emphases that are consistent with other findings in the literature. The leitmotiv of socialization practices for boys across the several age levels studied reflects a stress on achievement and competition, an insistence on control of feelings and expressions of affect, and a concern for conformity to rules. There is a differential emphasis on enforcing the "thou shalt nots" of childrearing; authority and control seem to pose the vital issues between parents, particularly fathers, and their sons at this age.

For girls, in contrast, emphasis is placed, particularly by their fathers, on developing and maintaining close interpersonal relationships; they are encouraged to talk about their troubles and to reflect on life, are shown affection physically, and are given comfort and reassurance. Whereas the issues between parent and son appear to be those of authority and control, the parent/daughter theme at the several age periods reflects an emphasis on relatedness, protection, and support.

Apart from the substantive socialization issues, the data from these studies suggest that, to a greater degree than has been supposed, the father appears to be a more crucial agent in directing and channeling the sex typing of the child, both male and female. In each of the four studies, fathers more than moth-

ers were consistently found to treat sons and daughters differently. A discussion of the several implications of these findings
is beyond the scope of this chapter other than to recognize the
critical role of the father in encouraging sex typing and enforcing sex differences. Although maternal childrearing orientations
do differ depending on the sex of the child, paternal attitudes
appear to be even more strongly determined by the child's sex.
Clearly, additional studies focusing on paternal influences and
attitudes are required.

The longitudinal study being conducted with my husband, still underway, further supports the findings of a differential emphasis on achievement for boys and for girls, even at the
preschool age. Fifty mothers and thirty-seven fathers of nursery
school children were observed interacting with their children as
each parent individually taught the child a variety of cognitive
tasks. One task, singled out for the present analysis because of
its emphasis on divergent thinking, required the parent to encourage the child to construct squares (or posts) to the same dimensions as a specified standard, using a variety of geometric
shapes that were available and could be combined in many different ways. The task permitted a variety of different solutions
as well as a number of redundant solutions. Parental behavior in
this teaching situation was rated by two independent observers
on a number of task-related dimensions, including three dimensions relevant to the achievement expectations of parents: (1)
the extent to which the parent rejected inadequate solutions
produced by the child, (2) the extent to which the parent pro-
hibited non-task-oriented play, and (3) the extent to which the
parent set high standards of achievement for the child. When
scores on the three achievement-related dimensions were composited, significant parental differences as a function of the sex
of the child were found ($p < .05$, one-tailed t test), indicating
that parents of boys were more concerned with task-oriented
achievements than were parents of girls.

These analyses suggest that boys, even at the preschool
level, are more pressed for achievement by their parents than
are girls, from whom less is expected and from whom less is
acceptable.

The differential socialization emphases that have been described appear consistent with Bakan's (1966) formulation in that agency in boys is encouraged, though mitigated somewhat by behavioral proscriptions. For girls, the interpersonal, communal aspects of being are fostered, and agentic concerns with achievement and extension are not encouraged.

The effects of unmitigated agency or communion on intellectual achievement are reflected in Maccoby's (1966b) comprehensive analyses of sex differences in cognitive functioning. She concluded that optimal cognitive functioning depends on a balance between the feminine/passive and masculine/active orientations. Children manifesting extreme sex role typing are handicapped intellectually because hyperpassivity (the supposedly feminine mode) interferes with concept formation and manipulation, while hyperactivity (the supposedly masculine mode) militates against sustained and concentrated analysis. Maccoby's conclusions have clear implications for the way the socialization of young children might be changed, suggesting that the tempering of sex role typing may benefit cognitive functions in important ways.

In a survey of ethnographic material describing mostly nonliterate cultures, Barry, Bacon, and Child (1957) found a widespread pattern of greater socialization pressure toward nurturance, obedience, and responsibility for girls and toward self-reliance and achievement strivings for boys. These differential socialization emphases seem to derive, in these primitive societies, from the different biological and socioeconomic functions the sexes must assume in their adult roles. Thus, when hunting or conquest is required for societal survival, the task naturally and functionally falls on the male because of his intrinsically superior physical strength. Consequently, boys, more than girls, receive training in self-reliance, achievement, and the agentic corollaries. Childbearing is biologically assigned to women, and because, in marginally surviving societies, men must be out foraging for food, childrearing, with its requirement of continuous responsibility, is assigned to women. Thus, girls, more than boys, are socialized toward nurturance, responsibility, and other qualities of communion.

The heritage and functional requirements of sex typing in

early or marginal cultures seem clear. The question for our times, however, is to what extent past socialization requirements must or should control current socialization emphases in our complex, technological, affluent society, where, for example, physical strength is no longer especially important and procreation can be under some control. Under present conditions, and for the future, we might ask What is necessary? What is "natural" in regard to sex typing? Some perspective on these questions is gained when we evaluate American sex stereotypes and those of some other Western and highly advanced societies.

Sex Role Stereotypes Across Cultures

In six countries—Norway, Sweden, Denmark, Finland, England, and the United States—I sought to study sexual stereotypes and their generality as they are projected in the values underlying an individual's conceptualizations of the "idealized self"—the description of the "kind of person I would most like to be." In defining one's ideal self, one necessarily sets forth one's values; in establishing the culturally modal definition of the ideal male and ideal female, we have a projection of the values of that culture. When the ideal self-descriptions of samples of male and female university students of six countries are compared across the sexes and across countries, we find impressive cross-cultural stability in masculine and feminine ideals as well as empirical verification of differential emphases on agency and communion between the two sexes. The findings are presented in Tables 1.3 and 1.4.

To gain some understanding of these results, the adjectives used for the descriptions of the ideal self were independently categorized by four psychologists instructed to identify those adjectives clearly expressing agency, those clearly expressing communion, and those neutral or irrelevant with respect to these concepts. Definitions of the concepts, taken from Bakan (1966), were given to each judge to guide decision making. Agreement among the judges was high. The results of this classification are indicated in the first column of Tables 1.3 and 1.4; the unclassified adjectives are blank. A few adjectives judged agentic or communal are not included because they were nondifferentiating.

The adjectives characteristic of the masculine ideal include ten agentic adjectives and none that were identified as communal. Six of the adjectives discriminating masculine ideals did not meet the specified criteria for either agency or communion. With respect to the feminine ideal as it is reflected in the adjectival ideal self-descriptions, we find seven adjectives judged to represent communion, one agentic adjective (vital, lively), and nine adjectives that were unclassified. Clearly, concepts of the masculine and feminine ideals are distinguished by their differential emphasis on agency and communion. This study replicates the findings of Carlson (1971a), who found that the self-images of males and females, scored according to Gutmann's (1965) impersonal/interpersonal dimension, differed as predicted. The self-images of men were represented in impersonal, individualistic terms, while the self-images of women were represented in interpersonal terms.

The stereotypes surrounding masculine and feminine ideals among these six Western, technological societies appear to be general and to manifest the agency/communion distinction. But there are some additional implications to be drawn from these data. Bakan (1966) has commented on the inevitable relationship of agency to capitalism, which requires the exaggeration of the agentic orientation. It is interesting that both fewer sex differences and less emphasis on agency appear to characterize the two countries, Sweden and Denmark, with long- and well-established commitments to social welfare. Explicit cross-cultural comparisons among the countries reveal that American males are distinguished, at or beyond the .05 level of significance, from the males of other countries in that, in their conceptualizations of the masculine ideal, they place greater emphasis on the following adjectives: *adventurous, self-confident, assertive, restless, ambitious, self-centered, shrewd,* and *competitive*—adjectives reflecting greater agency. Interestingly, American women also described their ideal in more agentic terms than did women in the other countries studied. The descriptions of the American feminine ideal incorporated to a significantly greater extreme the following adjectives: *practical, adventurous, assertive, ambitious, self-centered, shrewd,* and *self-confident.* The greater endorsement of agentic adjectives by American students, both males and females, is in accord with Bakan's suggestion of a relationship between capitalism and agency.

These cross-cultural differences in conceptions of masculinity and femininity are reflected in a corollary analysis of students' perceptions of parental childrearing orientations in these same countries. Via factor analysis, three primary dimensions were found to distinguish American childrearing values from those of the other five societies. Significantly greater emphasis was placed on early and clear sex typing in the United States; significantly more emphasis was placed on competitive achievement; and significantly less importance was attached to the control of aggression in American males. From this cross-cultural perspective, then, current American childrearing values appear both to foster agency through emphasis on competition and aggression and to magnify the culturally determined differences between the sexes.

These conclusions must be tempered to some extent by the recognition that since our samples were not fully representative of the national populations, the data cannot be considered normative. However, because the data were obtained from intellectually elite and culture-shaping groups in each of the several countries, the data seem to me to assume an importance transcending, to some extent, the restricted nature of the samples.

What does all this imply? For me, the important implication of the differences between American sexual stereotypes and childrearing orientations and those characterizing the European nations studied is that there *can* be differences, differences that begin to abandon narrow definitions of sex roles held over from harsher and less civilized times.

Developmental Implications

The last and theoretically most important test of the hypotheses deriving from Bakan's formulation is concerned with the developmental implications of his remarks. In this model,

personal maturity is associated with greater integration of agency
and communion within the personality. If this is true, it would
then be expected that the self-descriptions of individuals at
higher levels of maturity would reflect both agency and communion—that is, would be more androgynous.

Fortunately, data from two studies were available, permitting a test of this hypothesis. In the first study (Haan,
Smith, and Block, 1968), students who had participated several
years ago in a study of student activism were evaluated with respect to their level of maturity of moral reasoning, according to
criteria developed by Kohlberg (1964). The subjects also completed adjective Q-sort self-descriptions, and these were compared across the several levels of moral reasoning. The results
are shown in Table 1.5.

Kohlberg's conceptualization of moral reasoning, like
Loevinger's, employs a hierarchical model in which the characteristics of moral reasoning at different stages are specified and
objectified. His several levels of moral reasoning may be seen in
Table 1.5, where the adjectives are shown that significantly differentiated persons at different levels of moral reasoning. The
items significantly distinguishing students at the premoral level,
where moral decisions are guided by opportunism and hedon-
ism, are, for *both* men and women, essentially agentic adjectives: *individualistic, rebellious, not orderly,* and *unresponsive,*
for males; *stubborn, rebellious, aloof,* and *nonaltruistic,* for
females. At the conventional level, where moral decision making
is governed by the desire for personal concordance (Stage 3)
or acceptance of existing rules and laws (Stage 4), we find an
emphasis on adjectives denoting conformity and conventionality: *ambitious, foresightful, conventional, practical, orderly,
nonrebellious.* At the highest level of moral reasoning, the post-
conventional Stage 6, in which moral decisions are guided by
universal principles of justice and concern for human worth, we
find greater heterogeneity in the self-descriptions. Males at this
level do not endorse fewer agentic adjectives, but they do diverge
in their greater acceptance of communal adjectives: *sympathetic,
responsive,* and *idealistic.* The women at the highest, principled
level do not differ from their peers at other stages of moral

reasoning by being less communal but, rather, differ in that they see themselves as more *restless* and *impulsive,* suggesting a tendency toward agency. These data, then, lend some support, stronger in the case of males than females, to the hypothesis that greater maturity—in this instance as indexed by Kohlberg's Moral Judgment Test—is accompanied by more androgynous, less sex-typed definitions of self.

The second study, based on a sample of high school students reliably classified by Loevinger, Wessler, and Redmore's (1970) Sentence Completion method to index maturity of ego functioning, yielded essentially similar results when the self-descriptions of students scoring at the more mature ego levels and those scoring at lower levels of ego development were compared (Table 1.6). (Students scoring at the impulse-ridden and self-protective levels were combined for purposes of this analysis.) Both males and females scoring at the least mature levels of ego functioning embraced adjectives that strongly bespeak agency and appeared to reject aspects of interpersonal functioning that indicate relatedness and communion. Among the differentiating adjectives descriptive of males are *adventurous, ambitious, competitive, aloof,* and *effective;* and those descriptive of females include *assertive, courageous, stubborn,* and *proud.* The items differentiating students at the conformity level appear to be traditionally conventional adjectives: *optimistic, tolerant,* and *rational* for males; and *proud, tolerant, responsible,* and *responsive* for females. At the highest level measurable in the sample of high school students—the conscientious level—we find the males diverging from their peers at the lower ego levels in their endorsement of adjectives valuing interpersonal relationship and expressing communion: *idealistic, sensitive,* and *sympathetic.* The adjectives that differentiated high school girls at the highest ego levels clearly combine agency (*self-centered, effective, restless*) with communion (*sensitive, altruistic*).

The results of these two independent studies, though not definitive, are nevertheless consistent and support the hypothesis that the achievement of higher levels of ego functioning is associated with the development of self-concepts reflecting an integration of the agentic concerns (self-enhancement and self-extension) with the satisfactions deriving from communion and mutuality. The implications of these findings for the sex role socialization of the child are several and important. The present cultural emphasis in the United States on masculine machismo and feminine docility appears to impede the development of mature ego functioning. Because children are socialized early into culturally defined sex-appropriate roles, introspection and self-evaluation, which appear to be essential catalysts for psychological growth, are discouraged. Further, there appear to be significant personal costs paid by both sexes when the socialization of sex-appropriate behaviors, defined in such narrow terms, is "successful."

Longitudinal Findings

In the last section of this chapter, I wish to examine the costs of rigid sex typing by reference to the Institute of Human Development's longitudinal archives, which provide abundant data about the influences and adaptations in the lives of people followed over a thirty- to forty-year period. My remarks are the product of analyses completed in collaboration with two colleagues: Jack Block of the Department of Psychology, Berkeley, and Anni von der Lippe, now at the University of Oslo (Block, von der Lippe, and Block, 1973). For present purposes, only the conclusions of these analyses are included here; I do not attempt to present fully the empirical evidence on which these assertions are based. I shall, however, describe briefly some methodological features that are important in providing a context for understanding the implications of the study. (For a fuller account of the methodology, sample, and substantive findings, see Block, 1971.)

The subjects were drawn from two of the ongoing longitudinal studies being conducted at the Institute. The one study was initiated by Harold and Mary Jones and has been known as the Oakland Growth Study; the second study was begun by Jean Macfarlane and has been known as the Berkeley Guidance Study. All the subjects in these two samples, between thirty and forty years of age, who had responded to the California Psychological Inventory (CPI), a 480-item test scored on eighteen personality-relevant dimensions, were included in the analyses to be summarized here. Sixty-five men and sixty-eight women are represented.

Within the male sample and separately within the female sample, four subgroups of subjects were formed on the basis of two of the CPI scales, the Femininity scale and the Socialization scale. The Femininity scale, according to Gough (1968a), defines a personological continuum that is conceptualized as conservation-oriented at one pole and initiation-oriented at the other pole. The Socialization scale reflects the degree to which an individual has internalized societal standards—that is, the extent to which he is "able to govern internally his thought and behavior in accordance with the imperatives of his culture" (Gough, 1960, p. 24). Independent evidence indicates that individuals at the high end of the socialization continuum are conforming and "rule-respecting," while those at the low end are nonconforming and asocial.

Subjects scoring above and below the mean on the two scales were identified, providing the quadrants in Table 1.7. The upper left quadrant is composed of individuals expressing both socialized and sex appropriate attitudes (above the mean on the Femininity scale for women and below the mean on the Femininity scale for men), who are designated as the high-sex-appropriate, high-socialized group to reflect the patterning of their scores. Individuals in the upper right quadrant are designated the low-sex-appropriate, high-socialized group. The lower left quadrant is composed of individuals scoring high on sex appropriateness and low on the Socialization scale, designated the high-sex-appropriate, low-socialized group. Finally, those subjects scoring low on both the Socialization and Femininity scales (reflected for males) are designed as the low-sex-appropriate, low-socialized group.

The comparisons of character structures and the antecedent experiences of the individuals representing different sex role and socialization patternings yielded impressive differences among the groups. The personality qualities of the subjects were objectified by composited, independent ratings completed by clinically trained judges. The antecedent factors associated with the sex role socialization pattern at adulthood were identified by referring to the voluminous archives that describe the physical, psychological, and social development of the subjects from childhood on. Because the findings are so numerous, I only distill and summarize the essence of the results, relating them to Bakan's concepts and to his theorizing about personal maturity and the qualities of sex role definition.

First, many parallels were found to characterize the familial antecedents of individuals, both males and females, in equivalent quadrants. The high-sex-appropriate, high-socialized individuals in the upper left quadrant, both males and females, seem to derive from family contexts where there was clear and conventional role differentiation between the parents, where both parents appeared to be psychologically healthy, where both parents were available physically and psychologically to the child through adolescence, and where the like-sex parent appeared to be the more salient figure for identification. From this family milieu came men who were found to be relaxed, competent, and comfortable with self and sex role—men whose masculinity had been tempered by their acceptance of a rule-respecting, other-respecting value system. Women emerging from this context typify the traditional concept of femininity. They were judged dependable, feminine, conservative, and self-controlled and were not rebellious, aggressive, or unconventional. The psychological "costs" associated with stereotypic femininity are reflected, perhaps, in additional descriptive items that revealed these women to be somewhat dissatisfied, indecisive, vulnerable, and lacking in spontaneity. Both men and women in this quadrant appeared to have internalized parental values, with respect to both sex role and cultural proscriptions, through the process of identification with the same-sex parent in a context of familial harmony and traditional parental role definition.

The low-sex-appropriate, high-socialized individuals in the upper right quadrant had their origins in families where the parents offered more complex, less traditional sex role differentiations as models for their children. Parents of this group ap-

peared to offer a wider range of behavioral and attitudinal possibilities to their children as a function of their less stereotyped
definitions of masculinity and femininity. Both mothers and
fathers appeared to be psychologically healthy and had established emotionally satisfying and value-inculcating homes for
their children. Eventuating from this context were men described as conscientious, productive, ethically consistent, giving, self-controlled, and concerned about philosophical problems—a personality configuration that bespeaks mature ego
functioning and represents an amalgamation of agentic and
communal concerns. In adulthood, the women in this group
were described as poised, calm, nonintrospective, nonrebellious,
contented, gregarious, and conventional. Despite their relatively
low scores on the Femininity scale, the psychological characteristics of these women suggest that their sex role definition embodied an essentially outgoing and relaxed femininity, lacking,
however, the feelings of disquietude and tendency to passivity
characteristic of their peers in the high-sex-appropriate, high-
socialized group. The sex role definitions of both men and
women in the low-sex-appropriate high-socialized group are less
stereotyped and developed from a different pattern of identification—a pattern we have chosen to call "androgynous" to describe a parental pair in which neither mother nor father exemplifies the typical cultural sex role stereotypes, but rather where
both parents are salient and provide for their children models of
competence, tolerance, consideration of others, and a sharing of
familial responsibilities.

The high-sex-appropriate, low-socialized individuals in the
lower left quadrant derive from families in which the like-sex
parent was neurotic and rejecting and provided a poor model
for identification. The cross-sex parent was characterized, for
both males and females, as somewhat seductive. The homes
these parents established were transient, and the parents assumed little responsibility for the socialization of the child.
Young people growing up in this familial context appeared, in
adulthood, to exemplify exaggerated definitions of sex role.
The constellation of items descriptive of the males—hypermas-
culine, impulsive, aggressive, exploitative, self-centered, and

irresponsible—appears to represent the condition of "unmitigated agency" described by Bakan and suggests a less mature mode of ego functioning. Women in this quadrant were described as narcissistic and sexually preoccupied, eschewing both conventional and achievement-oriented values. Their sex role definitions include none of the nurturing, communal qualities, and their orientations to others are largely egocentric. Individuals in the group appear to have achieved their sex role definitions, not through identification, but by a process we term *reactivity*. According to this formulation, sex-appropriate behaviors are shaped by the reactions and behaviors of the child's cross-sex parent. Self-definitions and sex role definitions are molded by the responses of external agents, particularly those of the opposite sex.

Individuals in the last quadrant, the low-sex-appropriate, low-socialized group, emerge from families characterized by conflict and psychopathology. The like-sex parent of both males and females was emotionally uninvolved, in relation both to the child and to the spouse, while the cross-sex parent was salient and conflict-inducing. The behavioral characterizations of individuals in this group show important divergencies for the two sexes. The men were depicted as vulnerable, self-doubting, insecure, reassurance-seeking, hypersensitive, and feeling victimized. The descriptive data suggest a caricature of the less attractive characteristics often attributed to the "weaker" sex. Women in this group, in contrast, were described as assertive, critical, rebellious, expressive, and staunchly demanding of autonomy and independence—characteristics consistent with a strong agentic orientation. The personalities of the men and women in this group were found to be similar to the personalities of the cross-sex parent. Mothers of the males in this quadrant were seen as lethargic, lacking in confidence, depressed, neurotic, and brittle. Fathers of the females in this group were described as active, energetic, assertive, and both power- and status-oriented. In the absence of adequate same-sex models, and buffeted by family conflicts and recriminations, each sex appears to have rejected the traditional sex-appropriate values and to have emulated the proclivities of the cross-sex parent. This group is characterized,

for both men and women, by its extreme deviation from traditional definitions of appropriate sex role. The consequences of
this deviation appear more pernicious for the male sample, in
which psychological functioning seemed more impaired.

The foregoing analysis commands our attention because
it discloses the differential effects of socialization for males and
females. In the male sample, both masculine and less masculine
men in the highly socialized groups seem to have incorporated
positive aspects of both the masculine and feminine sex roles,
both agency and communion. They were productive, effective,
dependable, and conscientious. In contrast, both masculine and
less masculine men who scored lower on the Socialization scale
showed a differential internalization of the negative aspects of
the corresponding sex role: The less socialized, masculine men
manifested egocentrism, impulsivity, self-indulgence, aggressivity, and machismo—unmitigated agency. The less socialized and
less masculine men evidenced the full scale of vulnerabilities
that adversely colors the hyperfeminine role—dependence, anxiety, hypersensitivity, and gullibility.

For men, sex role socialization, when tempered by parental inculcation of ethical values, appears to expand the personal options available: The traditional masculine emphasis on
competence and instrumentality conjoins with the traditionally
feminine emphasis on the interdependence of individuals. Men
high on the socialization dimension appear to have achieved
some integration, or balance, of agency and communion, an integration essential for mature ego functioning.

The effects of socialization of women, however, are less
salubrious. Characteristics that are essential for individuation
and self-expression have been defined by the culture as "masculine," and so, progressively, these must be relinquished in female socialization. Socialization for women, therefore, regardless of level of femininity as indexed by the CPI, becomes
associated with control of impulse expression and the renunciation of achievement and autonomy. The occupational histories
of women in the four groups reveal a significant negative association between occupational commitment and socialization,
indicating that fewer women in the highly socialized groups

sought employment in their adult years. However, when the employment histories of those women who had been rather consistently employed over the years were examined, we found a different pattern of relationships. An *inverse* relationship between upward occupational mobility and femininity was found. Of those employed, 75 percent of the women in each of the two low-sex-appropriate groups were found to show a pattern of upward occupational mobility, while the comparable figures for the two high-feminine groups were 28 percent and 33 percent for the left-hand and right-hand quadrants, respectively. Socialization tends to militate against career interests in women, and for those women who do elect to enter the occupational arena, advancement in status is more likely to be achieved by those who diverge from the traditional feminine sex role stereotype. However, this advancement is achieved at some personal cost, since communal, interdependent connectedness with others is suppressed and agency is exaggerated. These findings cohere with the observations of Keniston (1971), who noted that successful professional women appeared more comfortable with their competence than with their interrelatedness.

To summarize, the socialization process—the internalization of values—appears to have differential effects on the personality development of males and females. For males, socialization tends to enhance experiential options and to encourage more androgynous sex role definitions, since some traditionally feminine concerns (conscientiousness, conservation, interdependency) are emphasized along with the press to renounce negative aspects of the masculine role: opportunism, restlessness, and self-centeredness. For women, the socialization process tends to reinforce the nurturant, docile, submissive, and conservative aspects of the traditionally defined female role and discourages personal qualities conventionally defined as masculine: self-assertiveness, achievement orientation, and independence. The sex role definitions and behavioral options for women, then, are narrowed by the socialization process, whereas for men the sex role definitions and behavioral options are broadened by socialization. The achievement of higher levels of ego functioning for women is more difficult because individuation involves conflict with our prevailing cultural norms. It is for this reason, perhaps, that few women of the generation studied here manifested androgynous sex role definitions: It was simply too difficult and too lonely to oppose the cultural tide.

Given these recognitions, it has seemed to me that the contemporary scrutiny of conventional definitions of masculinity and femininity is encouraging our society to reflect on the personal costs—to men and women alike—of adherence to the prevailing norms. Extant socialization patterns appear to attenuate the human possibilities residing in the individual, whether male or female, and both a redefinition of conventional sex role and a revamping of socialization practices are required if our societal goal is to encourage individuation and personal maturity for our young. If our social aim can become, both collectively and individually, the integration of agency and communion, the behavioral and experiential options of men and women alike will be broadened and enriched, and we all can become more truly whole, more truly human.

Table 1.1. Loevinger's Milestones of Ego Development and Extrapolations to Sex Role Development.

	Loevinger's milestones of ego development			Sex role development extrapolated
Stage	Impulse control	Interpersonal style	Conscious concerns	Conceptions of sex role
Presocial/symbiotic		Autistic, symbiotic	Self versus nonself	
Impulse-ridden	Impulse-ridden, fear of retaliation	Exploitive, dependent	Sexual and aggressive bodily feelings	Development of gender identity, self-assertion, self-expression, self-interest
Self-protective (formerly opportunistic)	Expedient, fear of being caught	Exploitive, manipulative, wary	Advantage, control, protection of self	Extension of self, self-extension, self-enhancement
Conformity	Conformity to external rule	Reciprocal, superficial	Things, appearance, reputation, self-acceptance	Conformity to external role, development of sex role stereotypes, bifurcation of sex roles
Conscientious	Internalized rules, guilt	Intensive, responsive	Differentiated inner feelings, motives, self-respect	Examination of self as sex role exemplar vis-à-vis internalized values
Autonomous	Coping with conflict, toleration of differences	Intensive concern for autonomy	Differentiated inner feelings, role concepts, self-fulfillment	Differentiation of sex role, coping with conflicting masculine/feminine aspects of self
Integrated	Reconciling inner conflicts, renunciation of unattainable	Cherishing of individuality	All of the above plus identity	Achievement of individually defined sex role, integration of both masculine and feminine aspects of self, androgynous sex role definition

Table 1.2. Sex Differences in Childrearing Values: A Comparison of Parental CRPR Descriptions Across Four Samples.

CRPR Items[a]	Parents of boys				Parents of girls			
	Sample[b] 1	Sample 2	Sample 3	Sample 4	Sample 1	Sample 2	Sample 3	Sample 4
I encourage my child always to do his best.	.01F[c]			.05M				
I feel a child should be given comfort when upset.	.10F	.10M .05F			.10F		.05F	
I feel physical punishment is best method of discipline.								
I express affection by holding, kissing, hugging my child.						.10M .05F	.01M .05F	.05F
I encourage my child to wonder and think about life.					.05F		.01M .05M .10F	
I take my child's preferences into account in making family plans.	.10M .05F	.10M			.05M			.05F
I find it difficult to punish my child.								
I do not allow my child to say bad things about his teacher.								
I am easygoing and relaxed with my child.	.05F			.01F		.10M	.10F	
My child and I have warm intimate times together.	.10F			.10F		.10M	.10F	
I have strict rules for my child.								
I expect my child to be grateful and appreciate his advantages.		.10M		.10M	.10M		.10M	
I believe praise gets better results than punishment.								
I make sure my child knows I appreciate his efforts.					.05F		.10M .05F	
I encourage my child to talk about his troubles.								

Table 1.2. Sex Differences in Childrearing Values: A Comparison of Parental CRPR Descriptions Across Four Samples, Cont'd.

CRPR Items[a]	Parents of boys				Parents of girls			
	Sample[b] 1	Sample 2	Sample 3	Sample 4	Sample 1	Sample 2	Sample 3	Sample 4
I teach my child to control his feelings at all times.	.05M	.05M						
I think a child should be encouraged to do better than others.			.05M .10F	.05M				
I believe scolding and criticism help a child improve.			.05M	.05F				
I sometimes tease and make fun of my child.		.05F	.01F	.05F				
I do not allow my child to question my decisions.	.10M .05M .01F	.05F	.01F					
I feel it is good for a child to play competitive games.			.05M					
I make sure I know where my child is.						.10M .01F	.05M .05F	
I don't go out if I have to leave my child with a stranger.								.10F

Note. Abbreviations: CRPR = Child-Rearing Practices Report. The CRPR items are in somewhat abbreviated form.

[a] Only items showing significant sex differences in two or more samples and consistent in direction are included.

[b] The four samples are all heterogeneous with respect to educational levels of parents, socioeconomic backgrounds, and ethnicity. The samples are described as follows: (1) parents of nursery school children—age range 3–4 years; mothers, $N = 90$; fathers, $N = 77$; (2) parents of children with physical illnesses (diabetes, asthma, congenital heart disease, hay fever)—age range 3–11 years; mothers, $N = 75$; fathers, $N = 44$; (3) parents of high school students—age range 15–17 years; mothers, $N = 120$; fathers, $N = 119$; (4) parents of university students—age range 17–20 years; mothers, $N = 183$; fathers, $N = 156$.

[c] Entries are probability levels obtained by t-test comparisons of parents of boys versus parents of girls. Letter following probability level (M or F) designates for which parent (mother or father) the item was differentiating.

Table 1.3. Sex Differences in Adjective Ideal Self-Descriptive Q-Sorts Among Students in Six Countries: Items on Which Males Are Significantly Higher.

Agency/ communion classification	Adjective	Country					
		United States	England	Sweden	Denmark	Finland	Norway
Agency	Practical, shrewd	.01[a]	.01	.01	.05	.01	.01
Agency	Assertive	.01	.05		.05	.05	.01
Agency	Dominating	.01	.05	.10		.01	.01
Agency	Competitive	.01	.05	.10			.10
Agency	Critical	.01	.10			.10	.05
—	Self-controlled	.05	.10			.05	.10
Agency	Rational, reasonable	.01				.01	
Agency	Ambitious	.10		.10	.10		
—	Feels guilty		.05				.05
—	Moody		.10				
Agency	Self-centered				.05		
—	Sense of humor					.01	
—	Responsible					.01	
—	Fair, just						
Agency	Independent						.05
Agency	Adventurous						.05

[a]Indicates level of significance for each comparison between males and females.

Table 1.4. Sex Differences in Adjective Ideal Self-Descriptive Q-Sorts Among Students in Six Countries: Items on Which Females Are Significantly Higher.

Agency/ communion classification	Adjective	Country					
		United States	England	Sweden	Denmark	Finland	Norway
Communion	Loving, affectionate	.01[a]	.01		.05	.01	.01
—	Impulsive	.01	.05	.01		.05	.01
Communion	Sympathetic	.10	.01			.05	.10
Communion	Generous	.10		.01	.10		.01
Agency	Vital, active	.01		.05			.05
—	Perceptive, aware	.10		.10			.05
Communion	Sensitive	.05	.05				
—	Reserved, shy	.01	.05				
Communion	Artistic	.10					
—	Curious			.10		.01	
—	Uncertain, indecisive		.10			.05	.05
—	Talkative					.05	.10
Communion	Helpful		.05				
—	Sense of humor		.01				
—	Idealistic				.05		
—	Cheerful						.05
Communion	Considerate						.01

[a]Indicates level of significance for each comparison between males and females.

Table 1.5. Adjective Self-Descriptions Differentiating Among
Kohlberg's Moral Reasoning Levels.

Moral reasoning stage	Males (N = 253)	Females (N = 257)
	Premoral level	
Stage 2 (Instrumental relativists) [Males, N = 16] [Females, N = 7]	More individualistic More rebellious More reserved More creative Less ambitious Less orderly Less responsive	More stubborn More rebellious More aloof, uninvolved Less altruistic Less impulsive
	Conventional level	
Stage 3 (Personal concordance) [Males, N = 57] [Females, N = 105]	More ambitious Less individualistic Less idealistic Less sympathetic	None
Stage 4 (Law and order) [Males, N = 109] [Females, N = 99]	More foresightful More conventional More practical More orderly Less curious Less rebellious Less creative	More ambitious More foresightful Less guilty Less rebellious Less aloof, uninvolved Less doubting, uncertain Less restless
	Principled level	
Stage 5 (Social contract) [Males, N = 54] [Females, N = 35]	Less foresightful	More fair More doubting, uncertain More altruistic Less ambitious
Stage 6 (Individual principles) [Males, N = 17] [Females, N = 11]	More curious More sympathetic More idealistic More responsive Less conventional Less practical Less reserved	More impulsive More restless More guilty Less foresightful Less fair, just Less stubborn

Adapted from Haan, Smith, and Block (1968).

Table 1.6. Adjective Self-Descriptions Differentiating Among Levels of Ego
Development as Defined by the Loevinger Sentence Completion Test.

Levels of ego maturity	Males (N = 144)	Females (N = 141)
Impulsive, self-protective levels [Males, N = 52] [Females, N = 19]	Adventurous Ambitious Competitive Fair Self-controlled Aloof, uninvolved Orderly Effective	Assertive Calm, relaxed Playful Courageous Proud Logical, rational Show off Stubborn
Conformity level [Males, N = 79] [Females, N = 101]	Optimistic Tolerant Logical, rational	Proud Tolerant Responsible Responsive
Conscientious level [Males, N = 13] [Females, N = 21]	Curious, questioning Needs approval Idealistic Sensitive Sympathetic	Self-centered Restless, discontented Sensitive Altruistic Worrying, fearful Effective

Table 1.7. Identification of Sex Role and Socialization Quadrants
Defined by Scores on the California Psychological Inventory.

CPI Socialization scale scores	CPI Femininity scale scores	
	Above-mean females Below-mean males	Below-mean females Above-mean males
Above mean	High sex-appropriate High socialization	Low sex-appropriate High socialization
Below mean	High sex-appropriate Low socialization	Low sex-appropriate Low socialization

Chapter Two

Issues, Problems, and Pitfalls
in Assessing Sex Differences:
A Critical Review of
The Psychology of Sex Differences

To survey, evaluate, and distill
the empirical evidence regarding psychological sex differences at
a time of intense, polarized debate on the issues of equality of
the sexes and changing sex roles is an awesome responsibility.
Eleanor Maccoby and Carol Jacklin were not intimidated by
this consequential challenge. Their book, *The Psychology of
Sex Differences* (1974), already has become a frequently cited
reference work because of the reputation of the authors, the
contemporary interest in the topic, the scope of the book's coverage, and the extensive bibliography provided. The authors'
conclusions about sex differences have received wide circulation
in both scientific journals and the lay press and have been accepted by many as an authoritative assessment of the nature

Originally published in *Merrill-Palmer Quarterly*, 1976, *22* (4),
283–308. Research supported by a National Institute of Mental Health Research Scientist Development Award.

31

and extent of psychological sex differences. Further, the Maccoby and Jacklin evaluation of the empirical literature may be expected to have important implications for psychological theorizing, for the direction of future research, and for the course of future social policy. Because of its potential influence, therefore, the work requires close scrutiny and careful evaluation as to its conceptual, empirical, and inferential adequacy. The positive contributions of the book have been discussed elsewhere (Emmerich, 1975); to avoid redundancy, I have defined my own task here as one of providing a critical appraisal of the evidential support for the authors' conclusions about sex differences.

The book, a sequel to Maccoby's *The Development of Sex Differences* (1966a), assays the results of approximately 1,600 studies published, for the most part, between 1966 and 1973. The authors surveyed the psychological journals that most frequently include findings about psychological sex differences and abstracted those studies analyzing between-sex differences for inclusion in their 233-page annotated bibliography. Additionally, other sources were referenced or contacted to extend the cast of their research net. The identified studies were then organized around eight broad topic areas ranging from perceptual abilities and learning to power relationships and parental socialization practices. Within these areas, studies were further classified for their relevance to particular psychological dimensions or constructs. A total of eighty-three extensive tables summarize analyses in which means and/or standard deviations were evaluated for sex differences. Each of these tables includes information about the investigator(s), ages of the subjects, sample sizes, specific variables analyzed, and the results of the between-sex statistical comparisons. Sex differences rejecting the null hypothesis at the .05 level of significance are noted; when sex differences do not reach the .05 level, the word *None* is entered into the "Difference" column of the table. Brief comments accompany each study tabled (for example, indications of trends toward significance where the sex difference achieved a p-value between .10 and .05 and identifications of samples composed of other than white, middle-class participants). Each table is extensively discussed.

In a final chapter, the authors summarize their conclusions from their survey and evaluation of the empirical literature. They cite a number of "unfounded beliefs about sex differences" (p. 349): that girls are more "social" than boys; that girls are more "suggestible"; that girls have lower self-esteem; that girls are better at simple repetitive tasks while boys excel at tasks requiring more complex cognitive processing and the inhibition of previously learned responses; that boys are more "analytical"; that girls are more affected by heredity and boys by environment; that girls are less motivated toward achievement; and that girls are more auditorially oriented while boys are more visually oriented.

"Sex differences that are fairly well established," according to Maccoby and Jacklin, include the following: that girls excel in verbal ability; that boys excel in visual-spatial ability; that boys are superior in mathematical ability; and that males are more aggressive.

The authors conclude that the evidence is equivocal in the areas of tactile sensitivity; fear, timidity, and anxiety; activity level; competitiveness; dominance; compliance; and nurturance and "maternal" behaviors.

Further, their "survey of the research on socialization of the two sexes revealed surprisingly little differentiation in parent behavior according to the sex of the child" (p. 338). Although noting, "There are some areas where differential 'shaping' does appear to occur," Maccoby and Jacklin "find very little evidence [for shaping], in relation to behaviors other than sex typing as very narrowly defined (for example, toy preference). The reinforcement contingencies for the two sexes appear to be remarkably similar" (p. 342).

Maccoby and Jacklin recognize the gap between their own sparse findings and the impressions held by parents, laypersons, and many psychologists that there are indeed pervasive psychological differences between boys and girls, men and women, and the further view that the sexes experience different developmental learning contexts. In explanation, they suggest that "many popular beliefs about the psychological characteristics of the two sexes . . . have little or no basis in fact. How is it possible that people continue to believe, for example, that girls are more 'social' than boys, when careful observation and measurement in a variety of situations show no sex difference? Of course it is possible that we have not studied those particular situations that contribute most to the popular beliefs. But if this is the problem, it means that the alleged sex difference exists only in a limited range of situations and the sweeping generalizations embodied in popular beliefs are not warranted. . . . A more likely explanation for the perpetuation of 'myths,' we believe, is the fact that stereotypes are such powerful things" (p. 355).

I suggest that many of the "popular beliefs" and "myths" to which Maccoby and Jacklin refer are not easily explained by pointing to the pervasiveness and persuasiveness of stereotypes. Earlier assessments of the literature on sex differences also sought to establish, via an evaluation of the empirical evidence, just what these differences are, with conclusions that appear to diverge in important respects from those of Maccoby and Jacklin. Thus, the considered conclusions of Terman and Tyler (1954), Tyler (1965), and Maccoby (1966b) *all agree* in finding evidence that scores of females, on the average, exceed those of males with respect to verbal ability, school grades, suggestibility, anxiety level, fears, social and affiliative interests, and fear of failure. These earlier reviews, in their empirical evaluations, also *all agree* that scores of males, on the average, exceed those of females with respect to quantitative ability, spatial ability, restructuring or breaking set, adult achievements, aggressivity, field independence, realistic assessment of own performance, and difficulty in controlling impulses.

This erosion in the evidence for sex differences over the past decade raises questions that are both puzzling and profound. Have newer and different data and newer and different criteria for evaluation shown the inadequacy of these earlier findings of sex differences?

Attempting to make sense of an inchoate field—and the

study of sex differences in such a field—is a difficult, complicated, arbitrary, and therefore inevitably premature undertaking. What shall we attend to and what shall we ignore? What decisional rules about methodologies and statistics should guide judgments and interpretations of studies? How shall we view areas where data are inconsistent? How shall the adequacy of the empirical data base be judged? It is difficult to find consensus on such issues; intellectual values, preferences, and biases therefore tend to direct inquiry and influence conclusions more than a little.

In a burgeoning field, successive integrations of knowledge can have great heuristic value in guiding the next wave of empiricism. However, an attendant risk in such structurings of data is that they may be regarded as more authoritative than is yet warranted. This problem is especially exacerbated if the field under review is of deep interest to publics not versed in the scientific and technical issues that complicate efforts at integration. Laypeople and even other scientists unfamiliar with the data being considered often will not recognize sufficiently the provisional and debatable character of a particular organization and interpretation of the available empirical findings.

I believe *The Psychology of Sex Differences,* although a monumental work, is nevertheless a controversial portrayal of the field. Valuable though the book will be to researchers because of its extensive documentation, the challenging questions raised, and the provocative explanations presented, it cannot serve as a definitive reference work because of certain problems in the Maccoby and Jacklin analyses. Interesting though the book may be to laypersons seeking the findings and knowledge of psychology, it can be misleading if the interpretations of Maccoby and Jacklin are accepted as the authoritative statement about the nature of psychological sex differences.

In the pages to follow, the reasons underlying my judgment will be brought forward and some revisions of the Maccoby and Jacklin conclusions suggested. Broadly stated, three sources of weakness or disputation can be said to characterize the book: (1) The research on sex differences to date often does not yet permit sensible conclusions of any kind to be drawn.

(2) Maccoby and Jacklin have employed various moot decision principles, some acknowledged and some not, that importantly shape the conclusions drawn. (3) In their sequence of surveying the literature, abstracting findings, tallying results, and then formulating conclusions, various "slippages" occurred that sometimes were of appreciable consequence.

Some Attenuating Factors in the Research
on Sex Differences

Maccoby and Jacklin express the opinion that, in the empirical literature on sex differences, "the omission of negative findings is considerably more frequent than the omission of positive findings" (p. 5), primarily because researchers do not bother to report negative findings. They are also bothered by "the tendency for isolated positive findings to sweep through the literature" (p. 6). Acknowledging these publication biases and concerns, it becomes important to note also some psychometric, methodological, and conceptual factors that *favor* the publication of findings that indicate the absence of sex differences. Whether these diametrical influences cancel each other or produce a decided tilt of the literature in one direction or another is difficult to say. Undoubtedly, different psychologists will have different views regarding the algebraic sum of the many considerations involved.

Unevaluated Quality of the Data Base. Maccoby and Jacklin elected to include all the studies uncovered in their bibliographic search because "there was no reasonable basis for selecting some studies and excluding others" (p. 11). Accordingly, there is a wide variability, as they acknowledge, in the statistical power of the studies on which they base their conclusions. More than one third of the comparisons between the sexes recorded in the Maccoby and Jacklin tables are based on samples of sixty or fewer, and about 20 percent of the comparisons involve samples of fewer than forty. Since factorial studies are heavily represented in the bibliography, many degrees of freedom are lost in the evaluation of main effects other than sex and in the evaluation of many simple and higher-order interactions. The result is that error terms for the evaluation of sex differences in many instances are based finally on rather few degrees of freedom. Such research tends to lack power in rejecting the null hypothesis when, in fact, the null hypothesis (that the sexes are not different) is wrong. Although the necessity of considering the power of a statistical test is not a new or questioned insight, little psychological research has been influenced by this recognition. Aware of the problem, Maccoby and Jacklin provided information about sample sizes in their tables so that readers who chose to do so would have some basis for assigning weights to the cited studies. In discussing their own tabled findings, however, Maccoby and Jacklin followed tradition in not considering how the poor statistical power of certain studies may have influenced adversely the trend of the findings they were attempting to integrate.

The question of reliability of psychological measures is too often ignored by experimentalists in psychology; the sufficiency of scores is often presumed rather than evaluated. Obviously, to the extent that sex differences are assessed with respect to scores that are undependable, differences that may exist in fact will go undetected. Because unreliable scores and indexes were encountered frequently in the studies forming the data base for the Maccoby and Jacklin conclusions, the extent of sex differences, particularly in those areas involving young children, may well be underestimated.

A further deficiency in many of the investigations referenced is conceptual insensitivity—wherein a measure may not be supportable as an indicator of the underlying construct supposedly being evaluated. Construct validation is a long and spiraling process, one too often evaded by the quicker stratagem of positing rather than ascertaining construct validity. The absence of sex differences when evaluated by casually constructed, construct-invalid measures does not mean that differences would not emerge when appropriate instruments or measures are used. When the broad field of psychology is being surveyed with respect to sex differences, the task of evaluating the conceptual quality of measures becomes energetically impossible for any one or two persons. Consequently, Maccoby and Jacklin, because of the very breadth of their coverage, were compelled to accept measures at their face value and could not delve into their conceptual merits.

Atheoretical Nature of the Data Base. Empirical psychological inquiry into sex differences has been essentially undirected and accidental. Most studies in developmental psychology include both sexes routinely and test for sex differences, not because theoretically such differences are expected, but rather with the hope that an *absence* of differences will provide justification for merging the samples of males and females, thus simplifying the statistical analysis and the reporting of results. Historically, investigators have not been interested in sex differences *per se* but, rather, in treatment effects, or in the interrelationships among variables; measures and procedures, therefore, often have been selected precisely because they either already have controlled for sex (as in intelligence tests) or have not demonstrated sex differences in pilot or other published studies. Whereupon, because investigators are encouraged or required to report, at least in some developmental psychology journals, the results of tests for sex differences even in the absence of a conceptual rationale for expectable divergence, the empirical literature is replete with null findings of inconsequential import.

For example, in the socialization realm, we have not yet developed a conceptual framework that permits specific and differentiated predictions about socialization practices as a function of the child's developmental level, the environmental context of the family, or parental role concepts. Accordingly, in our empirical efforts, research has tended to be of an ad hoc nature rather than targeted toward areas where, conceptually, sex-differentiated socialization practices might be expected. Emmerich (1973) has noted that the search for organizing processes in sex role socialization requires research studies designed to permit explicit age-related comparisons. Parental socialization emphases are dynamic and responsive to the enlarging geographic environment of the growing child, the emerging competencies and sense of responsibility of the maturing child, and reorganizing conceptions of parental roles over time. These different situational pressures may be expected to contribute to sex-related divergence in parental childrearing patterns. Unfortunately, our empiricism has been based on a static socialization model and has remained conceptually undifferentiated rather than seeking age- and stage-related shifts in parental socialization emphases for sons and for daughters.

Maccoby and Jacklin remark in their introduction that most of the findings reported on sex differences were incidental to the research interests of the investigator and suggest that the time has come for studies of sex differences to be guided by explicit hypotheses derived from considered conceptual schemata. No one can disagree with this recommendation; its implementation is long overdue. In the meantime, it must be recognized that the empirical data base with respect to psychological sex differences is unrepresentative in a number of ways that cannot be well assessed or allowed for by Maccoby and Jacklin or, of course, by anyone.

Overemphasis on the Null Hypothesis. The inferential inadequacy of the null hypothesis approach and its tendency to mislead interpretation of data have long been recognized (for example, Bakan, 1967; Cronbach, 1975; Rozeboom, 1960). Still, much of the psychological literature continues to embrace this way of reasoning. Cronbach (1975), in recommending that "the time has come to exorcise the null hypothesis," argues that the "canon of parsimony has been misinterpreted, has led us into the habit of accepting Type II error at every turn, for the sake of holding Type I errors in check" (p. 124). To avoid the "hopeless inconsistency" generated by the significant/nonsignificant dichotomy, Cronbach joins other statisticians in recommending the reporting of descriptive data and the use of confidence intervals to provide a proper interpretive perspective.

Maccoby and Jacklin "emphasize the null hypothesis because of the way most data on sex difference find their way into the psychological literature" (p. 4), assuming nonsignificant results are less likely to be reported. They "are aware . . . that no amount of negative evidence 'proves' that no sex difference exists" (p. 5). Unfortunately, although cognizant in their introduction that the statement "No sex difference has been shown" is fundamentally different from the statement "There is no sex difference" (p. 5), the authors subsequently use the latter shorthand phrasing on many occasions. Moreover, when studies are recorded in their tables, failures to reject the null hypothesis are noted by entering the word *none* in the column headed "Difference."

Inevitably, the omission of the tedious but necessary qualifiers has an insidious effect on the conclusions received by the reader and even on the interpretations offered by Maccoby and Jacklin. A positivistic conclusion, that there are no sex differences, tends to displace the more correct recognition, that no decision can yet be made. The interpretive perspective is distorted further when Maccoby and Jacklin use expressions like "unfounded beliefs" and "myths" in their summary evaluations of data bases yielding inconsistent findings with respect to sex differences. Thus, inconclusive results are transformed into strongly stated negative results.

Overrepresentation of Younger Age Groups. In the empirical literature on sex differences, there is great unevenness in the representation of various age groups. Thus, of the studies contributing to the Maccoby and Jacklin conclusions, 75 percent were based on research participants who were twelve years old or younger; almost 40 percent used preschool children. With respect to studies concerned with sex-differentiated socialization practices, 77 percent of all investigations cited are based on results of analyses comparing the socialization of boys and girls *five years of age and younger.* To the extent that sex differences are not all genetically or hormonally determined from birth but depend on maturation and socializing influences as well, considerable time may be required before sex differences in behavior would be manifested. The disproportionate representation of younger age groups may obscure those sex differences emerging at adolescence as a function of the physiological and anatomical changes occurring in response to sex-differentiated hormonal secretions of the reproductive glands. Further, it is widely believed that socialization efforts should be age-appropriate, and therefore, with respect to many behaviors, sex-differentiated tutoring would not be expected in the early years.

These observations suggest that with the increasing age of the child there will be increasing evidence of sex differentiation, at least through the first two decades of life. And such proves to be the case. When the studies cited by Maccoby and Jacklin are sorted into three categories according to the age of the subjects studied—infancy through age four, ages five through twelve, and age thirteen and over—the percentage of comparisons manifesting clear and significant sex differences shows a marked increase over time. In the earliest period, 37 percent of the comparisons reveal reliable sex differences; in the second period, 47 percent of the studies yield significant sex differences; and in the third age category, 55 percent of the studies show significant sex differences. This trend becomes even more striking if studies based on small samples are excluded. It is also pertinent to cite Carlson's (1971b) review of one year's issues of the *Journal of Personality and Social Psychology*, a journal in which research typically involves adult subjects. Fewer than half of the studies in that journal reported testing for sex differences (an interesting datum in its own right) but of those that did, 74 percent reported significant sex differences. Terman and Tyler (1954) report evidence for increasing sex differentiation with age in the areas of abilities, interests, preferences, and responses to personality inventories. Conclusions about the existence of sex differences, then, may well depend on the age mix in the set of studies in which sex differences are examined. Although Maccoby and Jacklin tabled their results according to subject age and occasionally comment on the influence of age on the presence or absence of sex differences, they do not advance the recognition that the finding of sex differences is powerfully contingent on the age of the subjects studied.

It should not be surprising that fewer sex differences are found in research studies based on infants and very young children. It is likely that parents respond to their infants and toddlers more as babies and young children than in terms of gender. In addition, behavioral assessments of infants and young children tend to be less reliable than psychological measurements of older individuals because of the short attention spans, the motivational flux, and the difficulties that the young have both in understanding and in communicating. And finally, in many areas of behavior, it is unreasonable to expect to find sex differences in young children because some areas have not yet become salient for sex-differentiated socialization (for example, achievement, competition, persistence, altruism), and in other areas parental tolerances perhaps have not yet been stressed (for example, dependency, aggression). Indeed, in the research studies cited by Maccoby and Jacklin assessing parental tolerance for dependency (Table 9.6) or parental responses to aggression (Table 9.7), *no* investigations have included subjects older than six years of age.

The age bias in the empirical literature needs to be recognized, and the Maccoby and Jacklin conclusions require qualification to indicate that *sex differences were evaluated predominantly in samples of preadolescent children.* Inclusion of more studies based on adolescent and adult samples would be expected to reveal substantially more evidence of sex differentiation.

The frequent incoherence of the psychological literature on sex differences is not surprising in light of the historical deficiencies discussed above—insensitivity of research design, undependability of measures, uncertain construct validities, atheoretical inquiry, misleading reasoning, and unincisive subject sampling—in addition to the factors noted by Maccoby and Jacklin. The unhappy consequence of the concatenation of these several kinds of shortcomings is that a tallying of findings and the resultant "box score" may not be sufficient for serious students of the nature of sex differences.

The Evaluational Framework of Maccoby and Jacklin

In this section, I consider some of the guidelines that Maccoby and Jacklin employed in their evaluational and integrative effort. Guidelines are inherently arbitrary, and arbitrariness itself should pose no problem if explicitly acknowledged. Maccoby and Jacklin have taken pains to indicate the decision rules and methodological values they followed. But other evaluational rules instead might as reasonably have been applied, resulting in very different summary conclusions. A chain of evaluation has many links, and even though anchoring points are initially known, the position finally reached at the end of the evaluative sequence may not be recognized as fundamentally constrained by earlier decisions. Therefore, it may be instructive to indicate some of the ways in which the reasonable but debatable decisions of Maccoby and Jacklin may have contributed to their conclusions.

The Problem of Conceptual Rubrics. In organizing research data, the classification scheme employed by research collators takes on critical significance. When research results achieved with a variety of instruments tapping different phenomena are brought together to assess the coherence of the empirical evidence surrounding a particular construct, what conceptual criteria shall be used to categorize the existing studies? In regard to such large constructs as, for example, "achievement emphasis," "impulsivity," "self-esteem," "conformity," or "compliance," how shall we decide which studies properly relate to which concepts?

For example, Maccoby and Jacklin brought together the following measures, all as indicators of parental pressures for achievement: amount of praise or criticism for intellectual performance; parental standards for intellectual performance, as expressed on a questionnaire item; expectation that the child will go on to college; pressure for competent task completion; expectation of household help from the child; responses to an "achievement-inducing" scale that reflects the ages at which parents feel it is appropriate to teach a child more mature behaviors; amount of direct help and number of task-oriented suggestions offered by the mother; number of anxious intrusions into the child's task performance; observed pressure for achievement (unspecified); pressure for success on a memory task; demands made on the child during a joint problem-solving task; and concern with the child's intellectual achievements.

Although many of these measures are clearly related to the achievement dimension, others are readily challengeable. Mothers' expectations for household help, or their anxious intrusions into the child's problem-solving attempts, or their demands on the child during a discussion in which consensus must be reached, or their pressures for competence in two-year-olds observed in the home setting, represent behaviors that lack both construct and discriminant validity with respect to achievement emphasis *per se*. Anxious interference, demands, and criticisms could as easily be construed as indicators of parental anxiety, impatience, sense of inadequacy, intrusiveness, and so on. With so heterogeneous a bag of supposed "achievement emphasis" measures, it may not be surprising that Maccoby and Jacklin found so little difference between the sexes in the socialization pressures each had experienced.

Organizing categories can be defined in ways that may be too limited as well. Thus, in Table 3.9 ("Impulsivity, Lack of Inhibition"), thirty-seven between-sex comparisons are listed. The Matching Familiar Figures Test and its variant, the Design Recall Test, contribute thirteen of these comparisons, Delay of Gratification tasks contribute ten, and the Motor Inhibition Task contributes five. Aggregated, 76 percent of the results tabulated are accounted for by these three procedures. Measures of persistence, decision speed, space utilization in drawing, and "dot" estimation compose the remaining experimental measures, while three rating studies complete the empirical data base from which Maccoby and Jacklin conclude the sexes do not differ with respect to impulsivity.

In her 1966 volume, Maccoby defined impulsivity to include the inability to delay gratification, distractibility, undirected activity, and lack of persistence (pp. 28-29), as well as temper tantrums, aggressiveness, and activity (p. 48). In *The Psychology of Sex Differences,* Maccoby and Jacklin have chosen a more restricted, cognition-emphasizing definition of impulsivity, placing the concept in the chapter "Intellectual Abilities and Cognitive Styles" rather than in the chapter on "Temperament: Activity Level and Emotionality." Many personologists would find their present definition too limited and would prefer the earlier and broader Maccoby conceptualization of impulsivity—to which well might be added measures of risk taking and daring, unrealistic goal setting, unmodulated expression of impulses and frustrations, and accident rates. For many psychologists, impulsivity is understood as a multifaceted concept, and its assessment therefore requires measures that tap its several aspects. With a broader view of impulsivity, the conclusion of Maccoby and Jacklin would be modified.

Finally, classification rubrics can be established that combine conceptually disparate behaviors. In evaluating sex differences with regard to the ability to "break set," or restructure, Maccoby and Jacklin consider together responses to problems requiring insight for solution (for example, Luchin's water-jar problem, the matchstick and two-string problems) *and* responses to the word game, anagrams, a "task calling for breaking set in a verbal context" (p. 103).

For many psychologists, the cognitive task demands involved in classical insight problems are fundamentally different from those involved in anagram solutions. Insight problems require the person to discover, *without instruction from the experimenter,* that a solution depends on the employment of a divergent strategy and that he or she must create or discern that new principle of solution. In anagram studies, however, the participant is *explicitly instructed* to make as many words as possible from the letters in the stimulus word, and no new principles of problem solution need to be created or discovered by the subject. Although both insight problems and anagrams require a recombination of stimulus elements for solution, at a deeper level of analysis these tasks differ in that the first requires the achievement of a new stratagem while the second requires only the more or less systematic application of an essentially recursive process.

If we examine the empirical evidence provided in the text and the annotated bibliography, we find that males scored significantly higher on twelve of fourteen problems requiring restructuring, the means on the two remaining tasks not being significantly different. In contrast, Table 3.10 includes between-sex comparisons with respect to anagram performance wherein females score significantly higher in four comparisons while no significant differences between the sexes are found in the remaining six contrasts. Conjoining both kinds of studies, Maccoby and Jacklin conclude that "results on set breaking, or restructuring, are equivocal" (p. 105) and that "it is by no means demonstrated that boys excel on tasks calling for restructuring or breaking set" (p. 132). Had Maccoby and Jacklin kept separate the two kinds of studies that they merged, a very different conclusion would have followed with regard to sex difference in problem restructuring.

So we have seen how aggregating measures of a construct in the absence of demonstrable convergent and discriminant validities, the omission or exclusion of construct-valid measures from a conceptual category, and/or the merging of conceptually dissimilar tasks into the same category can influence powerfully the nature of the conclusions subsequently drawn about a body of data. Obviously, theoretical preferences guide, and must guide, one's choice of a conceptual rubric, and I do not mean to suggest that Maccoby and Jacklin have been wrong in their selections. I *do* mean to emphasize that other, no less rigorous, conceptual viewpoints and classification schemata would place a different organization on the available empiricism and consequently issue conclusions of a very different cast.

The Problem of Stereotypes and Methodological Preferences. A theme encountered with some frequency in the Maccoby and Jacklin work is a concern about stereotypes and the ways in which stereotypes can constrain or influence ratings by parents, teachers, and other observers. Thus, for example, in discussing dependency, they say, "We can only reiterate now the warning that, although any measurement (including behavior observation) embodies the danger of observer bias, it would appear that ratings are especially susceptible to this problem, particularly where sex differences are concerned. . . . When rating studies and observational studies conflict, then, in the picture of sex differences they present, we believe it reasonable to rely more heavily upon the observational ones" (p. 199).

Or, again, in their concluding chapter: "We have repeatedly encountered the problem that so-called 'objective' measures of behavior yield different results than ratings or self-reports. Ratings are notoriously subject to shifting anchor points . . . for example, in one study, teachers rated each child in their class on activity level; the boys received higher average ratings; but 'actometer' recordings for the same group of children did not show the boys to be engaging in more body movement. Obviously, the possibility exists that teachers are noticing and remembering primarily the behavior that fits their stereotypes" (p. 356).

Maccoby and Jacklin's interpretation of this last study is worth closer inspection because they highlight it in an earlier discussion (p. 175) and because it illustrates an orientation toward psychological data that many psychologists will find too narrow and otherwise bothersome. Although poorly collected and poorly analyzed ratings may be susceptible to stereotypes and observer bias, ratings that are carefully achieved and well analyzed may be able to reveal relationships beyond the current capacities of "objective" measures, plagued as such measures often are by unreliability and an absence of cogency. Indeed, going further, although stereotypes may only embody "myths," they also may have encoded certain culturally discerned and repeatedly validated truths. Rather than automatically giving precedence to one kind of data and devaluing another, the quality and inferential adequacy of *all* kinds of data must be evaluated closely in the weighting and integrating of findings. So, too, with stereotypes; they should be neither rejected reflexively nor accepted uncritically as we pursue the scientific task of evaluating sex differences.

Thus, in the example emphasized by Maccoby and Jacklin (a study by Loo and Wenar, 1971), teacher ratings of activity based on prolonged observations of children over many different situations indicated sex differences in activity, while a *single* mechanical recording of activity in the classroom did not. Perhaps teachers were unduly influenced by culturally held stereotypes in making their individual and experience-based ratings, but perhaps not; the question is confounded and should not be prejudged. Perhaps the solitary actometer score, because it is "objective," deserves the greater credence, but perhaps not, because it was a one-time measurement in an activity-limiting (classroom) situation; again, the question is confounded and should not be prejudged.

It so happens that the low reliability of actometer scores

is well known and, indeed, was acknowledged by Loo and Wenar. For this reason, most studies employing the actometer take several activity recordings rather than only one and, typically, when multiple actometer recordings are used, these more reliable activity scores reveal sex differences (for example, Halverson, 1971; Halverson and Waldrop, 1973; Pedersen and Bell, 1970). Further, Maccoby and Jacklin's stereotype interpretation of the Loo and Wenar rating results is itself directly challenged by Halverson and Waldrop's additional finding that, within each sex, composited actometer scores correlated appreciably with composited teachers' rating of activity-related variables (for example, correlations with "vigor in play" were .72 and .64 for boys and girls, respectively). The Halverson and Waldrop findings are supported by similar results obtained in a longitudinal study (Block and Block, 1973) in which composited actometer scores were found to correlate highly with composited teacher scores on Q-sort items reflecting activity in a sample of 106 three-year-olds. Within-sex correlations with the item "Is physically active" were .51 and .49 for boys and girls, respectively; with "Is vital, energetic, lively," the correlations were .54 and .56 for boys and girls, respectively. Correlations of similar magnitude were obtained one year later when composited actometer scores of four-year-olds were correlated with composited teacher Q-sort ratings obtained from a completely different set of nursery school teachers. So the example introduced by Maccoby and Jacklin to support their view of the pervasive and determining role of stereotypes has a more parsimonious explanation. More generally, I suggest that Maccoby and Jacklin, because of their concerns about stereotypes and their possible influence on ratings, may well have relied too heavily on "objective" measures unable to bear this weight and unduly neglected valid information available from raters.

Worrying further about the possible influence of stereotyping in rater-based studies, Maccoby and Jacklin introduced and emphasized a second example, a study by Meyer and Sobieszek (1972). In this experiment, adults observed and rated the videotaped play of two toddlers selected so as not to be easily distinguished by gender. Each of the two children was sometimes identified as a boy and sometimes as a girl, the analysis seeking to evaluate the effects of general labeling on ratings. Commenting on the results, Maccoby and Jacklin say, "One possible outcome of the study might have been, of course, that raters would tend to see children as conforming to raters' stereotypes, so that boys would be seen as more aggressive and girls as more cooperative or shy. *In fact, however, the reverse was true* [italics added], at least for the subsample of subjects who had previous experience with children. If a child behaved in a vigorous, uninhibited way on the screen, the behavior was more likely to be labeled aggressive if the actor was thought to be a girl than if the same actor was thought to be a boy. In other words, behaviors were especially noticed if they ran counter to sex role stereotypes" (pp. 345-346).

Whatever the conceptual merits of these assertions by Maccoby and Jacklin, they again do not follow from the study cited. The scores used by Meyer and Sobieszek were distressingly unreliable and, if only for that reason, their analysis of variance found no differences even approaching statistical significance between observers as a function of previous experience with children ($p = .31$), sex of the observer ($p = .17$), or in the interaction of experience with children and sex of the observer ($p = .70$). It is therefore disconcerting when Maccoby and Jacklin attribute counterstereotypic effects to observers in such strong and incautious terms on the basis of this one, inconclusive study.

Certainly, stereotypes (and counterstereotypes) are a problem in the scientific evaluation of sex differences, and their influence must be carefully weighed in the integrative and interpretive balance. Just as stereotypes (and counterstereotypes) should not be permitted to constrain findings, the valid variance they contain should not be discarded along with the invalid variance. The issue is complex; judiciousness is required. To many psychologists, it will appear that Maccoby and Jacklin, in their determination not to be misled, directly or reversely, by the influence of stereotypes, have been too willing to presume such influences operate powerfully, even in well-conducted, carefully controlled studies based on observer ratings. Consequently, they have tended to minimize and even dismiss findings that would importantly modify their conclusions.

Sex as a Moderator Variable. The focus of Maccoby and Jacklin is on sex differences in mean level and/or variability of scores. They have elected to ignore sex as a moderator variable —that is, to ignore differences between the sexes in the patterning or organization of cognitive or personality characteristics. Earlier, Maccoby (1966) introduced a section on correlational differences in the two sexes by noting, "We have been summarizing the known differences between the sexes in their average performance on a variety of tasks. But this, of course, does not provide a complete account of sex differences. Even on tests where the distribution of scores is the same for the two sexes (in mean and standard deviation), the array of scores will often correlate differently with other variables for boys and girls" (p. 28). After presenting some ten pages of evidence showing reliable sex differences in linkages between intellectual task performance and personality characteristics, Maccoby (1966) concluded, "Whether or not there is a difference in average performance on a given task, there are some substantial sex differences in the intercorrelations between intellectual performance and other aspects of the individual or his environment" (pp. 38-39). Maccoby then went on to discuss possible causal factors contributing to these differences. In all, almost half of her chapter in the 1966 volume was concerned with pattern differences between the sexes.

Maccoby's earlier attention to differences in the organization of variables for the two sexes was shared by Tyler (1965), who reported, "Evidence is rapidly accumulating that the traits measured are *linked together differently* in the two sexes. It may be that these differences in personality organization are more important than the differences in average scores" (p. 264). In the current book, however, Maccoby and Jacklin devoted a total of three pages to discussion of differences in the patterning or organization of variables as a function of sex, and most of that discussion represents a recanting, perhaps premature, of Maccoby's earlier explanatory attempts.

Research workers frequently encounter reliable correlational or covariance differences as a function of sex. It is likely that these differences ultimately will have appreciable theoretical and practical import in understanding, for example, the different motivational systems that may characterize the sexes. Although the firm establishment of these sex-moderated relationships is complicated by the cumbersome research procedures and statistical manipulations required, the relative neglect of differences in the patterning of variables for the two sexes in the volume under review may discourage investigators from undertaking the formidable tasks of reliable identification and integration of such findings. To the extent that sex is or will prove to be a moderating influence on psychological relationships, the conclusions about sex differences offered by Maccoby and Jacklin may require revision when placed in this larger context.

Slippages in the Evaluational Sequence

It is inevitable, in so extended and complicated an effort, that errors, omissions, and other deficiencies will occur. Inevitability accepted, it is nevertheless required, if a work like *The Psychology of Sex Differences* is to be useful, that the inaccuracies be few and of small consequence. It is therefore a most unhappy responsibility to have to report finding more flaws in Maccoby and Jacklin's documentation and interpretations than are, I believe, acceptable in a reference volume. Only a sampling of the "slippages" I happen to have encountered or recognized will be presented.

Insufficiencies of the Annotated Bibliography. Some studies published in journals within the designated purview and time span of the search for studies of sex differences were not identified. Errors of this kind are inescapable and difficult to estimate, and hence their significance is difficult to evaluate. More immediately serious is the question of the sufficiency of the summaries of the research identified, as abstracted in the annotated bibliography. These research summaries are sometimes erroneous and, with some frequency, fail to include mention of significant interactions with sex, do not recognize the existence of consistent trends over several studies conducted by an investigator, and do not record clear differences in the patterning of relationships as a function of sex.

Thus, a study by Cruse (1966), based on samples of children at four age levels (three through six years), is summarized in the annotated bibliography as having found significant sex differences only at ages four and six. Reference to the original article reveals a significant main effect for sex ($p < .01$) and a near-significant age-by-sex interaction ($p < .10$) among the results. Statistical comparisons between the sexes at each of the different age levels are *not* reported and are not inferable from the tabled results.

The Manheimer and Mellinger (1967) study on childhood accidents is tersely summarized by the statement "Boys' accident rate was higher than girls' " (p. 533). The original article reveals that, in a sample of almost 9,000 successive admissions to one hospital's emergency ward, boys had significantly more accidents at *every* age level between four and eighteen years and that the frequency of accidents *increased* for boys with age and *decreased* for girls. Such information adds immeasurably to the power and implications of these findings.

A study by Staub (1971) is summarized by the statement "No sex differences were found in *S*s' helping responses" (p. 594). The original article reveals striking differences between boys and girls in the *pattern* of relationships between helping behavior and other personality variables. Teacher ratings (of initiation of activity, need for approval, expression of positive affect, and competence) were all *positively* related to helping behavior in boys but were all *negatively* related to helping behavior in girls. The *differences* between corresponding correlations for boys and girls were significant in three of the four comparisons. Although complicating enormously the task of evaluating sex differences, the consideration of reliable sex differences in the patterning of relationships seems essential if our aim is to understand the *psychology* of sex differences.

Omission of Relevant Studies from Tables. Numerous instances can be cited of articles in the annotated bibliography that were not included in the appropriate tables. Thus, I happened to encounter nine studies pertinent to "Activity Level" (Table 5.1) that were not tabled therein. In *each* of these nine studies, males were found to be more active than females. Because omissions were found to be a significant problem in other tables as well, the sense of the omitted studies will be presented here. Halverson (1971) found boys significantly more active as measured by actometer readings; Omark, Omark, and Edelman (1973), using samples from three different countries, found boys consistently engaged in significantly more physical interaction; Emmerich (1971) reported two separate experiments in which he found boys engaged in significantly more gross motor behavior; Battle and Lacey (1972) and Macfarlane, Allen, and Honzik (1954) reported that boys were rated as more hyperactive than girls; Wolfensberger and others (1962) found boys were more "hyperkinetic" when activity level was assessed with a ballistograph; Stein and Lenrow (1970) reported that men preferred motoric activities more than did women; and Kurtz (1971), using a self-report scale, found activity scores to be higher for men than for women. The omission of these nine studies clearly affects importantly the conclusions to be drawn about sex differences in activity level.

Table 7.5 of Maccoby and Jacklin, "Compliance with Adult Requests and Demands," omits eight studies from the annotated bibliography (Baumrind, 1971; Berk, 1971; Emmerich, 1971—two experiments; Shipman, 1971—two experiments; Whiting and Pope, 1973—two age groups). Five of the omitted comparisons found girls more compliant than boys, one comparison found boys more compliant than girls, and in two comparisons the differences were not statistically significant.

Table 4.5, "Curiosity and Exploration," also omitted eight studies related to exploration of the environment that appear in the annotated bibliography. These studies include four observational studies (Bronson, 1971; Kaminski, 1973; Pedersen and Bell, 1970; Torrance, 1965); responses to Cattell's High School Inventory (Baltes and Nesselroade, 1972); peer nominations (Tuddenham, 1971), and self-ratings (Kenney and White, 1966; Longstreth, 1970). The results of each of these omitted studies found boys significantly more curious, adventurous, manipulative, and/or exploring. Again, the inclusion of these studies changes the nature of the conclusions to be drawn about sex differences in curiosity.

In assessing sex differences in dependency, Maccoby and Jacklin elected to include only studies of proximity seeking and social responsiveness and interaction (including bids for attention) with parents, nonfamily adults, and peers. Studies relying on global measures of dependency and those in which the targets of dependency bids are unspecified have been omitted from their tables (Tables 6.1 through 6.4). It should be noted that studies assessing *specific* requests for help and reassurance also are not tabled. Even within Maccoby and Jacklin's restricted definition of the domain of dependency, however, I noted numerous omissions (Baltes and Nesselroade, 1972; Golightly, Nelson, and Johnson, 1970; Greenglass, 1971; Kenney and White, 1966; Munroe and Munroe, 1971; Omark and Edelman, 1973; Omark, Omark, and Edelman, 1973—two age groups in each of three countries; Speer, Briggs, and Gavalas, 1969; and Whiting and Pope, 1973). In each of the above studies, girls manifested more dependent behaviors in the sense of seeking help and/or information, maintaining closer proximity to teacher or to home, or scoring higher on dependency scales in standard inventories. Additionally, Santrock (1970), defining dependency as a subordinate, leaning relationship on parents in a structured doll-play situation, found girls scoring significantly higher on dependency so defined. The empirical results of these several studies are consistent and do not fit with the conclusions Maccoby and Jacklin derived from an incomplete data base.

Examples of relevant but untabled studies are numerous. Table 2.1, at the end of this chapter, identifies a number of other omissions. There does not appear to be a rationale or systematic reason for these various exclusions since, in most instances, the omitted studies employed dependent measures similar (or even identical) to those tabled. Obviously, the clerical work involved in sorting and tabling studies was enormous, and some error was unavoidable. What is unfortunate, however, is that the overlooked studies seem to change importantly the tenor of several of the tables on which Maccoby and Jacklin based their conclusions. I must also add the sobering note that although my comparison of the annotated bibliography with tables was exhausting, it was by no means exhaustive; there may be further omissions that I did not notice.

Discrepancies Between Discussion and Tabled Results. Most readers rely on the authors' discussion of tabled results, not wanting to assume the burden of integrating the findings cited. For this reason, discrepancies between the discussion in the text and information contained in the tables are disquieting. Some of the disparities I encountered will be described to illustrate this problem.

Maccoby and Jacklin note that when sex differences are found in general intellectual abilities between ages two and seven, the difference usually favors girls. They urge caution in interpreting this finding and indicate that "the higher scores of girls tend to be found in studies of 'disadvantaged' children" (p. 65). The data referenced (their Table 3.1) contain eighteen between-sex comparisons in the two-to-seven-year age range. Six of these eighteen studies employed "disadvantaged" samples, and of these, two, or 33 percent, found girls scoring significantly higher. Twelve of the eighteen studies employed conventional middle-class samples, and of these, four, or 33 percent, found girls scoring significantly higher. Since these percentages are identical, the suggestion that the observed trends are attributable to the "disadvantaged" origin of certain samples is quite unjustified.

As another example, consider the discussion of Maccoby and Jacklin in their concluding chapter of the findings on task confidence and a corollary issue, locus of control. "One interesting age trend emerged in our survey that is probably *not* a reflection of changes in methods of measurement: this is the tendency for young women of college age to lack confidence in their ability to do well on a new task, and their sense that they have less control over their own fates than men do. These trends are not seen among *older or younger women*" (p. 359; italics added). Reference to the relevant tables for the basis of this implicative statement raises some disconcerting questions.

First, consider the evidence for the assertion that this difference in confidence is not characteristic of younger persons. Table 4.8, "Task Confidence," includes three comparisons between boys and girls at younger ages (seven to fourteen years). In two of the three comparisons, boys are more confident, and in addition, an untabled result of the third study found boys significantly higher in their performance expectations in English than girls, while no significant sex difference in performance expectations for mathematics were found. These data suggest that the difference between the sexes at college age extends to the younger age range as well. Table 4.9, "Locus of Control," includes twelve comparisons of younger subjects (ages six to seventeen). No differences were found between boys and girls in eight of these twelve studies, suggesting that conclusions about locus of control in younger persons are, at best, equivocal. Now, consider the evidence for the assertion that the difference in confidence and sense of control over one's life is not sex-differentiating among adults beyond college age. Neither Table 4.8 nor 4.9, the two relevant tables, includes *any* comparisons of adult men and women over the age of twenty-one. Thus, there are no empirical grounds for the authors' assertions that "these trends are not seen among older or younger women."

A common effect of these discrepancies between empirical data and discussion is the minimization of possible sex differences by relegating the differences observed to a particular brief developmental period or to a specific subgroup. What may be a tendency to rationalize sex differences is reflected in other ways as well. In discussing the sex differences frequently found to exist with respect to both general anxiety and test anxiety (Tables 5.4 and 5.5), Maccoby and Jacklin note that the "greater general anxiety of girls and women is fairly consistent across studies . . . [while] measures of test anxiety frequently find no sex difference, but when there is a difference, girls score higher" (p. 186). Reference to the data indicates that five of the eight tabled studies of test anxiety found significant sex differences, with women scoring higher; only three studies failed to reject the null hypothesis.

Maccoby and Jacklin then question the validity of the anxiety measures and suggest that boys score lower on anxiety because of their greater tendency to lie and to be defensive, while candidness is more characteristic of girls and women, thus increasing their scores on anxiety scales. This explanation of these data is unsatisfactory. Maccoby and Jacklin are able to cite only one study where males scored higher on a Lie scale and acknowledge two studies where the sexes did not differ in Lie scores. In the annotated bibliography are five additional studies that fail to find sex differences on the Lie scale.

There is some evidence that males do score higher on scales measuring defensiveness, but if these few studies are invoked to explain the lower anxiety scores of males, it would seem reasonable to introduce as well the frequent finding (seven of nine studies) that females score higher on social desirability scales. Maccoby and Jacklin do not do so. However, by the same reasoning that they employ to explain the lowering of males' anxiety scores, scores of females are lowered because of their greater tendency to respond in socially desirable ways. In explaining the often obtained sex differences with respect to anxiety, all salient interpretive options should be discussed.

Tracking a Conclusion Back to the Original Data

In previous sections, examples of "slippage" have been reported more or less in isolation. But errors can compound, their cumulative effect thus distorting seriously our understandings of sex differences and sex similarities. Consider, for example, Maccoby and Jacklin's comment in their summary chapter regarding "instances in [their] review where a difference was evident only briefly, during a limited age period. This appears to be true, for example, on certain measures of 'impulsivity' where boys are more impulsive only during the preschool years" (p. 357). What is the basis for this assertion regarding male impulsivity during the preschool period?

This summary statement was heralded in an earlier interpretation, this time employing a more restricted notion of "impulsivity": "The reader may recall that this is the age [that is, preschool] at which boys were found to be more 'impulsive' in the sense that they were less able than girls to wait for a delayed, more attractive reward" (pp. 144-145).

This interpretation, in turn, may be traced back still further to the authors' discussion of the tabled evidence for sex differences in impulsivity: "As may be seen in Table 3.9, there is *some* [italics added] evidence that boys are more impulsive on this measure [that is, delay of gratification] during the preschool years" (p. 101).

Reference to Table 3.9 reveals three studies employing the delay-of-gratification paradigm with preschool children—two studies based on samples of largely black, lower-socioeconomic-status children, which yielded no significant sex differences, and one study by Mischel and Underwood (1973), in which a significant sex difference was found.

In consulting the original article by Mischel and Underwood, I noted in their reference list three other investigations conducted by Mischel and his associates studying preschool children with a similar experimental paradigm. In the Mischel and Moore study (1973), sex differences were evaluated but were *not* significantly different. The two remaining studies made no mention of testing for sex differences. The Mischel and Moore study, despite its inclusion among the references cited by Mischel and Underwood, was not picked up by Maccoby and Jacklin's research scan and therefore was neither tabled nor included in the annotated bibliography.

Thus, Maccoby and Jacklin's willingness to attribute greater impulsivity to boys during the preschool years is predicated on the results of only one study together with neglect of the findings from three other studies. A single, unreplicated result based on a specific and narrow experimental paradigm (waiting time for a preferred reward) has, through an erosion of qualifications, been converted to a positive conclusion about age-limited sex differences in "impulsivity." More substantial standards of evidence would seem to be required before such a conclusion is warranted.

Relationship Between the Evidence and the Conclusions

In formulating their conclusions, Maccoby and Jacklin employed a "box-scoring," or "tallying," approach. It is informative to examine the tallies of the empirical evidence for sex differences as they relate to the conclusions they have drawn. In Table 2.1 of this chapter, Maccoby and Jacklin's conclusions regarding the various cognitive and personality areas are recapitulated, together with the ratios and the proportions of the sex-differentiating findings reported in their tables.* Where studies were omitted by Maccoby and Jacklin, both the data as tabled by Maccoby and Jacklin and as extended to incorporate those omissions discovered in the course of preparing this review are provided. It should be noted that there is an inconsistency running through the tables in that results of comparisons *within the same study* of multiple measures are sometimes reported separately and sometimes as a single, combined finding. Further, when an investigator has included several samples (for example, various age, subcultural, or cultural groups), the results are again sometimes presented separately and sometimes combined. Finally, when an investigator has used the same procedure in multiple studies, the mode of reporting is again sometimes inconsistent. These variations obviously complicate recognizing the "units" of analysis to be tallied. I have not sought to disentangle these complications, and accordingly the totals shown in Table 2.1 are based on the number of *comparisons* reported by Maccoby and Jacklin. No attempt has been made to weight studies, and for the most part the tabled data include only the areas selected by Maccoby and Jacklin for discussion in their summary conclusions.

As the reader will note, there is wide variability in the standards of evidence—that is, in the ratios influencing the conclusions about a particular empirical data base. The results of this table suggest that sex differences may be more pervasive than the conclusions of Maccoby and Jacklin imply. In particular, those personality-relevant findings characterized by them as "equivocal" seem often to be as uniform in their implications as those findings said by them to be "well established," especially when the studies they omitted are included. Thus, for example, dominance is included among those personality characteristics said to be "open questions." However, earlier in their discussion of dominance, the authors concluded: "We have seen that males

*The table appears at the end of the chapter.

tend to be the more dominant sex in the sense of directing more dominance attempts toward one another, toward authority figures, and perhaps toward females as well; it does not follow that females are submissive. It is possible, in fact, that dominance/submission is not a single continuum" (p. 265). In the context of studies on dominance, the introduction of submissiveness is irrelevant and in no way alters the balance of findings suggesting a sex difference in dominance. In terms of the authors' summary evaluation of the empiricism quoted above, it is perplexing that dominance is included among the "open questions."

As I read the evidence included in Table 2.1, I would agree with Maccoby and Jacklin that these data suggest boys and men have greater spatial and quantitative abilities and also are more aggressive. But the data also impress me as indicating that males are better on insight problems requiring restructuring; are more dominant and have a stronger, more potent self-concept; and are more curious and exploring, more active, and more impulsive (when impulsivity is not narrowly construed). I would agree with Maccoby and Jacklin that girls and women score higher on tests of verbal ability. In addition, however, the available data suggest to me that females express more fear, are more susceptible to anxiety, are more lacking in task confidence, seek more help and reassurance, maintain greater proximity to friends, score higher on social desirability, and, at the younger ages at which compliance has been studied, are more compliant with adults. With respect to the issue of sex-differentiated socialization, my extended consideration of the available evidence (Block, 1976a; see Chapter Three) leads me to disagree with Maccoby and Jacklin's view that "the reinforcement contingencies for the two sexes appear to be remarkably similar" (p. 342). Overall, it seems clear that importantly different conclusions can be drawn from the evidence accumulated by Maccoby and Jacklin and that many psychologists will wish to do so.

What shall one conclude about this monumental, yet ambivalence-inducing work? Serious students of sex differences will want to read Maccoby and Jacklin. Their discussion of the problems besetting research on sex differences is perceptive;

their identification of areas of psychological functioning which have been underresearched, or where findings appear especially inconsistent, should motivate and direct investigators toward fruitful new studies; their developmental perspectives, embodied in their discussion of the acquisition of sex role concepts, extend previous theorizing. By attempting to systematize and to order, by raising questions both incisive and intriguing, Maccoby and Jacklin have generated new and provocative hypotheses about sex role development and have helped move the psychological study of sex differences toward the necessary next stage of scientific investigation, the testing of hypotheses. These are consequential contributions.

But insofar as the book is offered, and received, as a reference work, the large problems discussed in preceding pages surround it. Some of these problems derive from the fact of life that reasonable people can disagree, even when science and objectivity are shared values. Also, the very magnitude of the task of identifying sex differences in all major areas of psychological functioning inevitably makes it a risky endeavor. The long, arduous, complicated, technical evaluational process undertaken by the authors in their effort to impose organization on a sprawling, unruly body of data is vulnerable to error and reasonable argument at every step along the way. Unhappy though the task, I have felt compelled, because of the consequentiality of the issues involved, to note errors I have encountered and to introduce alternative interpretations of the data where I believe them warranted. Readers seeking the state of knowledge regarding sex differences and sex similarities will find the Maccoby and Jacklin book a valuable entry point to the scientific literature, but they will need to be wary and discriminating in accepting its conclusions.

Table 2.1. Tallies of Significant Sex-Differentiated Findings
Based on the Maccoby and Jacklin Literature Review.

| | Ratio of significant comparisons to total number of comparisons | | | |
| | Girls and women significantly higher | | Boys and men significantly higher | |
Behavior assessed	Ratio	Proportion	Ratio	Proportion
Sex differences said to be well established by Maccoby and Jacklin				
Verbal abilities				
Tested abilities	37/131	.28	12/131	.09
Spontaneous verbal	8/29	.28	2/29	.07
Spatial abilities				
Analytic	3/64	.05	25/64	.39
Visual nonanalytic	2/36	.06	10/36	.28
Quantitative abilities	6/35	.17	14/35	.40
Agressiveness	5/94	.05	52/94	.55
Evidence said to be equivocal by Maccoby and Jacklin				
Tactile sensitivity	5/13	.38	0/13	.00
Fear, timidity, and anxiety				
Fear and timidity	7/22	.32	0/22	.00
Omissions (3)	10/25	.40	0/25	.00
General anxiety	14/24	.58	0/24	.00
Test anxiety	5/8	.62	0/8	.00
Activity level	3/50	.06	15/50	.30
Omissions (9)	3/59	.05	24/59	.41
Competitiveness	3/24	.12	6/24	.25
Omissions (2)	3/26	.11	8/26	.31
Dominance	2/42	.05	15/42	.36
Omissions (5)	2/47	.04	20/47	.42
Strength and potency of self-concept	0/8	.00	7/8	.88
Compliance	8/16	.50	0/16	.00
Omissions (8)	13/24	.54	1/24	.04
Resistance to temptation (compliance studies only where experimenter instructs subject "don't touch")	5/11	.45	0/11	.00
Nurturance and maternal behaviors				
Helping	4/29	.14	4/29	.14
Donating to charities	3/13	.23	1/13	.08
Sharing	3/16	.19	2/16	.12

Table 2.1. Tallies of Significant Sex-Differentiated Findings
Based on the Maccoby and Jacklin Literature Review, Cont'd.

| | Ratio of significant comparisons to total number of comparisons | | | |
| | Girls and women significantly higher | | Boys and men significantly higher | |
Behavior assessed	Ratio	Proportion	Ratio	Proportion
Beliefs about sex differences said to be unfounded by Maccoby and Jacklin[a]				
Sociability				
Proximity to friends	10/21	.48	2/21	.10
Omissions (2)	12/23	.52	2/23	.09
Positive sociability — adults	3/25	.12	3/25	.12
Positive sociability — peers	1/26	.04	10/26	.38
Omissions (4)	4/30	.13	10/30	.33
Reports of liking for others	11/28	.39	2/28	.07
Omissions (3)	12/31	.39	4/31	.13
Empathy; sensitivity to social cues	7/31	.23	3/31	.10
Suggestibility				
Conformity, compliance with peers	13/53	.25	4/53	.08
Omissions (6)	19/59	.32	4/59	.07
Spontaneous imitation	4/13	.31	0/13	.00
Self-esteem				
Self-esteem (low)	9/40	.22	6/40	.15
Omissions (4)	11/44	.25	7/44	.16
Confidence in task performance	0/15	.00	11/15	.73
Omissions (3)	0/18	.00	14/18	.78
Analytic abilities				
Impulsivity, lack of inhibition	3/37	.08	8/37	.22
Omissions (6)	3/43	.07	14/43	.33
Breaking set responses to "insight" problems (data from text and annotated bibliography only)	0/14	.00	12/14	.86
Anagrams — breaking up words to form new words	4/10	.40	0/10	.00
Descriptive, analytic sorting style (data from test only)	0/6	.00	1/6	.17
Achievement orientation	5/23	.22	4/23	.17
Auditorially oriented	6/26	.23	2/26	.08

Table 2.1. Tallies of Significant Sex-Differentiated Findings
Based on the Maccoby and Jacklin Literature Review, Cont'd.

| | Ratio of significant comparisons to total number of comparisons | | | |
| | Girls and women significantly higher | | Boys and men significantly higher | |
Behavior assessed	Ratio	Proportion	Ratio	Proportion
Areas not included in overall summary				
Dependency				
Proximity to parent	8/48	.17	7/48	.15
Proximity to nonfamily adult	5/21	.24	2/21	.10
Attention seeking	2/6	.33	1/6	.17
Other studies of dependency from annotated bibliography, including rating studies	13/13	1.00	0/13	.00
Curiosity and exploration	4/21	.19	6/21	.29
Omissions (8)	4/29	.14	14/29	.48
Social desirability	7/9	.78	0/9	.00

Note: Comparisons yielding nonsignificant sex differences are not included.
[a]Two areas, "Differential Effects of Heredity and Environment" and "Repetitive vs. Complex Task Performance," included in this category are not tabled. Hereditary and environmental influences are discussed in the text and the data do not lend themselves to tabling. The evaluation of sex differences in task performance is given in numerous tables, where, in each case, few differences were found.

Chapter Three

Parental and Societal Influences on Sex Role

It has been prevalently believed, by professionals and laypersons alike, that boys and girls in our society are socialized differently and in ways that encourage behavior consistent with our cultural definitions of appropriate sex role behaviors. Sex differences in the socialization emphases of parents (mostly mothers) have been described and discussed by many researchers over the years (Barry, Bacon, and Child, 1957; Biller, 1971; Block, 1973; Hartley, 1959a, 1964; Hetherington, 1965, 1967, 1972; McCandless, 1969; Minton, Kagan, and Levine, 1971; Moss, 1967; Mussen, 1969; Sears, Maccoby, and Levin, 1957). However, after their comprehensive review of the literature with respect to the differential socialization hypothesis, Maccoby and Jacklin (1974) offered the summary evaluation that "our survey of the research on socialization of the two sexes has revealed surprisingly little differentiation in parent behavior according to the sex of the child. However, there are some areas where differential 'shaping' does appear to occur" (pp. 338-339).

Originally published in F. L. Denmark and J. Sherman (Eds.), *Psychology of Women: Future Directions for Research* (New York: Psychological Dimensions, Inc., 1979), under the title "Another Look at Sex Differentiation in the Socialization Behaviors of Mothers and Fathers." Reprinted, revised, and adapted, by permission of the publisher.

These conclusions by Maccoby and Jacklin will be com-
forting to some but are startling to many. Because of the reputation of these researchers, the large number of studies reviewed,
and the expressed caution surrounding their conclusions, it may
be expected that their evaluation of the empirical literature will
come to be the prevalent view of this important psychological
issue and will influence subsequent directions of research, theoretical conceptualizations, and even social policy. Because of
the potential impact of Maccoby and Jacklin's conclusions, it is
important to evaluate closely and carefully the empirical base
from which their interpretations derived. Unfortunately, psychological research on socialization has been characterized by
problems and deficiencies that permit the conclusions drawn by
Maccoby and Jacklin. Some recognition of these deficiencies,
therefore, is useful for keeping open inquiry on the existence
and nature of socialization differences.

The first section of the present chapter will develop additional perspectives on the studies bearing on differential socialization summarized by Maccoby and Jacklin. The quality and
cogency of the evidence will be evaluated. The second section
of the chapter will present data on sex-differentiated socialization derived from the self-reports of both mothers and fathers,
as well as from the perceptions of parental rearing practices
held by young adults. The results of these studies will then be
compared to the Maccoby and Jacklin conclusions. Finally, I
will offer some suggestions for new directions in research in the
area of socialization—directions informed by our past failures
and catalyzed by the provocative summary of Maccoby and
Jacklin.

The Evidence as Evaluated by Maccoby and Jacklin

In collating the results of studies that bear on the differential socialization of boys and girls, Maccoby and Jacklin reviewed close to 200 published studies and evaluated parental behaviors in eleven different domains. Their conclusions about the
empirical support or lack of support for the differential socialization hypothesis in each domain are summarized as follows.

1. No systematic differences are found in the amount of total interaction parents have with girls and with boys (although they note a "consistent trend" for parents to stimulate gross motor activity more in sons than in daughters) or in parental responses to the child's manifestations of sexuality (asking questions, engaging in sex play, masturbating).

2. Inconsistent findings are said to characterize studies assessing the amount of verbal interaction when parent/son and parent/daughter dyads are compared; studies of parental reactions to aggression; and investigations of parental pressures for achievement in boys and in girls.

3. Little or no evidence of sex-differentiated parental behaviors is reported in relation to parental warmth and nurturance, parental restrictiveness, and parental reactions to the child's dependent behaviors.

4. Significant differences in parental behaviors as a function of the child's sex were found in only three socialization areas: parental encouragement of sex-typed activities, greater pressure for appropriate sex role behavior being exerted on boys; the use of negative reinforcements, both physical and nonphysical, which was found to be significantly more characteristic of parents of boys; and the use of praise and other positive reinforcements, which also was more characteristic of parents of boys.

On the basis of the review of the socialization literature offered by Maccoby and Jacklin, few differences appear to characterize parental socialization emphases for the two sexes. Despite these negative conclusions, however, the authors did find evidence that parents tend to "shape" their male and female children in sex-appropriate ways by dressing them differently, by encouraging sex-typed interests, by providing sex-appropriate toys, and by assigning sex-differentiated chores. After searching the empirical data for evidence of sex-differentiated techniques used in the "shaping" process, the authors concluded, "We must summarize our analysis of this [shaping] hypothesis with the conclusion that we have been able to find very little evidence to support it, in relation to behaviors other than sex typing as very narrowly defined [for example, toy preference].

The reinforcement contingencies for the two sexes appear to be remarkably similar" (p. 342).

Parental sex-typing behaviors, however, even narrowly defined when viewed in the context of self- and sex role development, may have important implications. For example, Whiting and Edwards (1975) described one process by which sex-assigned chores may contribute to later behavioral differences noted between boys and girls. Citing data obtained from field studies in six cultures, they noted that girls, more frequently than boys, are assigned domestic and childcare chores (looking after young children, cooking, cleaning, food preparation, grinding) and that girls are assigned responsibilities at an earlier age than boys. Boys, in contrast, are assigned chores that take them from the immediate vicinity of the house, and are given responsibility (albeit at a later age) for feeding, pasturing, and herding animals. For boys and girls, these sex differences in assigned work are associated with different frequencies of interaction with various categories of people (for example, adults, infants, peers). Girls interact more often with both adults and infants, whereas boys interact significantly more often with peers. Whiting and Edwards suggested that to some extent the observed behavioral differences between boys and girls in their samples might be a function of sex distinctions in assigned chores. Younger girls in all cultures were found to be significantly more nurturant (offering help and giving support) and significantly more responsible than boys. In later childhood, girls remained more nurturant, but responsibility no longer differentiated girls from boys, because boys showed a significant increase in initiative—an increase occurring after they began to take care of the pasturing and herding of animals. Although conjectural, this analysis is highly plausible and draws attention to the possibility that a seemingly peripheral aspect of sex-typed socialization—chore assignments—may have broader implications.

Viewed from another, quite different perspective, these parental shaping behaviors urging the child toward sex-appropriate interests, activities, tasks, and the like may be seen as *labeling* behaviors. According to the cognitive-developmental theory of sex typing as explicated by Kohlberg (1966) and endorsed by

Maccoby and Jacklin (1974), sex typing is initiated by the very early labeling of the child with respect to gender. The gender label becomes an organizing rubric around which the child actively, selectively, and with increasing complexity constructs a personal sex role definition. Through experience with parents, siblings, and peers, with the outside world, with the media, and with books, the child learns—through a variety of techniques including environmental manipulation, tutoring, and reinforcement—those responses, interests, activities, clothes, play materials, and tasks that are deemed consistent with sex role categorization. Viewed from this perspective, the process of parental sex typing conveys information to the child that is essential for the cognitive construction of his or her sex role concept. The consequences of parental sex role "shaping" behaviors—conjoined with other documented differences in the use of positive and negative reinforcement and parental pressures exerted on boys to avoid sex-inappropriate behaviors—constitute important evidence for sex-differentiated socialization emphases. It would be most unfortunate to conclude that because of the incoherence of the available research literature and the ephemerality of the specific processes parents use in shaping their children, differences in the way parents socialize their sons and daughters do not exist. Rather, the empirical inconsistencies characterizing studies of sex-differentiated parental socialization behaviors should stimulate close diagnostic evaluation of the adequacy of the literature in the socialization domain. The conceptualizations, operational indexes, and research designs employed must be scrutinized closely. It is to this task we turn.

A Second Look at the Evidence

Several general problems—both theoretical and methodological—besetting the socialization literature have contributed to a premature embracing of the null hypothesis about divergence in childrearing emphases as a function of sex. At a conceptual level, we have not yet developed a coherent formulation of the socialization process that permits specific and differentiated predictions about socialization practices as a function of the child's developmental level, the environmental context of the family, or parental role concepts. And, in our empirical efforts, research has tended to be of an ad hoc or after-the-fact nature rather than targeted toward areas where, conceptually, differences might be expected. Socialization studies frequently have depended on globally defined concepts, which may operate to obscure differences that might be revealed if more differentiated criteria were used. Because these shortcomings have implications for the ways in which we may interpret the Maccoby and Jacklin compilation of the socialization literature, they will be discussed in some detail.

Theories of socialization (including sex role socialization) make implicit assumptions about developmental shifts in socialization emphases, as a function of both age and sex; however, research efforts have only infrequently been concerned with documenting and articulating these developmental trends. Emmerich (1973) noted that the search for organizing processes in sex role socialization calls for research studies designed to permit explicit age-related comparisons. Parental socialization emphases are dynamic and responsive to the changing environmental demands, to the emerging competence and responsibility of the child, and to reorganizing conceptions of the parental role over time. The particular circumstances in our society that contribute to different environmental contexts for boys and girls as they progress from nursery school to elementary school, to high school, and to the threshold of adulthood also create different situational "press" for parents that may be expected to contribute to sex-related divergence in their childrearing patterns over time.

In one of the few longitudinal studies documenting changes in maternal behaviors as a function of the child's development between nine and eighteen months, Clarke-Stewart (1973) reported significant changes. The child's increasing independence was accompanied by a decrease in maternal attention, as reflected by less physical contact, less caretaking, less social stimulation, and more leaving the child alone. Mothers were observed to institute more negative sanctions (punishment and scolding) with increasing age of the child. As the children ap-

proached eighteen months of age, mothers became more directive, more effective in their interventions, and more responsive
to their children's behavioral expressions, particularly in the social realm.

Reference to the Fels Institute longitudinal data, which
assessed maternal behaviors at three time periods (zero to three
years, three to six years, six to ten years), provides additional
evidence of changing socialization foci with the increasing age
of the child (Kagan and Moss, 1962). Not only is a shift shown
in the salience of particular childrearing practices associated
with age-related demand characteristics of the child from birth
to age ten, but with time maternal behaviors became more stable, and sex-differentiated patterns of maternal behavior are
suggested (pp. 207–209).

Two later studies have extended the sparse literature related to developmental trends in socialization. In a cross-sectional study including 342 children in grades one through four
who were administered the Child's Report of the Parental Behavior Inventory (PBI) (Schaefer, 1965), changes in children's
perceptions of parental childrearing behavior as a function of
age were found (Burger, Lamp, and Rogers, 1975). Perceptions
of both maternal and paternal behaviors on the acceptance/
rejection factor showed a significant decrease in acceptance
with age (from grades two to four for fathers and from grades
three to four for mothers); perceptions of parental behaviors on
the autonomy-versus-control factor showed a significant decrease in psychological control with age, with scores at each
level lower than those of the preceding grade level for both
mothers and fathers; and on the firm-versus-lax-control factor, a
significant increase in the firmness of both parents was found
from grades two through four. The results of this study show
significant developmental shifts in the children's perception of
parental rearing practices on each of the three factors constitut-
ing the PBI.

In the other study, parental socialization values were assessed among parents of forty-four preadolescent and adolescent boys by recording a discussion between parents and son
about the meaning of the proverb "A rolling stone gathers no

moss" (Jacob and others, 1975). A growth interpretation of the proverb, emphasizing the value of development through mobility, exploration, and striving, was more frequently endorsed by parents of preadolescent boys than was a stability interpretation, emphasizing the attainment of security through maintaining close and long-lasting relationships. Among parents of adolescent boys, however, there was a shift, primarily among upper-middle-class parents, toward the stability interpretation of the proverb. This shift is interpretable, according to the authors, as an expression of parental anxiety occasioned by challenges to their value systems by questioning adolescent sons for whom it is feared the alternative life-styles of the counterculture may be seductive. These results are intriguing, and therefore the study deserves replication with larger samples to include daughters as well. The findings suggest a shift in the focal anxieties and concerns of parents as they become older and as their children become older and are exposed to more, different, and less controllable (by parents) influences.

In commenting on the existing studies of differential socialization, Maccoby and Jacklin (1974) noted the predominance of studies in which parental socialization orientations were assessed while children were still quite young. They suggest that this age bias derives in part from an assumption of declining parental influence once the child enters school, where teachers and peers become salient socialization agents, and in part from an assumption that greater plasticity characterizes the young child. These assumptions imply that parental socialization is conceived by many researchers as a relatively static phenomenon, more readily observable during the child's early years. In Maccoby and Jacklin's comprehensive listing of studies, 77 percent of all investigations cited were based on the result of analyses comparing the socialization of boys and girls five years of age and younger.

But perhaps such young human offspring are treated more as children than as boys and girls. I suggest that it is simply unreasonable to expect that sex-related *differences* in socialization will be expressed by parents toward very young children in the areas of emphasis on achievement, control of aggression, amount of parental interaction, parental supervision of the child's activities, tolerance for sexuality, or responses to dependency. Some areas (for example, achievement emphasis, tolerance for sexuality) have not yet become salient for differential socialization, and in other areas (for example, dependency, aggression), tolerances perhaps have not yet been strained.

If we consider the results issuing from only the minority of studies (23 percent) assessing the socialization behaviors of parents of older children (age six or older), we may find a clear trend toward more frequent sex-differential parental behaviors. This trend becomes more pronounced when studies based on very small samples are excluded. However, with respect to certain psychological dimensions, age trends cannot be evaluated for two reasons: No subjects older than five have been included in research studies assessing total parental interaction with the child or stimulation of gross motor behavior, and no subjects older than age six have been included in studies assessing parental tolerance for dependency or parental response to aggression.

This age range limitation in socialization research suggests that an important qualifier be appended to conclusions drawn from this body of data, to wit: *The differential socialization hypothesis has been examined primarily (and for some areas exclusively) in samples of parents whose children were six years old and under.* The Maccoby and Jacklin review starkly reveals the disproportionate research emphasis on socialization of young children and suggests the need for systematic studies of differential socialization among parents of older children. These studies would seek to identify the nature of the relationship between socialization emphases, the stimulus value of the child (of which sex and age are determinants), and the situational press (of which sex and age are determinants).

A second factor contributing to the essentially null conclusions drawn from studies evaluated by Maccoby and Jacklin is the tendency of most socialization research to focus on the mother as the critical socializing agent. Maccoby and Jacklin note the lack of information about fathers and recognize that this omission could be a source of bias because fathers may differentiate between the sexes in their childrearing orientations to a greater extent than do mothers. Inferences drawn from studies of the effect of father absence on sex role typing in males (for example, Biller, 1971; Hetherington, 1966; McCord, McCord, and Thurber, 1962; Tiller, 1958) and the impact of the father on personality and sex role development in males (Mussen and Distler, 1959; Nash, 1965; Payne and Mussen, 1956) and in females (Block, von der Lippe, and Block, 1973; Heilbrun, Harrel, and Gillard, 1967; Hetherington, 1972) underscore the importance of the father and suggest that his socialization emphases for boys and for girls be studied more systematically.

In the studies contributing to the Maccoby and Jacklin evaluation of differential socialization for boys and girls, mothers as respondents account for 49 percent of the studies, fathers as respondents are the focus of inquiry in only 9 percent of the cited studies, and 30 percent of the studies, including those based on child reports, have attempted to document the socialization orientations of both parents. The remaining 12 percent of the studies summarized depended on teacher or caretaker responses to the child. Since fathers themselves were involved in only a small percentage of the total number of research studies reported, it could well be that evaluations of differential socialization effects are underestimated by virtue of the undersampling of paternal behaviors that has been typical of socialization research. References to the data pertaining only to fathers' socialization emphases as reflected in the results of the studies reviewed by Maccoby and Jacklin suggest that the father/daughter relationship is characterized by more warmth than is the father/son relationship; that fathers of boys are more firm, in contrast to fathers of girls; that fathers appear more concerned about the welfare of their daughters than of their sons; that fathers tend more to provide comfort when their daughters are upset than when their sons seek comfort; that fathers tend more to expect aggressiveness and competitiveness in their sons than in their daughters; and that fathers are more accepting of verbal aggression directed against them by their daughters than by their sons. By focusing explicitly and solely on the socialization emphases of fathers, some trends obscured in the results of studies aggregating both parents become apparent, suggesting that fathers may be more sex-differentiating than mothers in their interpersonal and socialization behaviors.

It is insufficient, however, only to conclude that fathers as well as mothers should be included in socialization studies. It is required, as well, that our theories of socialization become more articulated with respect to the particular contribution of each parent to the socialization process. If parental socialization roles vary in their degree of sex differentiation with respect to specific areas, then our failure to sample the behaviors of the parent who primarily assumes responsibility for socialization in a particular area represents another source of potential bias. Investigations of differential socialization using a teaching strategy paradigm, for example, have only infrequently included fathers as well as mothers.

The results of a study by Block, Block, and Harrington (1974) suggest that the failure to find consistent differences in the socialization of boys and girls in the achievement domain may be a function of the failure to study fathers' behaviors in the achievement-relevant context. These investigators assessed the teaching behaviors of both mothers ($N = 117$) and fathers ($N = 96$), who each separately taught their child a battery of four cognitive tasks varying in their convergent/divergent demand characteristics. Two parallel test batteries were developed for use by parents, and a counterbalanced design was used to control for order of teaching and test battery. In all cases a minimum of five weeks separated the experimental teaching situations of the two parents, each of whom was always interviewed by different examiners.

The data of interest in the study are the Q-sort observations completed by the examiners to describe the parents' behaviors in the teaching situations. Summarizing the results of t-test comparisons between mothers of girls and of boys, we found that the teaching style of mothers did not differentiate between the sexes; only one of the forty-nine Q-sort items significantly discriminated the sexes. Fathers, however, were found to manifest different teaching behaviors depending on the child's sex, and 14 percent of the t-test comparisons between fathers of boys and fathers of girls were significant at or beyond the .05 level. Fathers of sons were more concerned with achievement and emphasized the cognitive aspects of the teaching situation, whereas the fathers of daughters appeared to be more attuned to the interpersonal aspects and were less concerned with performance *per se*. The latter attempted to make the situation more fun, were more protective, and were less pressuring of their daughters. We concluded, "The items differentiating fathers of boys from fathers of girls clearly suggest that achievement emphasis [in the teaching strategy situation] is a more salient characteristic of the father/son than of the father/ daughter relationship."

The results from this study concur with the data summarized by Maccoby and Jacklin with reference to achievement, where mothers were found not to differentiate between the sexes in their pressures for achievement. Their results also agree with those of two of the three studies cited by Maccoby and Jacklin, in which fathers' pressures for *cognitive* achievement were evaluated. Together, these findings suggest an alternative interpretation of the data surrounding achievement emphasis, which recognizes that *cognitive* achievement may be a less salient socialization domain for mothers relative to fathers, that mothers are less sex-differentiating in their pressures for cognitive achievement, and that fathers tend to be more pressuring of their sons than of their daughters for cognitive achievement. Generally, these results emphasize the importance of differentiating not only the sex of the child but also parental roles with respect to particular areas of socialization.

Another source of potential bias in the accumulated findings bearing on the differential socialization issue is concerned with construct definition and operationalization. In collating research findings derived from heterogeneous measures tapping different domains of childrearing behaviors, a two-stage sequence of construct definition is involved. At the first stage, the operations of the investigator are crucial. Having decided to study a particular phenomenon or process, the investigator must define the construct, specify its expected behavioral manifestations, and select appropriate procedures of measurement. If a construct is too globally or equivocally defined, subsequent results may be blurred and inconclusive. Consider the concept of dependency, for example. This umbrella concept is not unidimensional, but as usually conceived, it embodies components of the inability to sustain oneself without aid from others, the inability to cope with a problem, lack of psychological autonomy, subordination, and docility (Block and Christiansen, 1966). As operationalized, measures of dependency include proximity seeking, attention seeking, reassurance seeking, and help seeking; the resulting correlations among these various aspects of dependency are uniformly low (Martin, 1975). The low interrelations among these different behavioral expressions of dependency are hardly surprising if one considers that behaviors may be alternatively manifested. That is, the expression of dependent behaviors in one domain may render unnecessary (particularly in the case of a responsive environment) their expression in other ways, thus accounting for the low correlations typically observed. In the case of the low relationship among variables presumed to index different aspects of a concept, the use of differentiated measures becomes crucial if we are to find consistencies in our empirical data.

In a study cited by Maccoby and Jacklin, Hilton (1967) noted, in summarizing the findings derived from observing mothers' behaviors while their first- or later-born children were completing a puzzle task, "The sex differences which do arise do not lend themselves to parsimonious explanation. In some areas boys were more dependent and in others the girls were. It may be that parents tolerate dependency in boys in some areas (asking for help) but not in others (clinging). The dependency is present in both sexes, but the form in which it is manifested varies" (p. 228). When parental behaviors in response to the child's request for help and in response to the child's clinging are *both* taken as indicators of dependency, cross-sex comparisons of mean scores will issue null findings as a function of the global nature of the concept definition. If, however, parental behaviors were studied *separately* with reference to help seeking and to clinging, significant differences previously obscured would have the opportunity to emerge.

At the second stage of construct definition, the classification scheme developed by the collators becomes crucial. When research results achieved with a variety of instruments, tapping different phenomena, are brought together in order to assess the empirical data base surrounding a particular construct, what criteria should be used for categorizing the existing studies with reference to the construct? In grouping studies under the rubric of "achievement" or "permissiveness for dependency" or "restrictiveness," how should we decide which studies properly relate to which construct? Should studies assessing parental pressures for developing competence be merged with those evaluating parental concerns for the achievement of long-range goals? As demonstrated in cognitive-style studies of categorization behavior, the clarity and cohesiveness of a category are a function of the width of category boundaries. With broad category boundaries, cohesiveness is more difficult and even impossible to achieve.

In the present context, the category boundaries established for the inclusion of particular studies in a domain can powerfully affect subsequent interpretation. The task of sorting studies is not an easy one and, generally, Maccoby and Jacklin attempted to stay close to the data. Nevertheless, the null conclusions they reported for some areas of socialization might simply be a function of the heterogeneity of the dependent measures they grouped together. (One example, discussed in detail in Chapter Two, is the Maccoby-Jacklin handling of studies nominally relating to parental pressures for achievement.)

It is imperative, therefore, that the posited interpretations of a particular measure be supported by evidence of both convergent and discriminating relationships that exclude alternative interpretations. When one considers how infrequently the validity of psychological instruments is established rather than declared, it is little wonder that many of the findings in the socialization literature are inconsistent and even incoherent.

I suggest further that evidence for differential socialization can be obscured by aggregating and weighting equally studies widely divergent in statistical power. In reaching conclusions about sex-differentiated socialization pressures, Maccoby and Jacklin relied on a "box score" approach wherein both the positive and the null findings issuing from comparisons between parents of girls and parents of boys on dependent measures are grouped together without regard for the psychometric quality or statistical power of the respective studies.

The power of a statistical test is a function of three parameters: the "effect size," which in this context means the size of the difference between the population of parents of boys and the population of parents of girls with respect to a measured phenomenon; the number of cases being evaluated; and the significance criterion set for the rejection of the null hypothesis (Cohen, 1969). To the extent that measures of parental socialization attitudes and behaviors—whether indexed by interviews, questionnaires, or laboratory or home observations—are unreliable or irrelevant, the effect size will become small and therefore undetectable.

When this source of power reduction is compounded by the employment of small samples, the power of a statistical test is further reduced, increasing the likelihood of falsely accepting the null hypothesis of no difference. A false acceptance of the null hypothesis will lead us to conclude, in the present context, that no differences (have been proved to) exist between parents of boys and parents of girls in their socialization behaviors. However, improvement in the quality of the measures employed, and the use of efficient research designs, could well result in the discernment of relationships not presently observed, or noted only inconsistently.

When the studies listed by Maccoby and Jacklin as dealing with differential socialization are evaluated with respect to only one aspect of statistical power (sample size), wide differences in the power of the studies are apparent. Of all studies contributing to the conclusion that there is little evidence for sex-related socialization, 43 percent are based on total sample sizes of sixty or fewer, yielding a maximum of thirty cases per subgroup. Coupled with the unreliability or irrelevance of many of the measures employed, these small sample sizes make it probable that many of the studies are so lacking in power that they are incapable of reflecting "true" population differences, thus leading us down the path of the Type II error.

I suggest that, in the absence of socialization theories that articulate differences in childrearing practices expectable as a function of age, sex, the child's environmental context, and parental role definitions, the critical research studies have not been completed. It is unrealistic to expect that similar socialization emphases will be characteristic of mothers and fathers across a variety of areas—across age levels, across contexts, and across sex of the child. A more complex model of socialization is required in order that we may develop differentiated hypotheses about differential socialization emphases. Methodological problems also have limited the implications of many of the studies cited. Small sample sizes, unreliability of instruments, and lack of construct validity have operated, both singly and conjointly, to reduce the power or cogency of many studies. Finally, it should be emphasized that the fact of *inconsistency* in research findings surrounding the differential socialization hypothesis does not imply that there are no differences in parental behavior. Rather, the inconsistency implies that we do not understand the reasons for this inconsistency.

With more differentiated hypotheses, with more reliable and construct-valid measures, with more appropriate sampling, and with better statistical design, we can reasonably expect that the findings on differential socialization will become more coherent. If well-executed comparisons of the socialization emphases of parents of boys and of girls uniformly yielded null (in contrast to inconsistent) findings, then the null hypothesis could be accepted more comfortably as a reasonable summary position. But on the basis of the research evidence now available, as reported in the Maccoby and Jacklin (1974) review volume, I suggest that the question remains moot.

Some Data to Encourage Exploration
of New Directions

I turn now to consider some data comparing the childrearing orientations, values, and techniques of both mothers and fathers from two different perspectives: parental self-report and perceptions of parental rearing practices by young adults. A standard instrument, the Block Child-Rearing Practices Report (CRPR) (Block, 1965) was administered to samples varying with respect to cultural and subcultural origins, age, sex, and health status of the child. In all, data from seventeen independent samples comprising 696 mothers, 548 fathers, and 1,227 young adults were brought together for the present analyses and evaluation.

The CRPR consists of ninety-one socialization-relevant items, which the respondent evaluates with reference to a specific, designated child in the case of the First-Person Parent form and with reference to a designated parent in the case of the Third-Person Parent form of the test. To minimize the operation of response sets, the CRPR is administered using a Q-sort format. Each of the ninety-one items is assigned to one of seven categories, depending on its salience to the respondent.

The CRPR was administered to six samples of mothers and to five samples of fathers whose children ranged in age from three to twenty years and who were heterogeneous with respect to ethnic and socioeconomic backgrounds. Additionally, the CRPR was administered to six samples of young adults attending universities and technical colleges in each of six countries (United States, England, Finland, Norway, Sweden, and Denmark). These young people described the childrearing emphases of their mothers, using the third-person form, and in the case of the United States sample only, they described the childrearing emphases of their fathers as well.

The kind of information generated by the CRPR is heavily represented in the research on differential socialization reviewed by Maccoby and Jacklin, where 40 percent of the studies cited depended on parent or child responses to a questionnaire or interview. In the present context, the use of a standard instrument for evaluating childrearing orientations has a distinct advantage. Maccoby and Jacklin were faced with the problem of interpreting data derived from noncomparable procedures varying in domain coverage, format, vulnerability to response sets, and psychometric quality. It may be instructive, therefore, to look again at the differential socialization hypothesis, using an instrument that has extensive domain coverage and good relia bility, which minimizes response sets and has been applied widely.

My purposes in presenting these data are three: (1) to examine sex-related socialization behaviors from the differing perspectives of mothers, fathers, and children, (2) to present a data base that may suggest some more-differentiated hypotheses about the socialization of boys and girls, hypotheses differentiated with respect to developmental trends, construct definition, and parental roles, and (3) to keep open and stimulate further inquiry into the question of differential socialization until the more inclusive and systematic studies required in this field have been completed.

The CRPR data were analyzed within each of the six samples of mothers by comparing, by means of t tests, the responses of the mothers of sons and the mothers of daughters for each of the ninety-one items. Similarly, within each sample of fathers, t-test comparisons of the responses of the fathers of sons and the fathers of daughters were completed. The results of these comparisons within each of the eleven parent samples, as well as the combined probabilities calculated across the six independent samples of mothers and the five independent samples of fathers (Winer, 1971), are presented in Table 3.1.*

To guide the reader through Table 3.1 some explanation is in order. The column entries indicate the direction of the mean difference between parents of sons (S) and parents of daughters (D); trends toward significance, indicated by S+ or D+, designate t ratios in excess of 1.00 but less than the 1.67 required for $p < .10$; when appropriate, the probability levels of the t-test comparisons (.01, .05, and .10) are given as cell entries. This method of data presentation was adopted in order to reveal cross-sample consistencies that might otherwise be neglected by the usual dichotomous practice of reporting only those results wherein the null hypothesis is rejected.

In order to facilitate the detection of age trends that might characterize the data, Samples 1 through 5 are ordered according to the increasing mean ages of the children. Sample 6

*Tables appear at the end of the chapter.

includes mothers and fathers from the Netherlands; the mean age of children in these samples is between those of Samples 3 and 4. The numerical designations of the samples of parents denote mother/father dyads; that is, the mothers and fathers in Samples 1, 2, 4, 5, and 6 are, for the most part, spouses, but some single parents are represented as well. Sample 3 includes only mothers. Sample 2 comprises parents of children with chronic illnesses. Sample 5 has the highest socioeconomic level and is composed of parents of college and university students.

Before abstracting the results based on parents' self-described childrearing orientations, I shall present the data derived from the study of college and university students in six countries. These students described their perceptions of their mothers' childrearing values and practices, and the students in the United States sample also gave their perceptions of paternal childrearing orientations. These data are presented in Table 3.2, and the same conventions used in Table 3.1 for reporting results are applied. Combined probabilities are reported only for the descriptions of maternal practices, since father descriptions were obtained from one student sample only.

In order to bring together the data from the four perspectives (mothers' self-descriptions, fathers' self-descriptions, young adults' perceptions of mothers, and young adults' perceptions of fathers) in a form that permits an overall comparison of the consistencies and inconsistencies of sex-related socialization emphases, a summary of the significant results is presented in Table 3.3. In reviewing this table and in evaluating the results of the several analyses, it is critical to recall that the young adults sampled are *not* the children of the parents participating in the study. Therefore, consistencies across data sources—because of the lack of correspondence between the parent and young adult samples and because of the cultural and subcultural heterogeneities characterizing the samples—are underestimated in the present analyses. Obviously, a more desirable research paradigm would examine consistencies in socialization viewed from the different perspectives of parents and their *own* children. Although cross–data source (parents and students) consistencies are more difficult to discern in the present analyses because of the differences between and unrelatedness of the samples, the results (if achieved) are probably rather robust and permit broader generalizations.

Inspection of the results of these several analyses (*within* the several independent samples of parents presented in Table 3.1, *within* the several independent samples of students presented in Table 3.2, and the combined results summarized in Table 3.3) suggests the following generalizations, which will be discussed later in greater detail.

1. *There is evidence for differential socialization of males and females.* Based on the results of the combined probabilities analyses across the samples of mothers presented in Table 3.1, twenty-six (29 percent) of the CRPR responses are significantly sex-differentiated ($p < .05$) (Block, 1965). For fathers, twenty-three (25 percent) of the CRPR items reveal significant differences between the socialization emphases of fathers of sons and fathers of daughters. For samples of young adults describing the childrearing practices and attitudes of their mothers, fifty-two (57 percent) of the items reflect significant sex-differentiated perceptions of maternal socialization behaviors, as shown in the analyses of combined probabilities presented in Table 3.2. The comparable figure based only on the sample of American students describing their mothers is thirty-one significant items (34 percent). For the American students only, who described their fathers' childrearing practices and values, thirty-three (36 percent) of the items were significantly sex-differentiated.

2. *There is evidence that sex-related socialization emphases are appreciably consistent when viewed from the differing perspectives of mothers, fathers, sons, and daughters.* As shown in Table 3.3, thirty-one (34 percent) of the CRPR items are consistent in the direction of response across all four subject groups, while twenty-nine of these items are both consistent in direction across all samples *and* significantly differentiating in at least one of those analyses. Were we to consider *only* the directional effects, the probability of four independent events occurring in the same direction, as calculated according to the binomial expansion, is $p < .07$, a minimal estimate of the probability in this case because twenty-nine items are also signifi-

cantly different (five items discriminate between sons and daughters in one analysis; eleven items significantly discriminate in two independent comparisons; six significantly differentiate in three independent comparisons; and seven CRPR items significantly differentiate between sons and daughters in all four independent comparisons).

3. *There is evidence of specific, consistent sex-of-parent and sex-of-child effects.* In Table 3.3 the items reflecting specific sex effects are grouped under headings of cross-sex influences, same-sex influences, and specific mother/son, mother/daughter, father/son, and father/daughter influences. An overall summary of the degree of consistency characterizing the data with respect to parental self-reports and the perceptions of independent unrelated samples of students is presented in Table 3.4. Based on all ninety-one CRPR items, we find strong evidence of consistency across independent data sources for both mothers and fathers. For mothers, 49 percent of the items are consistent in direction and significantly differentiating in at least one comparison when their self-reports are compared with the perceptions of maternal practices offered by the samples of unrelated students. The comparable data for fathers reveal that 11 percent of the items are consistent in direction and significant in at least one analysis. Looking at the discrepancies between parental self-reports and the perceptions of students using similar evaluative criteria, only 17 percent of the items for mothers and 12 percent of the items for fathers diverge significantly in direction of response in at least one analysis. These figures represent minimal estimates of agreement, as pointed out earlier, because the parent and student samples are not correspondent.

4. *There is some evidence suggesting that sex differentiation in socialization emphases appears to increase with the age of the child, reaching a maximum during the high school years.* Evidence for this assertion is found in Table 3.1, where the trend toward greater sex differentiation is shown to be consistent in the data for both mothers and fathers (Block, Block, and Harrington, 1974). Only in Sample 2 for fathers, where the power of the statistical test is weak because of small sample size, is there a small departure from the monotonic trend.

5. *There is evidence of consistency in sex-related sociali-*

zation emphases among samples of mothers and samples of fathers heterogeneous with respect to socioeconomic level, education level, cultural origins, and the health status and age levels of their children. Across the six samples of mothers representing the rather diverse backgrounds shown in Table 3.1, sixteen (18 percent) of the CRPR items were answered in the same direction by all six samples. The probability of an item's showing a consistent directional effect across six samples is less than .02. Comparable consistency in response among the five samples of fathers was found on twenty-seven (29 percent) of the CRPR items, yielding a probability with respect to directional effects alone of $p < .03$ for each of these twenty-seven items.

6. *There is evidence of cross-cultural similarities in the sex-differentiated socialization patterns as reflected in students' perceptions of maternal rearing practices.* The relationships observed in student samples—which are relatively homogeneous within each country and comparable across countries (all college students)—are, despite the differences among the participating countries, relatively consistent and coherent. As shown in Table 3.2, nineteen (21 percent) of the items are consistent in direction across all six countries, yielding a probability for the directional effects alone of $p < .02$. When it is also considered that fifteen of the nineteen items yielded sex differences in perceptions of maternal practices that are significant in two or more of the six countries, the cross-cultural consistencies are even more impressive. It is difficult to attribute these consistencies across nations to cultural similarity, since the countries represented vary widely on many demographic indexes—such as the number of employed women (Holter, 1970), suicide and homicide rates (Block and Christiansen, 1966; Hendin, 1965), degree of industrialization and urbanization (Hendin, 1965)—as well as differences in sociopolitical and human values.

7. *There is an indication that the countries represented in the study differ in the extent of emphasis on sex-role differentiation.* If we take as a guide the number of significant differences between sons and daughters in the CRPR descriptions of their mothers, as presented in Table 3.2, the Danish, Swedish, and Finnish students saw fewer distinctions in the socialization

emphases of mothers of sons and mothers of daughters. American, English, and Norwegian students, however, perceived their mothers as engaging more distinctively in sex-related socialization behaviors.

The thrust of these several generalizations underscores the importance of taking a more differentiated view of sex-determined socialization practices. Although there are impressive consistencies in these data, there are differences as well, differences that ultimately may prove lawful.

Having outlined the results from the various comparisons of parental socialization orientations, I can now discuss these substantive findings and relate them to the Maccoby and Jacklin conclusions summarized earlier.

Differential Socialization of Sons

The CRPR data from several independent samples demonstrate first that both mothers and fathers appear to emphasize *achievement and competition* more for their sons than for their daughters. Second, there is strong evidence that both parents encourage their sons, more than their daughters, to *control the expression of affect.* Third, *punishment orientation* is a more salient concern of parents of males than parents of females. Fourth, the differentiating CRPR items suggest a greater emphasis on *independence* or the *assumption of personal responsibility* by parents of males than of females, an emphasis, however, that is more apparent in the responses of fathers than of mothers. Fifth, fathers appear more authoritarian in their rearing of their sons than of their daughters; they are *strict and firm,* believe in physical punishment, and are *less tolerant of sons' aggression* directed against them. Sixth, mothers encourage their sons, more than their daughters, to *conform to external standards,* wanting their sons to make a good impression and to be conforming. Although the particular standards are not elaborated, it may be that these items are manifestations of the generally observed greater parental concern for sex-appropriate behavior in males than in females.

Together, these data support the Maccoby and Jacklin

conclusions that punishment orientation, negative sanctions, and emphasis on conformity (at least in the area of sex appropriateness) is stressed more by the parents of males than by the parents of females. However, the present findings with respect to achievement and competition, independence in the sense of the assumption of personal responsibility, and parent-directed aggression appear stronger, more coherent, and more consistent than in the summary results offered by Maccoby and Jacklin. Control of the expression of affect, an important area of sex-differentiated socialization not addressed in the researches included in the Maccoby and Jacklin volume, emerges strongly from the results of the analyses presented here. Considering the widely held assumption that males in our society are less able to express deeply felt affects, it is surprising that so little empirical attention has been directed to the study of sex-differentiated socialization influences on the expression of affect.

Differential Socialization of Daughters

The parent/daughter relationship is characterized, first, by greater *warmth and physical closeness,* according to the CRPR items significantly differentiating across the several independent samples of the parents of daughters and the parents of sons. Second, both mothers and fathers appear to have greater confidence in the *trustworthiness and truthfulness* of their daughters than of their sons. Third, there is greater expectation by mothers and fathers alike of *"ladylike" behavior* on the part of their daughters. They discourage rough-and-tumble games, mothers particularly expect their daughters to stay clean while playing, and fathers discourage fighting in their daughters more than in their sons. Fourth, there is expressed by both parents a *greater reluctance to punish* their daughters than their sons. Fifth, mothers' childrearing practices are more sex-differentiated with respect to *restrictiveness and supervision* of their daughters than of their sons. Sixth, daughters, more than sons, are encouraged by both parents to *wonder and think about life.* Interpretation of this last, isolated finding is a bit hazardous, but when considered in combination with fathers' expressed attempts to include daughters, more than sons, in discussions of family plans, the greater perception of tolerance for daydreaming by women students, and parental encouragement for daughters to discuss their problems, what may be being expressed is a focus on communal familial concerns in the socialization of females, a focus that has been described by other investigators (Bakan, 1966; Carlson, 1971a).

The findings on the differential socialization emphases of parents of daughters and parents of sons accord with the results of Barry, Bacon, and Child (1957), who reported significant and consistent sex-related socialization emphases in a variety of cultures, with girls more pressured to be nurturant, obedient, and responsible and boys more pressured to achieve and be self-reliant. However, the present findings diverge from the summary conclusions about differential socialization offered by Maccoby and Jacklin. Parental warmth, a salient characteristic of the mother/daughter relationship as assessed by the CRPR, was not found to differentiate the sexes in the studies forming the data base for the Maccoby and Jacklin conclusions. The present findings of restriction and supervision for daughters are both more clear and more implicative than is apparent in the results and discussion of chaperonage provided by Maccoby and Jacklin. Restrictive parental behaviors are associated, especially in the perceptions of daughters, with parental anxiety, worry, and concern about the misfortunes that can befall young women as they grow up. The affective implications of restrictiveness-in-the-context-of-anxiety might be expected to have pervasive and persistent consequences, urging caution as women seek self-definition and project long-term goals. Finally, the greater discouragement of aggression in girls compared with boys represents another area in which the present findings diverge from the summary conclusions of Maccoby and Jacklin.

Perceptions of Parental Rearing Practices

Comparing the childrearing orientations of mothers as they are perceived by male and female students in several countries has provided evidence of both cross-cultural and cross-perspective (parental self-descriptions and student perceptions) continuities. According to the perceptions of students, sons more than daughters described *both parents* as emphasizing *competition,* encouraging *control of the expression of affect,* demonstrating more concern about *punishment,* emphasizing *control of impulse* with respect to sex, being uneasy about the *consequences of affection on the development of masculinity,* concerned about *health issues,* emphasizing *early achievement of particular developmental landmarks* (weaning in the case of mothers, toilet training in the case of fathers), and *obtaining satisfactions* from the parent/son relationship. Additionally, mothers were described by their sons, more than by their daughters, as being more proscriptive, as exerting more *control on the expression of aggression,* as being concerned about *others' impression of their sons,* and as attempting to *isolate their sons from values diverging from their own.* Fathers were also perceived by their sons, more than by their daughters, as *emphasizing responsibilities* and as *sacrificing some of their own interests* for their children. Overall, the relationship between parents and sons, viewed from the vantage point of the son, is characterized by a variety of expectations—insistence on the control of both impulse and affect expression, salience of punishment-related concerns, and anxiety about health-related issues.

Looking now at the depictions of the parent/daughter relationship through the perceptions of young women students, we find that daughters, more than sons, described *both parents* as *emphasizing affection and physical closeness, believing in* their daughters' *truthfulness, encouraging introspection* (wonder and daydreaming), *keeping close track* of their daughters, *being relaxed about sex typing,* having a more *playful relationship* characterized by both joking and teasing, and being more *indulgent.* The mother/daughter relationship is described as somewhat *ambivalent.* Mothers are seen as warm, trusting, interested in and respecting of their daughters, encouraging discussion of problems at the same time that they are perceived as forgetting promises, expressing anger, feeling conflicted, and being somewhat disappointed in their daughters. Mothers are also seen as *encouraging independence,* both as differentiation from the parent and in the making of decisions. Fathers are characterized by their daughters as encouraging the *develop-ment of "ladylike" behaviors,* as *being anxious* about them, as *sorry to see them grow up,* and as finding the *administration of punishment difficult.* Overall, the relationship between parents and daughters, viewed from the perspective of the daughter, is characterized by an emphasis on interaction, physical closeness, encouragement of introspection, and less concern with prohi-bitions and punishments. In the mother/daughter relationship, the mothers were also perceived both as ambivalent and as en-couraging differentiation. In the father/daughter relationship, the fathers were additionally described as encouraging feminin-ity, as regretful of seeing their daughters grow up, as reluctant to punish them, and as being anxious about them.

It is clear that many of the socialization themes charac-terizing the students' perceptions of the parent/son and parent/ daughter relationships have much in common with the self-reported childrearing emphases of parents. With sons, parents encourage competition, foster control of affect and impulse expression, urge the assumption of responsibility, are oriented toward punishment, and are concerned about the impression created by their sons. These parental qualities are also to be dis cerned in the descriptions given by independent and unrelated samples of sons characterizing the socialization emphases of their parents. With daughters, parents emphasize closeness, are trusting, display a vigilant interest in their activities, encourage "ladylike" behaviors, encourage introspection, and are reluc-tant to punish. These qualities are also to be found in the de-scriptions of parental socialization practices offered by the independent and unrelated samples of daughters.

Discrepancies Between Parent Self-Reports and Student Perceptions

Because few researches have explored the congruence be-tween parental self-reports and perceptions of parental child-rearing values held by offspring, it may be instructive to look explicitly at the items on which there are significant disagree-ments between the two data sources.

In the present study, as shown in Table 3.4, there are

rather few significant deviations in direction of response when parent self-reports are compared with student perceptions of parental childrearing orientations. The items where there are statistically significant discrepancies between the two data sources are collected in Table 3.5.

Looking at Table 3.5, it appears that when parental responses are significantly sex-differentiated and also deviate from the perceptions of students, the like-sex parent/child relationship is involved. Thus, mothers describe themselves as encouraging feminine behaviors in their daughters, as exerting authority and close supervision, and as being reluctant to administer punishment. These items suggest a more authoritarian mother/daughter relationship, when viewed from the mother's perspective, than is described by female students. Viewed from the vantage point of the diverging and sex-differentiated items characteristic of female students, perceptions of the mother/daughter relationship reflect more interaction (both positive and negative) than is expressed in the mothers' self-reports. Although some degree of ambivalence was ascribed to the mother/daughter relationship by mothers and daughters alike, these discrepant items suggest that ambivalent feelings are stronger in the perceptions of daughters than in the reports of mothers. Female students also perceive that they were granted somewhat greater freedom than is implied by mothers' self-characterizations of their childrearing practices. With reference to daughters' perceptions of fathers, paternal teasing and expectations of gratitude appear more salient than is suggested in the fathers' self-reported data.

For the father/son relationship, the significant sex-differentiating and deviating items characteristic of the fathers' self-descriptions stress the importance of achievement, acceptance of paternal authority, and acknowledgment of teasing. Again, these items suggest a more pressuring and authoritarian father/son relationship when viewed from the father's perspective than is perceived by male students. The significant sex-differentiating and diverging items characteristic of male students' perceptions of fathers extend the list of behavioral prohibitions (discouraging secrets from parents, forbidding teasing) and reflect fathers as encouragers of outdoor play and as defenders of their sons when others provoke trouble.

Socialization practices attributed to mothers by male students, which were not reflected in maternal self-reports, indicate maternal emphasis on the importance of cleanliness, maternal discouragement of participation in rough games, maternal anxiety about the health and eating habits of their sons, and maternal feelings of self-sacrifice.

When the inconsistently answered CRPR items are compared with the sex-differentiated socialization emphases, where there is some degree of agreement between parents and students, the overall thrust of the findings seems to indicate little actual discrepancy. Although differences exist both in emphasis and in specific item content, they seem relatively few, particularly when it is recognized that three factors have operated to attenuate agreement. First, because the young adults represented in the student sample are not the children of the parents represented, the extent of agreement is underestimated. Second, since the results derived from students are predominantly from countries other than the United States, while the parental self-reports were obtained primarily from parents in the United States, agreement between the two data sources would be expected to be lowered. The inclusion of samples from other countries makes it clear, however, that sex-differentiated socialization is a general phenomenon characterized by themes common across cultures and by emphases that appear culturally specific. The third source of attenuation with respect to agreement across data sources resides in age differences. Parents completed the CRPR when their children were, on the average, approximately twelve years old, whereas perceptions of parental childrearing approaches were obtained from students who were, on the average, twenty-one years old. If parental socialization practices and emphases do in fact change as a function of the different competencies, circumstances, and needs of children at different age levels, this age difference represents another important limitation on the agreement across data sources. Further, it must be remembered that these young people were describing their parents' rearing of them at a time when many of them were involved in defining their own identities and in differentiating themselves from their parents. Thus, their perceptions of parents during this period of personal flux and selfconscious examination might be expected to differ from those obtained when identity issues were less compelling. From the perspective of parents, the themes that were more salient in their self-reports, but not reflected in the students' perceptions of parents, appear to be appropriate socialization emphases when the average age of the child is considered. Parental authority and control undoubtedly are more salient childrearing concerns for parents of twelve-year-olds than for parents of students of college age. Future research comparing self-reported and perceived childrearing data will have to control for, or at least allow for, the age of the child being studied.

These analyses of agreements and disagreements across sources underscore the need for more studies in which socialization is viewed from multiple perspectives. In 1963 Yarrow called for studies of childrearing practices that would include systematically the mother, father, child, and observer as sources of information. Many years later, her recommendations are as cogent but have been largely ignored. However, in one of the research studies reported here (Sample 1 in Table 3.1), observerbased data describing mothers and fathers interacting individually with their children in a teaching/learning situation (Block, Block, and Harrington, 1974) were available, along with the CRPR data. Because the observer-based ratings of the mother's and father's interactions with the child in the teaching situation are not directly comparable to the CRPR data, it is difficult to quantify the extent of agreement between these two data groups. However, it will be recalled that mothers were less sex-discriminating in the teaching situation; the same trend characterizes the CRPR results for mothers in Sample 1.

Fathers of sons were found in the teaching situation to be more active, more pressuring, and more attuned to the cognitive demands of the situation than were fathers of girls, who were described by observers as more attentive to the interactional elements of the teaching situation. Fathers were seen as protecting their daughters from failure experiences, making the situation fun, and developing a comfortable working relationship, and both fathers and their daughters were described as enjoying the interaction. The sex-discriminating behaviors of fathers observed in the standardized teaching situation are consistent with the sex-differentiated socialization emphases expressed by Sample 1 fathers on the CRPR: Achievement pressures and firmness significantly differentiated fathers of sons, while fathers of daughters encouraged wonder, worried about their daughters, wanted their daughters to be independent of them, and found their daughters interesting.

Despite these indications of correspondence, however, these data do not speak adequately to the question of the validity of parental reports. Specifically designed studies are required in which self-reported behaviors of parents can be directly compared with observer reports of parental behaviors in situations designed to permit the self-described behaviors to become manifest.

Age-Related Socialization Emphases

One of the fundamental tasks of the developing individual is the mediation between internal impulses, desires, wishes—both biological and physiological—and the external socialization forces of the society. This developmental requirement implies different socialization emphases at different stages, depending on the developmental level of the child and the tolerance of society and its socializing agents for impulse expression in particular areas (Block, 1973). In the present analysis, there is the suggestion that socialization becomes more sex-differentiated with the increasing age of the child, reaching a maximum during the high school years. The observation is consistent with results obtained in England by Newson and Newson (1968), who found relatively little sex differentiation in the socialization practices of parents of four-year-olds but did find more evidence of sex-related socialization at age seven, particularly with respect to greater restrictiveness of girls (Maccoby, 1975). Both the findings reported here and the observations of Newson and Newson are consistent with the results of studies cited by Maccoby and

Jacklin, who found sex differentiation to be more characteristic of older than younger children. These age-specific socialization emphases must be specified and understood, and for this task longitudinal studies are required. It is sufficient here simply to underscore the importance of age as a determiner of parental socialization emphases. Perhaps the data presented in Table 3.1 can provide a source of hypotheses for this needed research.

Overview of Sex-Differentiated Socialization

I find there is considerably more evidence of differentiation in parental rearing practices as a function of the sex of the child than was reported or summarized by Maccoby and Jacklin. My results are consistent with theirs in finding that punishment orientation, negative sanctions, and sex typing are more characteristic socialization concerns of parents of sons than of parents of daughters. Further, the results presented here agree with the studies focusing explicitly on fathers in the Maccoby and Jacklin work when those studies are disembedded and examined separately. Thus, fathers are more accepting of aggression directed against themselves by their daughters than by their sons, provide comfort to their daughters more than to their sons, and characterize their relationship with their daughters as warmer than the relationship with their sons. Fathers of sons, in contrast, tend to accept aggressiveness and competition more than fathers of daughters.

There appear to be several reasons for the discrepancies between the results of the present series of studies and the research findings reviewed by Maccoby and Jacklin. First, the discrepancies appear greater in those areas where they have employed concepts defined globally. With respect to the large concept "restrictiveness," for example, the *area* of restrictiveness is all-important. Parents tend to be restrictive of their daughters in the sense of maintaining closer supervision of their activities; however, parental restrictiveness of sons appears to be focused on assertiveness toward parents and expression of feelings. With respect to the globally defined concept of independence, the relationships issuing from the present study suggest that parental encouragement of independence may have somewhat different meanings for sons than for daughters. Parents appear to encourage their sons to be independent in the sense of taking chances and assuming responsibility; for daughters, however, it appears that parental encouragement of independence may be in the service of encouraging differentiation from the parents. With respect to aggression, parents again appear to make more distinctions than are typically reflected in our measures. For sons, aggression in the sense of competition is encouraged, and participation in rough games is tolerated by both parents; fathers are more accepting of fighting in their sons than in their daughters. Teasing and expressions of sibling rivalry in sons do not elicit significant parental reactions, despite their aggressive implications. However, fathers of sons discourage expressions of anger toward themselves.

Obviously, the classification of conceptually distinct behaviors into one large category tends to suggest inconsistencies or to level differences that would otherwise be seen. Greater articulation of the global concepts on which much socialization research has depended in the past is essential if we are to discern clear and reproducible evidence of sex differentiation in parental socialization.

A second source of the discrepancy between the present findings and the conclusions summarized by Maccoby and Jacklin concerns the role of the father. The systematic information obtained about the childrearing attitudes of fathers has revealed sex-differentiated socialization emphases obscured in the Maccoby and Jacklin conclusions as a function of several factors—the paucity of information about fathers; the secondary informational sources about fathers on which many researchers have depended; and the aggregation of results derived from mothers, fathers, and perceptions of parents. The opportunity to compare directly the childrearing orientations of mothers and of fathers has provided clear evidence of parental role specialization in some socialization areas, while in other areas the two parents appear to have similar reinforcement emphases.

Third, the appreciable sex-related socialization differences observed in the research reported here, as compared with the rather limited evidence reported by Maccoby and Jacklin, may be viewed as a function of differences in domain coverage. The socialization literature has tended to concentrate on relatively few childrearing dimensions (such as warmth, dependency, aggression, achievement, positive and negative reinforcements). Some of the significant and consistent differences emerging in the present study, however, have been found on dimensions only infrequently studied. Specifically, these are the emphasis on control of affect expression in sons, the encouragement of introspection (wonder, daydreaming, reflection on personal problems) in daughters, the sense of their trustworthiness conveyed to daughters, the explicit valuing of competition separate from achievement in sons, and the greater parental concern about the impression made on others by sons. All these represent socialization emphases of parents that have been given relatively little attention in previous studies of parental influences on children.

Finally, the differing conclusions about the extent of sex differentiation in parental socialization practices reported by Maccoby and Jacklin and those suggested by the present series of studies are a function also of age differences in children at the time parental childrearing orientations were assessed. If sex differentiation in socialization practices becomes more marked with the increasing age of the child, as suggested by our analyses and the observations of Newson and Newson (1968), then the generally young age of the children in the studies forming the data base for the Maccoby and Jacklin conclusions is responsible for the sparseness of their findings.

By attending to childrearing behaviors frequently ignored, by using more differentiated concepts, by assessing the socialization emphases of parents when children are older, and by including fathers uniformly in our studies of childrearing practices, it may be anticipated that we will establish more precisely the ways in which sons and daughters are differently socialized by their fathers and mothers.

Our discussion of the leveling conclusions drawn by Maccoby and Jacklin and the sharpening ones emerging from the present series of analyses requires, finally, that we consider the educational and social implications of these diverging views of the empirical situation.

Currently, there is a strong movement, deriving from various considerations of the connections between character and society, toward changing the traditional, culturally prescribed definitions of sex roles. In this context, the summary view of Maccoby and Jacklin that there are few differences in parenting as a function of the sex of the child can readily lead to the inference that there are few points of entry for change in the socialization process. The appreciable differential parenting as a function of the sex of the child found in the present analyses, however, lends encouragement to current concerns and suggests specific directions and ways in which socialization emphases might be modified.

With regard to the rearing of sons, agentic interests (competition, aggression, egocentrism) would be leavened by the encouragement of a more communal orientation (expression of deeply felt affects, sociocentrism). With regard to the rearing of daughters, the interlacing of a communal focus (interpersonal orientation, compromise, and sacrifice for the general welfare) with a greater sense of agency (self-assertion, self-valuation) can be expected to benefit ego development. Machismo dissimulates manhood; hyperfemininity feigns womanhood. The socialization changes now feasible within our civilization can permit self- and sex role definitions that can transcend the stark and limiting conceptions of masculinity and femininity imposed in the past (Block, 1973).

Table 3.1. Differential Socialization Emphases Reflected by Parents of Sons and Parents of Daughters.

CRPR Item (abridged)	Self-descriptions											Analyses of combined probabilities			
	Mother samples[a]						Father samples					Mothers		Fathers	
	1	2	3	4	5	6	1	2	4	5	6	Direction	p	Direction	p
	62M 65F	43M 32F	31M 32F	75M 46F	100M 83F	73M 54F	46M 55F	26M 18F	58M 61F	90M 66F	73M 55F				
Respected C's opinions	D	D	D	.05D	S	S	D	D	D+	D+	S	D		D	
Encouraged C to do well	S	S	.05D	S+	.05S	S	.01S	S	S+	S+	S	S	.10	S	.002
Put spouse's wishes first	.10D	S+	S	S	S	S	S+	D	S+	D	D	S		S	
Helped C when teased	D	S+	D	S	D+	D+	D	D	D+	D+	S	D		D	
Felt angry with C	S	S+	S	S	D+	D	D	D+	S	S	D+	S		D	
Wanted C to handle own problems	S+	S	S	S	S	S	S	S	S	S	S+	S		S	.05
Punished by isolating C	D	S	S	S	D	.05S	S	D	D	.05S	S+	S		S	
Watched C's eating habits	D+	D	D	S	D+	S	D	S	D	S+	D	D		S	
Didn't think young C should be naked with other children	S+	S+	D	S	S	D	S+	D	D	S	D	S		D	

Item														
Wished spouse more interested in C	D	S+	.01S	D	S	D	D	.10D	S	D+	S	.02	D	.08
Gave C comfort when upset	.10S	.05D	D	S	.05S	D+	D+	.05D	D+	D	S		D	.008
Kept C away from families with different ideas	S+	S	D	D	S+	S+	D	S	S	S+	S		S	
Didn't allow rough games	D	D+	.05D	D+	D	S	D	D+	D	D+	D	.003	D	.10
Believed physical punishment best	D	D	.10S	D	S	S	S	.05S	S	.10S	S		S	.01
Thought C should be seen, not heard	S+	D	S+	S	S		S	S	S	S	S		S	
Sometimes forgot promises to C	D+	D	D	D	D	S	.05D	S	D	S	D		D	.08
Thought it good for C to perform	.10S	D+	D	S	D+	S	D	S	D	S	D		S	
Expressed affection physically	S	D	.10D	D+	D+	D	.05D	.05D	.05D	.10D	D	.005	D	.0003
Obtained great satisfactions from C	S	S	D	S	S+	D	D	D	.10S	D	S		D	

Table 3.1. Differential Socialization Emphases Reflected by Parents of Sons and Parents of Daughters, Cont'd.

CRPR Item (abridged)	Self-descriptions												Analyses of combined probabilities			
	Mother samples[a]						Father samples						Mothers		Fathers	
	1	2	3	4	5	6	1	2	4	5	6		Direction	p	Direction	p
	62M 65F	43M 32F	31M 32F	75M 46F	100M 83F	73M 54F	46M 55F	26M 18F	58M 61F	90M 66F	73M 55F					
Protected C against failure	S	S	D	S	S	S	D+	D	D	D	D		S		D	
Encouraged C to wonder about life	D	D	D	.01D	D	D	.05D	D	D+	D	D		D	.02	D	.04
Included C in making plans	.05D	S	.05S	.05D	S	.10S	D+	D	.10D	D	D		S		D	.04
Was sorry to see C grow up	S	S	S	D	S	D+	S	D	D+	D	D+		D		D	
Allowed C to daydream and loaf	D	S	D	D	S	D	D	S	S	D+	D		D		D	
Found it difficult to punish C	D+	D	D+	D+	D	D	D	D	D	.05D	.10D		D	.03	D	.02
Let C make decisions	S	.10S	.10S	S	S	D	D+	D	D+	D	D		S	.10	D	.04

Item														
Didn't allow C to say bad things about teachers	S+	.10S	D+	D	D+	S	.05S	S+	D	D	D	S	S	S
Worried about C	S	D+	S	S	S	S	D	S	.01S	S	.01D	D	D	D
Taught C punishment would come if bad	.10S	S	S+	S	S	S	S	S	S	S	D	S	S .02	S
Didn't blame C if others provoked trouble	D	D	D+	D	D	D+	D+	S+	S	.10D	S	S	D	D
Felt C a disappointment to me	S	D	D	S	D+	D	S	S+	S+	S	S	D	D	S
Expected a great deal of C	S	D	S	S	S	S	S+	S	S+	S+	S+	S	S	S .01
Was relaxed with C	S	S	S	.05D	S	D+	S+	S+	D	S+	S+	D	D	D
Gave up my interests for C	.10D	D	S	S	D	D	S	D	D	S	S	D	D	S
Spoiled C	.10S	S	S	D	D	S	S	S	S	.05D	S	S	S	D
Believed C always truthful	D+	D+	D	D+	S	D+	S	.10D	D	D	D+	D .03	D	D .05
Reasoned with C	S	S	.10D	D	D	D	D	D+	D+	D	D	D	D	D
Didn't allow C to be angry with me	S	S	S	D	D	D	.10S	S+	S+	S	S	S	S	S .03

Table 3.1. Differential Socialization Emphases Reflected by Parents of Sons and Parents of Daughters, Cont'd.

CRPR Item (abridged)	Self-descriptions											Analyses of combined probabilities			
	Mother samples[a]						Father samples					Mothers		Fathers	
	1 62M 65F	2 43M 32F	3 31M 32F	4 75M 46F	5 100M 83F	6 73M 54F	1 46M 55F	2 26M 18F	4 58M 61F	5 90M 66F	6 73M 55F	Direction	p	Direction	p
Trusted C for proper behavior	D	D+	D	.10D	D	D	S	D	.10D	D+	D	D	.009	D	.10
Joked and played with C	S	D+	S	D	.10S	S	D+	D	D+	D+	S+	S		D	
Gave C responsibilities	S+	S	S	S	D	S	S	S	S	S	.05S	S		S	
C and I shared warm times together	S	.10D	D+	D+	D+	.05D	D	D+	.10D	D	S	D	.001	D	.05
Had firm rules for C	D	D	D	D	D	S	.05S	S+	S	.01S	.05S	D	.0001	S	.0001
Let C take chances	D	S+	S	S	S	.10S	S+	.10S	S+	S	S+	S	.08	S	.006
Encouraged curiosity	D	S	D	D	S	.01S	D	D	D	D	S	S		D	
Explained by using the supernatural	D	S	S+	D+	.05D	S	D+	D	S	D	.10D	D		D	
Expected gratitude from C	S	S	D	D	S	.10S	S+	S	D	.10S	D	S		S	

Was too involved with C	S+	D	D	S	S	S	D	S	.05S	S	D+	S	S
Believed in early toilet training	D	D	S	S	S	S	S+	D	S+	S	D	S	S
Threatened more than punished	D	S	.01S	S	D	.10S	D	S	S	D	S	S .03	S
Praised more than criticized	D+	D	.05S	.10D	S	D	D+	S	S	S	S+	D	S
Appreciated C's efforts	S	.10S	D	D+	.10S	S	D	D	D	D	D	S	D
Encouraged C to talk of troubles	D	D+	S	.10D	S+	S	D+	D+	.05D	D+	D	D	D .009
Didn't want C to have secrets from parents	S+	D+	D	D	S+	D	S	D	D	S	.05D	S	D
Encouraged C to control feelings	S+	.05S	S	D	.05S	S	S	S+	S+	S+	.05S	S .005	S .004
Tried to keep C from fighting	D	.10S	D	D	D	S	D+	D	.01D	D	S	S	D .007
Dreaded answering sex questions	S+	D	S	D+	S	S	S	D+	D+	S	D	S	D
Let C know when I felt angry	S	D+	S	S+	D+	S	D	S	S	S	D	D	S
Encouraged competition	S	S	.05S	S+	.05S	S	S	D	S+	.10S	S	S .0002	S .08

Table 3.1. Differential Socialization Emphases Reflected by Parents of Sons and Parents of Daughters, Cont'd.

| | Self-descriptions | | | | | | | | | | | Analyses of combined probabilities | | | |
| | Mother samples[a] | | | | | | Father samples | | | | | Mothers | | Fathers | |
CRPR Item (abridged)	1 62M 65F	2 43M 32F	3 31M 32F	4 75M 46F	5 100M 83F	6 73M 54F	1 46M 55F	2 26M 18F	4 58M 61F	5 90M 66F	6 73M 55F	Direction	p	Direction	p
Punished by taking away privileges	S	S+	S	S	S	.10S	S+	S	S+	.10S	S+	S	.01	S	.02
Gave extra privileges for reward	S+	D+	.05D	S+	S	S+	D	S	D	D	S	S		S	
Enjoyed a houseful of children	D	S	S	S	S	D+	D	D	.10D	D	D	S		D	.08
Felt affection can weaken C	S	S	D	S	S+	S	S	S	S	D	S	S		S	
Thought scolding improved C	S	S+	D+	.05S	D	S	S	.01D	S	.05S	.10S	S	.02	S	
Sacrificed a lot for C	S	S	D	.10D	D	D	.05S	D+	D	S	D	D		S	
Teased C	D	D+	D	D	D	S	D+	.05S	.01S	D	.10S	D	.02	S	.02
Taught C to be responsible for self	S	D	D	D	D	S	S	S	S+	S	S	D		S	

Statement	1	2	3	4	5	6	7	8	9	10	11	12	13	14	15	16
Worried about C's health	S	S+	.05D	S	S	D+	S	.05D	S	.10S	.10S	S	.05S	.10D	D	D
Was conflict between us	S	D	D	S	.05D	S	S	S	S	.05S	.05S	D	D	D	D	S
Didn't allow C to question decisions	S	D	D	D	D+	.10S	D+	.10S	.01S	S+	S	S	S	D	D	S .0003
Believed competitive games good for C	S	S	.05S	S+	S+	S+	.0-S	S+	S+	S+	S	S	S+	S	S .0000	S .006
Liked time away from children	D+	D	D	S	D+	.10S	S	S	S	S+	D	D	D	D	D	S
Shamed C for misbehavior	D	D	S	S	D	S+	S	S-	S	S	S+	S+	D	S	S	S
Concerned with impression C makes on others	S	S	S	S	S	S	S	D	S	S	.05S	S	S	S	S .05	S
Encouraged C to be independent of me	S	D	D	D+	D	S	S	.01D	S	D	S	D	D	D	D	D
Kept close track of C	D	D	D	.05D	D	D	D	S	.05D	S	S	S	D	D	D .03	D
Found children interesting	S	D	D	D	D	D	D	.10D	D+	D	S	S	D	D	D	D
Believed in early weaning	D	S+	S+	.10S	S	S	S	S	.10S	D	D	S	S	S	S .03	S
Expected C to stay clean	D+	D	D	D	D+	D	D	D	D+	D	S	D	D	D	D .03	D

Table 3.1. Differential Socialization Emphases Reflected by Parents of Sons and Parents of Daughters, Cont'd.

| | Self-descriptions | | | | | | | | | | | Analyses of combined probabilities | | | |
| | Mother samples[a] | | | | | | Father samples | | | | | Mothers | | Fathers | |
CRPR Item (abridged)	1 62M 65F	2 43M 32F	3 31M 32F	4 75M 46F	5 100M 83F	6 73M 54F	1 46M 55F	2 26M 18F	4 58M 61F	5 90M 66F	6 73M 55F	Direction	p	Direction	p
Didn't like leaving C with stranger	S	.10D	D	S	S	.01D	D	.01D	D	.10D	D	D	.01	D	.007
Punished sibling rivalry	D	D	D	S	D	D+	.05D	.10S	S+	S	S	D		S	
Taught C early not to cry	S+	S	.10S	S+	S	D	S+	S	S+	S	S	S	.05	S	.07
Controlled C by warning of bad things	D	S	S	D+	S+	D+	D	D	S+	S	.01D	D		D	
Mother had most authority in family	S	S	.01D	D+	D	S	S+	D	.05D	D	D	D	.02	D	
Wanted C to be same as others	S+	D	S	S	S	S+	S+	S	S	S	S+	S	.008	S	.08
Believed sex information should wait until C older	S	.10S	S	S	S	S	S	S	S	D	D	S	.04	S	

												(p<.05) N=26	(p<.05) N=23
Felt important for C to play outside	S+	S	S+	D	S	.10S	S	S	S	D	D	S	S
Liked seeing C eat well	D	S	S	D	S+	S	S	S	S	D	D	S .01	S
Did not allow C to tease others	D	S	S	S	D	.01D	S	S	S	.10D	D+	D	D
Wrong to insist on different toys for boys and girls	D+	S	S	D	D	S	D	.10S	D	D	D+		D
Believed children need close supervision	D	D	D	D	D	D	S	S	D	S	D+	D .03	D
Total number of comparisons yielding p values <.10	6	10	13	16	7	14	12	10	20	16	13	(p<.05) N=26	(p<.05) N=23

Note: Entries represent the results of t-test comparisons between parents of sons and parents of daughters. S and D indicate the direction of the mean difference (sons and daughters). S+ or D+ indicates t-test values in excess of 1.00 but less than the 1.67 required for $p<.10$. For significant comparisons, p levels based on two-tailed tests of significance are given in cell entries. Combined probabilities are calculated across the independent samples of mothers and, separately, the independent samples of fathers according to Winer (1971, p. 50). CRPR = Child-Rearing Practices Report.

[a] Samples are described as follows:

Sample 1. Mothers and fathers of nursery school children participating in a longitudinal study. Age range of children 3–4 years.

Sample 2. Mothers and fathers of children with chronic illnesses varying in degree of severity (asthma, diabetes, congenital heart disease, hay fever). Age range of children 3–11 years (mean 7.2 years).

Sample 3. Mothers of sixth-grade children. Age range of children 11.5–12.5 years.

Sample 4. Mothers and fathers of urban high school students. Age range of adolescents 15–17 years.

Sample 5. Mothers and fathers of university students. Age range of students 18–20 years.

Sample 6. The Netherlands. Mothers and fathers of children living in Amsterdam. Age range of children 7–13 years.

Table 3.2. Differential Socialization Emphases Reflected by Comparisons of Young Adult Sons' and Daughters' Descriptions of Parental Childrearing Practices.

| CRPR Item (abridged) | Descriptions of mothers[a] | | | | | | Analyses of combined probabilities for mothers | | Descriptions of U.S. fathers |
| | United States | England | Finland | Norway | Sweden | Denmark | Direction | p | |
	238M 256F	95M 57F	58M 133F	84M 108F	40M 92F	30M 36F			234M 236F
Respected C's opinions	D	.10D	D	.10D	S+	D	D	.04	S
Encouraged C to do well	S	S	.05D	D	S	S	S		D+
Put spouse's wishes first	.05D	.01D	S	D+	D+	S	D	.004	D+
Helped C when teased	D	D	D	D	.10D	D	D	.03	S
Felt angry with C	.01D	D	S	D+	.10D	S+	D	.03	S
Wanted C to handle own problems	D	.01D	S	.05D	D	S+	D	.07	S
Punished by isolating C	D	D+	D	S	.10D	S	D		S
Watched C's eating habits	.01S	S	S	S	S	D	S	.04	.05S
Didn't think young C should be naked with other children	.10S	.05S	.10S	S	D	D	S	.008	D

	1	2	3	4	5	6	7	8	9
Wished spouse more interested in C	D	S	D	S	D	S	S		S
Gave C comfort when upset	D	D+	.10D	D+	D	S	D	.04	.05D
Kept C away from families with different ideas	D	.10S	D	.05S	D	S	S	.05	D
Didn't allow rough games	S+	S+	S+	.01S	S	.05S	S	.0002	.001D
Believed physical punishment best	D	D+	S	S	.10D	S+	D		S+
Thought C should be seen, not heard	D	D	S	—	.05D	S	D		D
Sometimes forgot promises to C	.05D	D+	D	S	D	D+	D	.006	S
Thought it good for C to perform	D+	D	D+	D	S	D	D	.07	S
Expressed affection physically	D	S	D	D	S	D+	D	.09	.001D
Obtained great satisfactions from C	S+	S+	S	D	.10S	S	S	.02	.10S
Protected C against failure	.10D	S	S	D	S	S	S		S

Table 3.2. Differential Socialization Emphases Reflected by Comparisons of Young Adult Sons' and Daughters' Descriptions of Parental Childrearing Practices, Cont'd.

CRPR Item (abridged)	Descriptions of mothers[a]						Analyses of combined probabilities for mothers		Descriptions of U.S. fathers
	United States	England	Finland	Norway	Sweden	Denmark	Direction	p	
	238M 256F	95M 57F	58M 133F	84M 108F	40M 92F	30M 36F			234M 236F
Encouraged C to wonder about life	D	.10D	D+	D	S	D	D	.05	.01D
Included C in making plans	D	D+	D+	D	S+	D+	D		D+
Was sorry to see C grow up	S	D+	D	S	S	D	D		.001D
Allowed C to daydream and loaf	.05D	.01D	.10D	D	.05D	D+	D	.0000	.01D
Found it difficult to punish C	.10S	D	D+	S	S+	D+	S		.05D
Let C make decisions	D+	.05D	.10D	.10D	S	S	D	.004	D
Didn't allow C to say bad things about teachers	S+	D	S	S+	.05S	.05S	S	.005	S

Worried about C	D+	S	D	S	S	D+	D		.01D
Taught C punishment would come if bad	.05S	.01S	S	.01S	S	D	S	.0005	.05S
Didn't blame C if others provoked trouble	S	S	D+	D	D+	D	D		.05S
Felt C a disappointment to me	.05D	.10D	S+	S	.05D	D	D	.03	D
Expected a great deal of C	S	.01S	D	S	S	S	S	.04	D
Was relaxed with C	S	D	D	D	S+	D+	D		D+
Gave up my interests for C	.01S	S	D+	S	D	D	S		.01S
Spoiled C	S	S+	D	.10D	S	.10D	D	.10	.001D
Believed C always truthful	.05D	D	D+	.01D	D	.05D	D	.0000	.01D
Reasoned with C	D	.05D	D	S+	.10S	S	S		S
Didn't allow C to be angry with me	.01S	S+	S	S	D	S	S	.009	S+
Trusted C for proper behavior	.05D	.10D	.05D	D	S+	D	D	.001	D+
Joked and played with C	D	D	D	.01D	S	.10D	D	.009	.05D
Gave C responsibilities	.05D	D+	S	D+	S+	S	D		.05S

Table 3.2. Differential Socialization Emphases Reflected by Comparisons of Young Adult Sons' and Daughters' Descriptions of Parental Childrearing Practices, Cont'd.

CRPR Item (abridged)	Descriptions of mothers[a]						Analyses of combined probabilities for mothers		Descriptions of U.S. fathers
	United States	England	Finland	Norway	Sweden	Denmark	Direction	p	
	238M 256F	95M 57F	58M 133F	84M 108F	40M 92F	30M 36F			234M 236F
Gave extra privileges for reward	.10S	S	S	D+	.10S	S+	S	.04	S
Enjoyed a houseful of children	S	D	S	.01D	D	D	D	.06	D
Felt affection can weaken C	.01S	.01S	.05S	S+	D+	.05S	S	.0000	.001S
Thought scolding improved C	.10D	S	S+	S	D	S	S		S
Sacrificed a lot for C	D	S+	S	.10S	D	.10S	S	.01	S+
Teased C	.05D	.05D	D	.01D	.01D	.10D	D	.0000	.001D
Taught C to be responsible for self	S	S	S	.01D	D	D	D	.10	.10S
Worried about C's health	.01S	.10S	.10S	S	S	D	S	.0000	.10S

Was conflict between us	.05D	.10D	D	.05D	D+	D	D	.0002	S+
Didn't allow C to question decisions	.10S	S+	D	S	.05D	S	S		D
Believed competitive games good for C	.05S	S	.01S	.05S	.01S	.05D	S	.0001	.001S
Liked time away from children	.01D	.10D	S	S+	S	S	D		.10D
Shamed C for misbehavior	S+	.10S	S	.10S	S	S	S	.02	.05S
Concerned with impression C makes on others	.05S	.01S	S	.01S	S+	S+	S	.0000	S+
Encouraged C to be independent of me	.01D	.01D	D	.01D	D+	D	D	.0000	S
Kept close track of C	.05D	D+	D+	.01D	D	D	D	.0000	.01D
Found children interesting	D	.01D	D	D+	S	S	D	.01	S
Believed in early weaning	S+	S+	.01S	D	S+	S+	S	.001	S+
Expected C to stay clean	.05S	S	.10S	.01S	S	.10S	S	.0000	D
Didn't like leaving C with stranger	D+	.10D	D−	D	D+	S	D	.003	D

Table 3.2. Differential Socialization Emphases Reflected by Comparisons of Young Adult Sons' and Daughters' Descriptions of Parental Childrearing Practices, Cont'd.

CRPR Item (abridged)	Descriptions of mothers[a]						Analyses of combined probabilities for mothers		Descriptions of U.S. fathers
	United States	England	Finland	Norway	Sweden	Denmark	Direction	p	
	238M 256F	95M 57F	58M 133F	84M 108F	40M 92F	30M 36F			234M 236F
C and I shared warm times together	.05D	.05D	D	.01D	D	D+	D	.0000	D+
Had firm rules for C	.05D	D+	.05S	S	D+	S+	D		S
Let C take chances	.10D	.01D	D+	.05D	.01D	D	D	.0000	S+
Encouraged curiosity	S	.10D	D	S	S+	S+	S		D
Explained by using the supernatural	S	S	.10S	S	D+	D+	S		S
Expected gratitude from C	D+	S+	D	.10S	D	.10S	S	.08	.05D
Was too involved with C	S	.10S	D	D	S	S	S		S+
Believed in early toilet training	D	S+	S	.01D	D	D	D	.03	.10S

	1	2	3	4	5	6	7	8	9
Threatened more than punished	S+	.01S	S	S	S+	S	S	.0005	S+
Praised more than criticized	S+	—	D	S	S+	D+	S		D
Appreciated C's efforts	S+	D	D	.10D	S	D	D		.10D
Encouraged C to talk of troubles	S	D+	D+	D+	S+	D+	D	.05	S
Didn't want C to have secrets from parents	.10S	.05S	S+	S	S	D	S	.01	.01S
Encouraged C to control feelings	.05S	S	.05S	S	S+	S	S	.001	.05S
Tried to keep C from fighting	S+	.05S	.05S	.01S	.01S	.01S	S	.0000	.05D
Dreaded answering questions about sex	.05D	S	S+	S	.10D	D	D		D+
Let C know when I felt angry	.01D	D	D	S	D	S	D	.06	D
Encouraged competition	.01S	.01S	D	.01S	S+	D	S	.0000	.01S
Punished by taking away privileges	S	S+	S	D	D	S	S		S+

Table 3.2. Differential Socialization Emphases Reflected by Comparisons of Young Adult Sons' and Daughters' Descriptions of Parental Childrearing Practices, Cont'd.

CRPR Item (abridged)	Descriptions of mothers[a]						Analyses of combined probabilities for mothers		Descriptions of U.S. fathers
	United States	England	Finland	Norway	Sweden	Denmark	Direction	p	
	238M 256F	95M 57F	58M 133F	84M 108F	40M 92F	30M 36F			234M 236F
Punished sibling rivalry	S	.10S	D+	D	D	D+	D		.01S
Taught C early not to cry	.01S	.05S	.01S	S+	S	S	S	.0000	.001S
Controlled C by warning of bad things	S	.10S	D	S+	D	S	S	.06	S
Mother had most authority in family	D+	S	S	.01S	—	D	S		S+
Wanted C to be same as others	S	.10S	D	S	S	D+	S		S+
Believed sex information should wait until C older	S	S	S	S+	D	S	S	.04	.05S
Felt important for C to play outside	S+	D	S	S+	.10S	S+	S	.02	.001S

Liked seeing C eat well	.01S	.01S	S	01S	01S	S+	S	.0000	.05S
Did not allow C to tease others	S+	S+	S	05S	S	S+	S	.001	.05S
Wrong to insist on different toys for boys and girls	.01D	.01D	D+	D	D	S	D	.0000	.001D
Believed children need close supervision	S	D	S+	S+	D	D	S		S
Total number of significant differences (p < .05)	31	22	9	23	10	6	52		33

Note: Entries represent the results of *t*-test comparisons of sons' and daughters' descriptions of the childrearing orientations of their mothers and, for the U.S. sample only, their fathers. S and D indicate the direction of the mean differences (sons or daughters). S+ or D+ indicates *t*-test values in excess of 1.00 but less than 1.67 required for *p* < .10. For significant comparisons, *p* levels based on two-tailed tests of significance are given in cell entries. Combined probabilities are calculated across the six independent samples of students (Winer, 1971, p. 50).

CRPR = Child-Rearing Practices Report.

[a]Samples are college and university students in each of the six countries.

Table 3.3. Summary of Results Suggesting Consistencies in Sex-Differentiated Socialization.

| CRPR Items[a] | Parental CRPR responses | | | | Students' descriptions | | | |
| | Mothers | | Fathers | | of Mothers | | of Fathers | |
	Direction	p	Direction	p	Direction	p	Direction	p
Items consistent in direction across all analyses								
Believed competitive games good	Sons	.000[b]	Sons	.006	Sons	.000	Sons	.001
Encouraged competition	Sons	.000	Sons	.08	Sons	.000	Sons	.01
Encouraged C to control feelings	Sons	.005	Sons	.004	Sons	.001	Sons	.05
Taught C early not to cry	Sons	.05	Sons	.07	Sons	.000	Sons	.001
Punished by revoking privileges	Sons	.01	Sons	.02	Sons	ns	Sons	ns
Taught punishment would come if bad	Sons	.02	Sons	ns	Sons	.001	Sons	.05
Thought scolding improved C	Sons	.02	Sons	ns	Sons	ns	Sons	ns
Threatened more than punished	Sons	.03	Sons	ns	Sons	.001		
Believed no sex information given until older	Sons	.04	Sons	ns	Sons	.04	Sons	.05
Wanted C to be same as others	Sons	.008	Sons	.08	Sons	ns	Sons	ns
Concerned with impression C makes	Sons	.05	Sons	ns	Sons	.000	Sons	ns
Believed in early weaning	Sons	.03	Sons	ns	Sons	.001	Sons	ns
Did not allow anger at parents	Sons	ns	Sons	.03	Sons	.009	Sons	ns
Did not allow C to say bad things about teachers	Sons	ns	Sons	ns	Sons	.005	Sons	ns
Felt affection can weaken C	Sons	ns	Sons	ns	Sons	.000	Sons	.001

Item						
Shamed C for misbehavior	Sons	ns	Sons	.02	Sons	.05
Gave extra privileges as reward	Sons	ns	Sons	.04	Sons	ns
Liked seeing C eat well	Sons	ns	Sons	.000	Sons	.05
Expressed affection physically	Daughters	.005	Daughters	.09	Daughters	.001
C and I shared warm times	Daughters	.001	Daughters	.000	Daughters	ns
Believed C is truthful	Daughters	.03	Daughters	.000	Daughters	.01
Believed C is to be trusted	Daughters	.009	Daughters	.001	Daughters	ns
Encouraged C to wonder	Daughters	.02	Daughters	.05	Daughters	.01
Didn't like to leave C with a stranger	Daughters	.01	Daughters	.003	Daughters	ns
Kept close track of C	Daughters	.03	Daughters	.000	Daughters	.01
Allowed C to daydream	Daughters	ns	Daughters	.000	Daughters	.01
Wrong to insist on different toys for boys and girls	Daughters	ns	Daughters	.000	Daughters	.001
Worried about C	Daughters	ns	Daughters	ns	Daughters	.01
Sorry to see C grow up	Daughters	ns	Daughters	ns	Daughters	.001
Items suggesting cross-sex effects						
Tried to keep C from fighting	Sons	ns	Daughters	.007	Daughters	.05
Didn't think young children should see each other naked	Sons	ns	Daughters	ns	Daughters	ns
Items suggesting same-sex effects						
Had firm rules for C	Daughters	ns	Sons	.000	Sons	ns
Punished sibling rivalry	Daughters	ns	Sons	ns	Sons	.01
Was conflict between parent and C	Daughters	ns	Sons	ns	Sons	ns
Taught C was responsible for self	Daughters	ns	Sons	ns	Sons	.10
Thought it good for C to perform	Daughters	ns	Sons	ns	Sons	ns

Table 3.3. Summary of Results Suggesting Consistencies in Sex-Differentiated Socialization, Cont'd.

CRPR Items[a]	Parental CRPR responses				Students' descriptions			
	Mothers		Fathers		of Mothers		of Fathers	
	Direction	p	Direction	p	Direction	p	Direction	p
Additional items suggesting mother/son agreement								
Important for C to play outside	Sons	.01	Daughters	ns	Sons	.02	Sons	.001
Did not want C to have secrets	Sons	ns	Daughters	ns	Sons	.01	Sons	.01
Obtained great satisfactions from C	Sons	ns	Daughters	ns	Sons	.02	Sons	.10
Wish spouse more interested in C	Sons	.02	Daughters	.08	Sons	ns	Sons	ns
Expected a great deal of C	Sons	ns	Sons	.01	Sons	.04	Daughters	ns
Encouraged C to do well	Sons	.10	Sons	.002	Sons	ns	Daughters	ns
Kept C away from families with different ideas	Sons	ns	Sons	ns	Sons	.05	Daughters	ns
Expected C to be grateful	Sons	ns	Sons	ns	Sons	.08	Daughters	.05
Additional items suggesting father/son agreement								
Let C take chances	Sons	.08	Sons	.006	Daughters	.000	Sons	ns
Believed physical punishment best	Sons	ns	Sons	.01	Daughters	ns	Sons	ns
Wanted C to handle problems	Sons	ns	Sons	.05	Daughters	.07	Sons	ns
Gave C responsibilities	Sons	ns	Sons	ns	Daughters	ns	Sons	.05
Believed in early toilet training	Sons	ns	Sons	ns	Daughters	.03	Sons	.10
Gave up own interests for C	Daughters	ns	Sons	ns	Sons	ns	Sons	.01
Watched C's eating habits	Daughters	ns	Sons	ns	Sons	.04	Sons	.05

Additional items suggesting mother/daughter agreement

Teased C	Daughters	ns	Sons	.02	Daughters	.000	Daughters	.001
Felt C a disappointment	Daughters	ns	Sons	ns	Daughters	.03	Daughters	ns
Let C know when angry	Daughters	ns	Sons	ns	Daughters	.06	Daughters	ns
Sometimes forgot promises to C	Daughters	ns	Daughters	.08	Daughters	.006	Sons	ns
Encouraged C to talk of troubles	Daughters	ns	Daughters	.009	Daughters	.05	Sons	ns
Respected C's opinions	Daughters	ns	Daughters	ns	Daughters	.04	Sons	ns
Found children interesting	Daughters	ns	Daughters	ns	Daughters	.01	Sons	ns
Helped C when teased	Daughters	ns	Daughters	ns	Daughters	.03	Sons	ns
Encouraged C to be independent of parent	Daughters	ns	Daughters	ns	Daughters	.000	Sons	ns

Additional items suggesting father/daughter agreement

Did not allow rough games	Daughters	.003	Daughters	.10	Sons	.000	Daughters	.001
Found it difficult to punish C	Daughters	.03	Daughters	.02	Sons	ns	Daughters	.05
Gave C comfort when upset	Sons	ns	Daughters	.008	Daughters	.04	Daughters	.05
Joked and played with C	Sons	ns	Daughters	ns	Daughters	.009	Daughters	.05
Spoiled C	Sons	ns	Daughters	ns	Daughters	.10	Daughters	.001
Included C in planning	Sons	ns	Daughters	.04	Daughters	ns	Daughters	ns
Let C make many decisions	Sons	.10	Daughters	.04	Daughters	.004	Daughters	ns
Enjoyed a houseful of children	Sons	ns	Daughters	.08	Daughters	.06	Daughters	ns
Appreciated C's efforts	Sons	ns	Daughters	ns	Sons	ns	Daughters	.10

aCRPR = Child-Rearing Practices Report. Items are in abbreviated form.

bp values reported are based on two-tailed tests of significance and represent combined probabilities across the several independent samples (mothers, fathers, and students describing their mothers' childrearing values). p values for student perceptions of fathers' childrearing orientations are based on t-test comparisons for the U.S. sample only.
The abbreviation ns = not significant.

Table 3.4. Summary of Statistical Comparisons Across Parents' and Student-Perceived Childrearing Practices.

	Comparisons of parent self-reports and student perceptions							
	Mothers				Fathers			
	Agreements		Disagreements		Agreements		Disagreements	
Criteria used to evaluate agreements and disagreements	No. of items	%	No. of items	%	No. of items	%	No. of items	%
Direction of response only	10	11	12	13	16	18	17	19
Direction *and* results significant in one comparison ($p < .10$)	5	5	4	4	6	7	5	5
Direction *and* results significant in one comparison ($p < .05$)	27	30	12	13	26	29	9	11
Direction *and* results significant in *both* comparisons	17	19	4	4	11	12	1	1
Totals	59	64.8	32	35.2	59	64.8	32	35.2

Table 3.5. CRPR Differences, for Sons and Daughters, Between
Parent Self-Reports and Student Perceptions.

CRPR Items	Direction of response		Level of significance	
	Parent	Student	Parent	Student
Mother/student comparisons				
Watched C's eating habits	D	S	ns	.04
Didn't allow rough games	D	S	.003	.000
Found it difficult to punish C	D	S	.03	ns
Sacrificed a lot for C	D	S	ns	.01
Worried about C's health	D	S	ns	.000
Expected C to stay clean	D	S	.03	.000
Believed children need supervision	D	S	.03	ns
Best if mother has most authority	D	S	.02	ns
Didn't allow teasing	D	S	ns	.001
Put spouse's wishes first	S	D	ns	.004
Felt angry with C	S	D	ns	.03
Gave comfort when upset	S	D	ns	.04
Let C make decisions	S	D	.10	.004
Joked and played with C	S	D	ns	.009
Let C take chances	S	D	.08	.000
Believed in early toilet training	S	D	ns	.03
Father/student comparisons				
Didn't blame C when others provoked	D	S	ns	.05
Encouraged C to talk of troubles	D	S	.009	ns
Didn't want C to have secrets from parents	D	S	ns	.01
Felt it important for C to play outdoors	D	S	ns	.001
Didn't allow C to tease others	D	S	ns	.05
Encouraged C to do well	S	D	.002	ns
Expected a great deal of C	S	D	.01	ns
Expected C to be grateful	S	D	ns	.05
Teased C	S	D	.02	.001
Didn't allow C to question	S	D	.000	ns

Note: CRPR = Child-Rearing Practices Report. C = child; D = daughter;
S = son; ns = not significant.

Chapter Four

*Psychological Development
of Female Children
and Adolescents*

Two goals of the socialization process have been stated eloquently by Hodding Carter, Jr., a journalist and philosopher: "There are two lasting bequests we should give our children. . . . One is roots, the other is wings." It will be contended in this chapter that conventional sex-differentiated socialization practices tend to encourage the development of roots in females and to minimize, for them, the importance of wings. For males, the pattern is reversed, wings being accorded greater emphasis in socialization and roots being viewed as less salient.

In focusing on the implications of socialization practices for psychological development, it should not be inferred that behavioral gender differences are being attributed solely to environmental conditions or to an individual's learning history. The scope of this chapter does not permit an extended discussion of the biological matrix from which we derive or considera-

Originally published in P. W. Berman and E. R. Ramey (Eds.), *Women: A Developmental Perspective.* Washington, D.C.: U.S. Government Printing Office, 1982.

tion of the role of biological factors in behavior. However, two brief observations are particularly pertinent here. First, the recognition of biological influences on behavior does not necessarily imply that behavior is thereby predetermined and immutable. Recent researches have shown that biological factors function with enormous complexity and are often dependent—in amplifying and dampening ways—on the ecological context and experiences encountered by the individual organism. The complexity of biological influences is reflected in the differential effects of hormones, for example, which have been shown to vary as a function of the timing of their administration (Beach, 1975; Goy and Resko, 1972; Money and Ehrhardt, 1972). That presumably biologically determined functions are influenced by ecological context has been demonstrated in studies showing the sexual behavior of primates to be responsive to characteristics of the rearing environment (Beach, 1980) or of the contemporary social grouping (Rose, Gordon, and Bernstein, 1972). These studies illustrate ways in which biological influences may be mediated by environmental considerations.

Second, in attempting to forge a conceptual scheme capable of encompassing the exquisite interplay of biological and ecological factors, we may be guided by certain recognitions that have proved useful in ethology. The concept of *modal action* patterns (Barlow, 1977) provides an enlarged perspective for viewing behavior. The concept implies that an action or action sequence may, in a statistical sense, characterize a species or subspecies while allowing for variation—perhaps great variation—about the statistical mode as a function of genetic variation and the demand quality of the particular ecosystem confronting the individual members of the species. It recognizes the existence of biologically grounded behavioral propensities but does not insist on the existence of uniform, almost reflexive behaviors as evidence of genetic influence. Most important, it recognizes that biological propensities may be manifested in behavior in diverse and complex ways, as organisms are shaped by, or selected by, or choose the (often changing) environment in which they must function.

Applied to the question of gender differences, the idea of

modal action patterns suggests that although biology lays down certain modal behavioral dispositions for males and for females, biology also allows for great variation about these behavioral modes. Moreover, and most important, the ways in which existing biological propensities issue into behavior is a complex (and largely unexplored) function of the structure of the environment impinging on individual males and females each seeking to construct a viable mode for living life. The ecological niche or learning environment in which development occurs thus becomes a salient focus for the study of developmental patterns. The socialization experiences of the child may be considered important definers of the learning environment that influences the child's constructions of reality and self.

With this perspective, we turn to consider the ways in which sex-differentiated socialization patterns serve to create different ecological niches for boys and for girls.

Evidence of Sex-Differentiated Socialization

Parental Reports of Childrearing Emphases. Looking first at the self-described socialization practices and values of parents, the evidence suggests that four conclusions are warranted (Block, 1979a):

1. Parental childrearing emphases socialize the child in sex-differentiated ways.
2. There are specific, consistent sex-of-parent and sex-of-child interactions.
3. Sex differentiation in socialization emphases appears to increase with the age of the child.
4. Many sex-related socialization values of mothers and of fathers appear to be relatively consistent across socioeconomic levels, educational levels, and cultural backgrounds.

Briefly, the following are specific areas in which the socialization of daughters and of sons appears to diverge: The self-described childrearing emphases of both mothers and fathers indicate greater encouragement of achievement and competition in sons than in daughters. In addition, both parents encourage their sons, more than their daughters, to control the expression of affect, to be independent, and to assume personal responsibility. Parents report punishing their sons more than their daughters. In addition, fathers appear more authoritarian in their rearing of sons, being stricter, firmer, more given to physical punishment, less tolerant of aggression directed against themselves, and less accepting of behaviors deviating from the traditional masculine stereotype (Block, 1979b). Examples of childrearing items endorsed more frequently by parents of boys are "I think one has to let a child take chances as he grows up and tries new things"; "I encourage my child to control his feelings at all times"; "I feel it is good for a child to play competitive games"; "I think a child should be encouraged to do things better than other children."

The self-described childrearing emphases of parents of daughters indicate that the parent/daughter relationship, in contrast to the parent/son relationship, is characterized by greater warmth and physical closeness, greater confidence in the trustworthiness and truthfulness of their daughters, greater expectation by mothers and fathers alike of "ladylike" behavior, greater reluctance to punish daughters, and greater encouragement to reflect on life. Additionally, mothers of daughters tend to be more restrictive of their daughters and to engage in closer supervision of their activities (Block, 1979b). Examples of childrearing items endorsed more frequently by parents of girls are "I express affection by hugging and holding my child"; "I find it difficult to punish my child"; "I have never caught my child lying"; "I don't go out if I have to leave my child with a sitter she does not know."

These results are consistent with the large-scale survey findings of Hoffman (1977a), which were that parents expected their sons, more frequently than their daughters, to be independent, self-reliant, highly educated, ambitious, hardworking, career-oriented, intelligent, and strong-willed. In contrast, parents more often expected their daughters to be kind, unselfish, attractive, loving, and well-mannered and to have a good marriage and be a good parent. The results also cohere with observa-

of socialization practices in other cultures (Barry, Bacon, hild, 1957; Whiting and Edwards, 1975; Whiting and Whit-975) as well as with findings from systematic studies of parent/child interactions, to which we now turn.

Observational Studies of Parental Behaviors. Studies of parent/child interactions provide additional evidence of sex-differentiated interaction patterns and also suggest that fathers appear to be more sex-differentiating in their behaviors with their children than mothers (Block, Block, and Harrington, 1975; Maccoby, 1980).

Even in the first year of life, sex-differentiated parental interactions with infants have been observed (Lamb, 1977; Lewis, 1972b; Moss, 1967; Parke and Sawin, 1976). Parents appear to provide more physical stimulation for boys than for girls. Male infants are held and aroused more and are also given more stimulation for gross motor activity (Lamb, 1977; Moss, 1967, 1974; Parke and O'Leary, 1976; Yarrow, 1975). In Yarrow and others' (1972) study of mother/infant interactions, mothers of males were observed to interact more frequently with their male infants, at higher levels of intensity, and with richer, more varied behaviors. These differences in parental behaviors, whereby boys are given more stimulation and more varied responses than girls, may be expected to predispose males to more active engagement of the world at a later age.

A second implicative area in which parents of boys and parents of girls have been observed to differ is in the frequency of their contingent responding to behaviors initiated by their child. In the feeding situation, mothers were observed to be more responsive and attentive to signals from their male infants than their female infants (Murphy and Moriarty, 1976; Walraven, 1974), modifying their behavior accordingly. Both mothers and fathers react more contingently to the vocalizations of boys than to the vocalizations of girls (Lewis and Freedle, 1973; Parke and Sawin, 1976; Yarrow, 1975). These apparent differences in contingent responding noted in infancy appear to continue throughout the childhood years. It has been shown in numerous studies at different age levels that boys receive not only more negative feedback from parents, including physical punishment, but more positive feedback as well (Maccoby and Jackl, 1974; Margolin and Patterson, 1975). Analyses of sequenti, interactions conducted by Margolin and Patterson revealed tha both parents responded contingently more to males than to females, fathers of boys responding contingently and positively to sons more than twice as often as fathers of girls.

Experience with contingency relationships has been shown to be related to general developmental level, goal direction, and exploratory behaviors of infants (Yarrow and others, 1972). These early experiences with contingency relationships, therefore, may be expected to benefit motivation and to encourage the development of awareness of the child's evocative role in eliciting effects from the environment. Experiences of efficacy (and of the sense of efficacy) help to build the personality and cognitive foundations on which later instrumental competence depends. It is posited that boys more than girls, as presently socialized in this culture, are helped by their contingency experiences to develop a premise system that presumes or anticipates mastery, efficacy, and instrumental competence.

Sex differences in the contingent responding of parents to their offspring are augmented by differences in the contingent experiences afforded by the toys parents provide. Boys are given a greater variety of toys than girls, and there are important differences as well in the kinds of toys parents provide for boys and girls (Rheingold and Cook, 1975; Yarrow and others, 1972). Boys' toys, more than girls' toys, afford inventive possibilities (Rosenfeld, 1975), encourage manipulation, and provide more explicit feedback from the physical world. Girls' toys, in contrast, tend to encourage imitation, provide less feedback, are more often used in proximity to the caretaker, and provide less opportunity for variation and innovation. Although differences in the toy preferences of boys and girls have been documented in numerous studies (Fagot, 1977; Fein and others, 1975; Goldberg and Lewis, 1969), the developmental implications of these differences in toy preference and availability have only recently begun to be explored (Block, 1981; Carpenter, 1983; Carpenter and Huston-Stein, 1980; Hoffman, 1977a). Differential exposure to toys with dissimilar characteristics may predispose boys and girls toward different play and problem-solving experiences, experiences with considerable implication for later psychological development.

A third area in which sex-differentiated parental socialization behaviors are found relates to exploratory behaviors and supervision of activities. Boys are given more freedom to explore and are allowed to engage in more unsupervised activities than girls. Girls are observed to play more proximally to their mothers (Lewis and Weintraub, 1974; Messer and Lewis, 1972), are allowed fewer independent excursions into the neighborhood (Callard, 1964; Saegert and Hart, 1976), are encouraged more by their mothers to follow them about the house (Fagot, 1977), are more closely supervised in their play (Newson and Newson, 1968), and are given more "chaperonage" (Maccoby and Jacklin, 1974). The differential assignment of household chores to boys and to girls also reflects the greater emphasis on proximity for girls. Boys more often are given chores taking them out of the house and/or farther away from home, while girls are assigned homebound chores of cleaning, "helping," babysitting. Not only do the chore assignments of girls limit their spheres of activity, but they also serve to increase the salience of the family milieu (Duncan, Schuman, and Duncan, 1973; Whiting and Edwards, 1975). Chodorow (1974) has argued that the different social contexts experienced by boys and by girls over the childhood years account for the development of many psychological sex differences, particularly those reflecting the greater embeddedness of women in social networks in contrast to the more individualistic, mastery-emphasizing activities of men. Sigel and Cocking (1976) have drawn attention to the effects of insufficient parental "distancing" on the development of children's representational thought. They propose that adult distancing behaviors serve to promote the child's active engagement in problem solving and increase the likelihood that the child will encounter discrepancies between experience and expectation that cannot readily be assimilated. Such discrepancies place demands on the child to alter approaches, reexamine earlier understandings, and modify premises. Data from several sources converge in suggesting that socialization practices that foster proximity, discourage independent problem solving by premature or excessive intervention, restrict exploration, and discourage active play may impede the child's achievement of the cognitive understandings and fluencies essential for problem solving. They may also constrain the child's experiences with mastery, which are an essential foundation for the development of self-esteem and confidence.

Turning to systematic studies of parent/child interactions in achievement-related situations, further evidence for sex-differentiated parental behaviors is found. When the separate teaching behaviors of fathers and of mothers were videotaped, observed, and independently rated, it emerged that greater emphasis was placed by parents on the achievements of sons than of daughters (Block, Block, and Harrington, 1975). With their sons, fathers set higher standards, attended to the cognitive elements of the tasks, took advantage of opportunities to engage in "incidental teaching," and placed greater emphasis on performance in the teaching/learning situation. With their daughters, fathers focused more on the interpersonal aspects of the teaching situation—encouraging, supporting, joking and playing, and protecting. A similar sex-differentiated pattern in adults' teaching behaviors was found by Day (1975) in an experiment in which the investigator manipulated the presumption of the sex of her two-year-old subjects. Adults, particularly males, provided more goal-directed reinforcements to presumed boys and expected them to do significantly better on the tasks than presumed girls. Presumed girls were given more compliments and encouragement. The lesser paternal emphasis on achievement and mastery in girls is also reflected in maternal behaviors. Mothers of girls have been observed to provide help in problem solving situations more than mothers of boys, even when their help was not required (Gunnar-vonGnechten, 1977; Rothbart, 1971; Rothbart and Rothbart, 1976). Mothers respond with more positive affect to bids for help from girls than from boys (Fagot, 1977) and provide girls more immediate physical comfort after a frustrating experience (Lewis, 1972b). Overall, these results indicate that adults, particularly fathers, act in more instrumental, task-oriented, mastery-emphasizing ways with their sons and in more expressive, less achievement-oriented, more dependency-reinforcing ways with their daughters (Cantor, Wood, and Gelfand, 1977; Hoffman, 1975; Radin, 1976; Stein and Bailey, 1973).

The differential emphasis on cognitive achievement and independent problem solving given by parents of boys serves to communicate early to the son parental expectations for later achievement. While this readiness to provide help and support to daughters may be well-intentioned, it also constrains their problem-solving experiences. Further, at a metacommunicative level, such help may convey the message to the daughter that her parents feel insecure about her ability to deal effectively with situations. Such messages, in conjunction with attenuated opportunities to engage in independent problem solving, would be expected to influence the development of self-confidence in females.

As the preceding studies indicate, evidence has been accruing suggesting that parents treat their sons differently from their daughters in a number of areas implicative for later development. Because fathers have been included more often in recent investigations, sex-differentiated socialization emphases, not identified in earlier studies, have been revealed. The divergencies in the socialization of males and females that have been discussed derive from studies based predominantly on white middle- or upper-lower-class families. There have been few systematic studies of parenting among other ethnic groups in our society, and until such investigations are completed, we cannot know the extent to which conclusions about sex-differentiated parenting discussed in this section can be generalized. Although the researches cited indicate differences in parental behaviors exist in a number of domains as a function of the sex of the child, more empirical efforts are required to evaluate the robustness of these effects, to define the limits of generalization, to identify factors influencing sex-differentiated parental behaviors, and to evaluate stringently the specific impact, over time, of these sex-differentiated parenting emphases on the personality and cognitive development of sons and daughters. Families, however, are not the only socializing institutions in our society, and we turn now to consider socialization in the context of the schools.

   Studies of Sex-Differentiated Teacher Behaviors. To the extent that sex-related differences in family socialization patterns are echoed in the behaviors of teachers, the sex-typed behaviors of males and females are given extensive reinforcement. There is considerable evidence for such reinforcement in the classroom. Observations of nursery school teachers' behaviors demonstrate in several studies that boys are given more attention, both positive and negative, than girls (Meyer and Thompson, 1956; Serbin and others, 1973; Felsenthal, 1970). Serbin and others (1973) also found differences in the responses given to boys and to girls in reaction to solicitation behaviors: Not only were teachers were likely to respond to boys, but they responded in more encouraging ways. Other researchers have reported similar findings (Cherry, 1975; Golden and Birns, 1975). The results of a recent study of teaching behavior with fifth-grade children solving concept evaluation problems are distressing in their implications for intellectually advantaged girls (Frey, 1979). The teaching behaviors of male and female tutors were recorded as they taught boys and girls assigned to one of two ability levels (high and moderate achievement). Of the four groups of pupils, *girls in the high-achievement condition received the lowest levels of supportive, ego-enhancing feedback;* they also received significantly fewer laudatory attributional statements and significantly more disparaging attributional statements. The findings from this study cohere with those from other studies of sex-differentiated teacher behavior where teachers have been observed to interact more with boys, to give boys more positive feedback, and to direct more criticism toward girls, even high-achieving girls (Cherry, 1975; Sears and Feldman, 1966; Serbin and others, 1973).

   At the university level, lesser reinforcement of the cognitive achievements of female students also has been reported. Survey studies of student and faculty attitudes reveal that the intellectual aspirations of female students are taken less seriously by professors (Carnegie Commission on Higher Education, 1973b; Feldman, 1974; Heyman, 1977; Hochschild, 1975). The greater attrition of women in higher education may reflect, among other factors, the pernicious effects of this pattern of discouragement and negative reinforcement of females' intellectual activities, a pattern identified at all educational levels—from nursery school through college.

These results from the home, laboratory, and classroom settings suggest that girls, even high-achieving girls, are given less encouragement than their male peers for cognitive efforts. The gender differences in confidence, self-concept, and problem-solving behaviors noted by Hoffman (1977a), Tyler (1965), and others may well derive from these home and classroom experiences, which often discourage and denigrate the efforts of females.

In addition to specific teacher behaviors, the larger school context plays a role in socialization as well, reinforcing gender differences and emphasizing traditional sex role behaviors. Males hold the more prestigious positions in the school system; at the elementary and secondary levels, female teachers are less professionally identified and committed; schoolyards tend to be sex-segregated as a function of the different activity preferences of boys and girls; and classroom chores tend to be allocated in a sex-differentiated way (Guttentag and Bray, 1977). Further, the games in which boys and girls spontaneously participate on the playground are sex-differentiated and diverge in their formal characteristics. Lever (1976) analyzed the formal characteristics of games played on the playground by boys and by girls and found that girls participated more in highly structured, turn-taking games, which are regulated by invariable procedural rules, include fewer players, and less often require contingent strategies. In contrast, boys more often participated in games that, though rule-governed, rewarded initiative, improvisation, and extemporaneity. Boys' games involved teams made up of a number of peers and encouraged both within-team cooperation and between-team competition. These differences in preferences of males and females for structured versus unstructured games and activities have important ramifications, as the research of Carpenter and Huston-Stein (1980) has demonstrated. In preschool classrooms, girls were observed by these investiga-

tors to spend more time than boys in highly structured activities (playing house, cooking, looking at books, playing with
puzzles), while boys spent more time than girls in low-structure
activities (playing with blocks or Tinkertoys, engaging in rough-
and-tumble play). Carrying their analysis one step further, these
investigators also examined the effects of structure on behavior
and found that both boys and girls manifested more compliance
and less novel behavior in high-structure than low-structure activities. Because girls spend more time from preschool on in
games and activities that are more highly structured than the
activities and games of boys, girls—even in their play—are learning compliance to rules and roles and adherence to the familiar.
Boys, in contrast, are learning to develop their own structures,
to generate rules, and to experiment with new approaches to
problems.

Differences in teacher behaviors, institutional arrangements, and experiences with peers in play activities operate to
accentuate differences between males and females from an early
age. They also reinforce the sex-differentiating socialization behaviors of parents by extending the network of stereotyped sex
role socializing agents beyond the family into the larger world.

Implications of Sex-Differentiated Socialization Effects

I suggest that the sex-differentiated socialization observed
in the home, at school, and on the playground acts to define
different learning environments and experiential contexts for
males and for females. The average expectable environment of
the male child is more extended, less structured, more tolerant
of active play, more accepting of aggression with peers, more
emphasizing of mastery. In addition, the context in which males
more typically develop provides more frequent and more certain feedback and encourages exploration, experimentation, and
independent problem solving. It is suggested that such socialization experiences, more often provided males, are conducive to
the development of "wings"—which permit leaving the nest, exploring far reaches, and flying alone.

In contrast, the average expectable environment created

by the socialization emphases and practices more often manifested by parents of girls appears to be more circumscribed, more closely supervised, more emphasizing of the proprieties. In addition, the milieu in which females typically develop is more socially interactive, is more structured, provides less feedback, and stresses familial interdependence and responsibilities. Such a learning environment would be expected to be more conducive to the development of "roots"—roots that anchor, stabilize, and support growth.

Roots and wings must be viewed as conjugate legacies, however. Wings without roots may eventuate in unfettered, adventurous souls—free spirits who, however, may lack commitment, civility, and relatedness. Roots without wings may issue prudent, dependable, nurturing, but tethered individuals—responsible beings who may lack independence, self-direction, and a sense of adventure. In reviewing the literature on the socialization of female children and adolescents, it is difficult to escape the conclusion that, at least until very recently, females in our society are "oversocialized," having been bequeathed roots without wings.

Some results emerging from our longitudinal study—started in 1968—of ego and cognitive development from the preschool period to late adolescence (Block and Block, 1980b) speak to the question of oversocialization. In evaluating the effects of different kinds of family experiences on male and female adolescents, it was found that particular family circumstances appear to be associated in a sex-differentiated way with personality characteristics in preadolescents. While family disruption (for example, separation, divorce, death of a parent) was significantly associated with a number of negative psychological characteristics in the sample of boys, family disruption was relatively independent of the quality of psychological functioning in the sample of girls. The personality characteristics of the children were assessed using the CCQ, the 100-item California Child Q-Set (Block and Block, 1980a), which was completed by the child's teacher(s), by four graduate students who separately saw each child in two one-hour testing sessions, and by a graduate student who viewed a twenty-minute color videotape of each child producing a dramatic production in a standardized free-play situation. All persons completed the Q-sort descriptions independently, and the individual Q-sort item placements were averaged to form a composite personality description of each child. Among the items significantly distinguishing boys from nonintact families were items suggestive of undercontrol of impulse (inability to delay gratification, lack of planfulness, inattentiveness, restlessness, rapidly changing moods) and of ego brittleness, or nonresiliency (lesser responsivity to reason, lesser competence). In contrast, and as the data in Table 4.1 indicate, few of the CCQ items significantly distinguished preadolescent girls from nonintact families.*

In a second analysis, the psychological characteristics at age eleven associated with less extreme changes in the family (moving to a new neighborhood, changes of school not part of the regular sequence, changes in the employment status of mother and/or father) were found once again to be sex-differentiated. In this analysis, family changes not involving object loss or disruption of affective relationships were found to be associated in the sample of preadolescent girls with a large number of CCQ items reflecting ego resiliency (for example, ability to cope with stress, tolerance of ambiguity, responsivity, creativity, self-reliance) and with moderate ego undercontrol (curiosity, testing or stretching limits, lesser inhibition and constriction, self-assertion). In all, 32 percent of the CCQ items were significantly associated ($p < .05$) with the family change score in the sample of girls, while *none* of the CCQ items produced significant correlations in the sample of boys, as the data in Table 4.2 indicate.

In reflecting on the meaning of these results with respect to preadolescent girls, I suggest that external events or circumstances that shake up the family system set in motion the possibility of compensations for the tendency to oversocialize females in our society. That is, moves, changes in school, mothers going to work may present more opportunities for girls to learn to be independent, to explore, to be self-reliant than they typically experience in their average expectable environment. Even in more serious family disruption, whereby only one parent re-

*Tables appear at the end of the chapter.

mains available on an everyday basis, young girls may not be as profoundly impaired as boys because family disruption, in its very nature, results in a diminution of supervision, restriction, and help giving. Although one would not wish to prescribe family change as an antidote to the tendency to oversocialize females, these results may encourage reflection on the qualities of "growth-encouraging" environments. The characteristics of environments favoring the realization of potentials for males and for females may not be the same. Because of the tendency to oversocialize females in our society, girls learn early to (over)control impulses, to be tractable, obedient, cautious, and self-sacrificing. Although these psychological characteristics may have been functional in yesterday's world of large families, a predominantly male work force, and shorter life spans, their functionalism in today's world is problematic. As Hoffman (1977a) has pointed out, the socialization of females, similar across many Western cultures, is guided by the assumption that women will spend most of their adult lives engaged in mothering activities. The decrease in size of the average family, the increasing numbers of women employed outside the home, and increased longevity have changed dramatically the nature of women's activities. Because more time is currently being spent by women in working than in mothering (Hoffman, 1977a), the process by which females are socialized requires review. The ego resiliency, spontaneity, and competencies that serve women well both at home and in the workplace may be facilitated by learning contexts that are somewhat less circumscribed, structured, supervised, and predictable—environments that permit more opportunity for independent problem solving. To accomplish these goals, greater parental "distancing," as suggested by Sigel and Cocking (1976), would be beneficial, affording girls greater freedom to explore the world, to engage in trial-and-error learning, to profit from their mistakes. In structured, sheltered environments, lessons are too often taught, a practice that deprives the child of the opportunity to "invent" solutions and educe principles. With appropriate "distancing," encouragement, and affirmation of competence, parents can bequeath wings as well as roots to their daughters.

Table 4.1. Significant California Child Q-Sort Correlates of the Stress Index
at Age Eleven: Disruption of Object Relations.

Sample of girls (N = 48)		California Child Q-Sort Item	Sample of boys (N = 50)	
r	p		r	p
.17	ns	Seeks reassurance from others	.32	.05
.04	ns	Is restless and fidgety	.33	.05
.28	.10	Has rapid shifts in mood	.29	.05
.19	ns	Unable to delay gratification	.28	.05
− .14	ns	Is attentive, able to concentrate	− .39	.01
− .04	ns	Is planful, thinks ahead	− .39	.01
− .14	ns	Appears bright	− .38	.01
− .27	.10	Uses and responds to reason	− .42	.01
− .31	.05	Has high standards for self	− .25	.10
− .10	ns	Is verbally fluent	− .30	.05
− .10	ns	Is competent, skillful	− .32	.05
− .08	ns	Is reflective	− .34	.05
.09	ns	Composite Ego Undercontrol Index	.24	.10
.00	ns	Composite Ego Resiliency Index	− .13	ns

Note: ns = not significant.

Table 4.2. Significant California Child Q-Sort Correlates of the Stress Index
at Age Eleven: Number of Family Changes.

Sample of girls (N = 48)			Sample of boys (N = 50)		
r	p	California Child Q-Sort Item	r	p	Difference between Z scores
.45	.01	Is an interesting, arresting child	.00	—	2.32
.43	.01	Is verbally fluent	−.10	—	2.69
.42	.01	Is curious, exploring	.02	—	2.05
.41	.01	Is self-assertive	−.14	—	2.76
.41	.01	Is talkative	−.07	—	2.42
.38	.01	Responds to humor	−.04	—	2.11
.38	.01	Tries to be center of attention	−.17	—	2.74
.36	.01	Is self-reliant, confident	−.14	—	2.48
.35	.05	Is vital, energetic	.07	—	—
.35	.05	Characteristically tries to stretch limits	−.02	—	—
.33	.05	Can recoup after stressful experiences	−.09	—	—
.32	.05	Becomes strongly involved in activities	−.05	—	—
.33	.05	Is aggressive	−.16	—	2.42
.30	.05	Is warm and responsive	.04	—	—
.29	.05	Is creative	.02	—	—
−.47	.001	Becomes anxious when environment is unstructured	.09	—	2.88
−.45	.01	Is shy and reserved	.02	—	2.42
−.45	.01	Tends to keep thoughts to self	.05	—	2.56
−.42	.01	Is inhibited and constricted	.05	—	2.39
−.42	.01	Tends to withdraw under stress	.03	—	2.29
−.41	.01	Tends to be indecisive, vacillating	.22	—	3.16
−.42	.01	Looks to adults for help and direction	.07	—	2.48
−.41	.01	Is fearful and anxious	.09	—	2.52
−.37	.01	Is physically cautious	.00	—	—
−.37	.01	Is neat and orderly	.04	—	2.05
−.36	.05	Is immobilized or rigidly repetitive under stress	.13	—	2.43
−.33	.05	Tends to go to pieces under stress	.14	—	—
−.34	.05	Tends to be distrustful	.02	—	—
−.36	.05	Tends to be sulky, whiny	.02	—	—
−.31	.05	Reverts to immature behavior under stress	.03	—	—
−.29	.05	Seeks reassurance from others	−.06	—	—
−.29	.05	Is obedient and compliant	.03	—	—
.39	.01	Composite Ego Undercontrol Index	−.01	—	2.03
.39	.01	Composite Ego Resiliency Index	−.05	—	2.23

Chapter Five

Background Factors Related to Sex Role Socialization and Personality

Conventional societal definitions of masculine and feminine behavior are under challenge by the new feminism and other social movements. Freud's dictum that "anatomy is destiny" is regarded by many contemporary women as a "male chauvinist" premise, to be categorically rejected. In the view of those seeking redefinition of traditional sex roles, the extant cultural forces powerfully shaping sex role socialization in the developing child attenuate the human possibilities residing in the individual, whether male or female. Concern with this issue is intense; the implications of the movement are profound.

Until recently, psychological research in this realm was

Originally published in *Journal of Consulting and Clinical Psychology*, 1973, *41*, 321–341, with the title "Sex-Role and Socialization Patterns: Some Personality Concomitants and Environmental Antecedents." Copyright 1973 by the American Psychological Association. Reprinted and adapted by permission of the publisher.

directed primarily toward the naturalistic description of sex role acquisition, the extent and nature of sex differences, and the defining characteristics and prevalence of sexual stereotypes. With only a few exceptions (for example, Keniston, 1971), the cultural prescriptions and proscriptions for appropriate sex role behavior for men and for women have been little studied in an empirical and systematic way to determine their characterological influence and the extent to which the way to personal integration is eased or burdened. The present study attempts to address this question from the context of longitudinal investigation by identifying some antecedent, historical variables associated with the achievement of different sex role and socialization patterns, as manifested in adulthood.

Explanations of the development of sex differences and what are commonly called sex role characteristics have been attempted from the viewpoints of social learning (Mischel, 1966), psychoanalysis (Bronfenbrenner, 1960), and developmental cognition (Kohlberg, 1966). Within each of these perspectives, the motivated modeling of another person, that is, the mechanism of identification, has been invoked as a means of explaining sex role development, albeit in different ways. The effectiveness of models has been attributed, for example, to their power over resources (Bandura and Walters, 1963), their consumption of resources (Whiting, 1959), their potential for aggression (Bronfenbrenner, 1960; Mowrer, 1950), and their warmth and affection (Sanford, 1955; Sears, 1957).

Essays and empiricism have attempted to establish the connections between the behaviors, attributes, and perceived characteristics of the persons principally responsible for the upbringing of the child—the parents or their surrogates—and the subsequent sex role development of the child.

Reviews by Maccoby (1966a) and Becker (1964) and specific research reports by Bronson (1959), Brown (1957), Heilbrun (1965), Lansky and others (1961), Lynn (1962), Mussen and Distler (1959), Payne and Mussen (1956), and Tiller (1958) suggest that children generally prefer association with their same-sex parent, like that parent better, and are more influenced by that parent—all indications of a strong motive for modeling the same-sex parent. A correspondence between liking for parents and the assumption of sex role manifestations has also received empirical support. There is further general agreement in the literature that appropriate sex role behavior and personal adjustment are positively related (Cava and Raush, 1952; Lazowik, 1955; Payne and Mussen, 1956; Rychlak and Legerski, 1967). Still other investigations call attention to the different behavioral manifestations associated with different levels of sex role learning (Bronson, 1959; Lansky and others, 1961). In particular, studies of boys from father-absent homes have suggested the existence of a compensatory masculinity on an overt level, with feminine tendencies existing on the covert level (Lynn and Sawrey, 1959; Tiller, 1958). It therefore cannot be assumed that overt attitudes and ideals correspond to the attitudes operating on a covert level; indeed, the overt manifestations may represent a defensive cover for an underlying rejection or failure to attain these manifest ideals. Further, discrepancies between overt and covert attitudes may most readily occur where the child's relationship to the same-sex parent is conflicted (see, for example, Bronson, 1959; Miller and Swanson, 1960).

Modeling of parents has been used to explain more than the establishment of sex role typing. From a societal standpoint, parental influence is the vehicle by which internalization of norms, values, and self-control—in short, the socialization of the child—is made to occur. Either parent may be influential (Jourard, 1957; von der Lippe, 1965), and his or her influence is facilitated by a positive affective relationship with the child. Sex role typing is only one aspect of these broader requirements of socialization, although a most fundamental one, which appears to be mediated by determinants similar to those already noted. For example, the sex role typing of the child has been found to correspond to the sex of the dominant disciplinarian in the home, if that parent is also affectionate (Moulton and others, 1966).

As the foregoing brief review suggests, previous research and thinking on sex role typing, socialization, and identification, although informative and convergent in many ways, nevertheless has tended to place these three aspects of growing up into one large conceptual grab bag. Sex role typing has been viewed as equivalent to identification, but, of course, it is not. The achievement of sex role typing does not require similarity in this regard between son and father; nor is a similarity in value orientation (the core meaning of identification) between son and father required even if there exists a similarity in sex role typing across the generations. In noting a positive (but not perfect!) relationship between identification and socialization, psychologists have failed to give due consideration to the many exceptions to this rule; one can identify, for example, without also being socialized, just as one can be socialized without having identified. Exceptions such as these, when studied rather than neglected, can be especially clarifying and advancing of our understanding of personality development.

It is from this last point of view that the present analysis derives. A distinction was enforced between sex role typing, on the one hand, and socialization, on the other. A sample of adult males and a sample of adult females were grouped according to their sex role and socialization pattern, and the empirical incisiveness or power of this conceptual separation was then evaluated. Because this analysis of the "contemporary," or concomitant, implications of distinguishing between sex role typing and socialization was found to be trenchant, further analysis proceeded to evaluate a variety of family and childhood data available for these subjects, seeking to comprehend the many relationships found in terms of a differentiated and extended concept of identification.

Measuring Sex Role and Socialization

As operational measures of the concepts of sex role typing and of socialization in adults, two scales were used from the CPI, the California Psychological Inventory (Gough, 1964), a well-developed and widely used personality assessment device. The two scales selected, the Femininity (Fe) scale and the Socialization (So) scale, are measures whose conceptual origins and established validities seemed especially appropriate for the purposes of this study.

The CPI Femininity Scale. The thirty-eight-item Fe scale, as developed by Gough (1952), has three purposes: (1) to differentiate males from females, (2) to distinguish between deviant and sexually normal persons, and (3) to define a personological continuum that could be conceptualized as "feminine" at one pole and "masculine" at the other (Gough, 1968a, p. 66). The scale has been employed extensively on large samples in the United States and in other countries, establishing its validity as a discriminator of the sexes and its usefulness as an indicator of the psychological nature of masculinity and femininity. In particular, the power of the Fe scale to differentiate the sexes in seven rather different cultures suggests that what is tapped by the scale goes beyond any narrowly defined and highly culture-specific view of sex role behaviors and values. Gough (1966) views the underlying but broad psychological dimension reflected by the Fe scale as one of *conservation versus initiation*, recognizing that other continua could be specified for other masculinity/femininity measures. That is, any measure of masculinity/femininity at the present state of psychological knowledge *must selectively emphasize* one or another of the continua on which sex differences can be empirically demonstrated.

Thus, whether the Fe scale identifies a single underlying dimension of "basic" femininity or a less basic subdimension is uncertain. The construct of masculinity/femininity is still evolving in psychology, and scales must therefore be seen as less than final. Moreover, for certain conceptual purposes it may be useful to view femininity and masculinity not as polar opposites of a single dimension but as polyfactorial categories employed (imperfectly) in cultural usage.

Although conceptual issues still remain, it seems safe to state that the Fe scale reflects the broadly held and culturally relevant sex role attitudes prevalent in the United States, and it is on this basis that the scale was used in the present study.

The CPI Socialization Scale. The fifty-four-item So scale attempts to measure the degree to which an individual has internalized societal standards—that is, is "able to govern internally his thought and behavior in accordance with the imperatives of his culture" (Gough, 1960, p. 24). Individuals at the high end of the socialization continuum are "rule respecting"; individuals at the very low end are asocial, even delinquent, and are "unperceptive concerning the inner needs and feelings of others, little guided by interpersonal nuances, and (thereby) given to rash and precipitate behaviors" (Gough, 1968a, p. 66).

Construction of the So scale was guided by an adaptation of Mead's (1934) role-taking theory of the development of the self, in which the self is seen as "the product of social interaction and of the capacity of the individual to view himself as an object, that is, from the standpoint of the other" (Gough, 1960, p. 23). Gough views socialization as a continuous, broadly valid psychological dimension varying inversely, but not perfectly, with sociological definitions of delinquency.

Research on the So scale has been extensive, with many studies testifying to its construct validity. Thus, cross-cultural research confirms that the So scale successfully separates delinquents from nondelinquents in a number of different cultural contexts (Gough, 1965), while other studies support the claim for the continuous dimensionality of the So scale (Gough, 1960). Because of the So scale's conceptual basis and the empirical support it has attained, the scale seemed especially pertinent for this study.

The subject samples were drawn from two of the ongoing longitudinal studies being conducted at the University of California at Berkeley. One was initiated by Harold E. Jones (1938, 1939a, 1939b) and has been known as the Oakland Growth Study; the second was begun by Jean Macfarlane and has been known as the Berkeley Guidance Study. Characteristics of the subjects in each of these studies, as children and as adults, have been described in Jones (1938, 1939a, 1939b), Macfarlane (1971a, 1971b), and Block (1971). All the subjects in these two studies between the ages of thirty and forty years who had responded to the CPI (sixty-six men and sixty-eight women) were included for the purposes of the present analysis.

The sex role/socialization subgroups were formed in the following way: Within the male sample, and separately within the female sample, four subgroups of subjects were formed on the basis of scores above and below the mean of the Fe scale and the So scale for that sample. For the present conceptual purposes, the Fe scale, when scored for the male sample, required reflection of its orientation, so that *a low Fe scale score, for a male, implies strong masculine sex role typing.* For labeling convenience, individuals scoring above the mean of the Fe scale are designated, if male, as low masculine and, if female, as feminine. Individuals scoring below the mean of the Fe scale are designated, if male, as masculine, and if female, as low feminine. Individuals, whether male or female, who scored above the mean of the So scale are designated as socialized, while those scoring below the mean are identified as relatively low in socialization. Table 5.1 presents the designations for the defined quadrants, their cutting points, means, and the sizes of the male and female groupings.* The disproportionate sizes of the several subgroups reflect the correlations (.33 and .34, respectively, for the two sexes) between the Fe and So scales. Fortunately, no subgroup was so small as to preclude statistical analysis.

Each adult in the sample was described by at least two, and usually three, clinical psychologists, using a slight variant of the 100-item California Q-Set (Block, 1961). The psychological descriptions were based on extensive in-depth interview proto cols. The judges worked independently, and their separately formulated Q descriptions were composited to form a more reliable characterization of each subject. These composite evaluations were used in the present analysis. A complete description of the rationale, procedure, reliability, and validity of these personality characterizations may be found in Block (1971). The reader should note that the Q character formulations are entirely independent of the inventory protocols on the basis of which the subjects were placed into sex role/socialization categories.

Three kinds of early environmental data were obtained, although complete data were not available for all subjects. These were the early family ratings, the ratings of mothers, and environmental Q-set descriptions. Only a brief description of these data sources is provided here; for fuller accounts, the reader is again referred to Block (1971).

*Tables appear at the end of the chapter.

The early family ratings were obtained between the twenty-first and thirty-sixth months of the lives of the subjects who participated in the Berkeley Guidance Study. Both parents were interviewed by staff psychologists and social workers, and parent/child interactions were observed in the home. The parents were then rated on forty-two variables, each scaled to five steps. The ratings covered an array of personality, attitudinal, and interactional characteristics. Consensus ratings were obtained by differentially weighting the several judgments of the raters according to the confidence of each judge in his or her evaluation.

The mother ratings were available for almost all the subjects and consisted of twenty-nine judgments about the mother's intellectual and emotional characteristics. The mothers in the two samples were assessed by psychologists at differing times. Four ratings were made of the Berkeley Guidance mothers during their children's second and third years. The mothers of Oakland Growth Study subjects were evaluated three times between their children's eleventh and fifteenth years. Evaluation of the two sets of data in another context (Block, 1971) indicated sufficient comparability to justify merging them.

The environmental Q-set consists of ninety-two Q items, developed by Block and Block (1967), which were used to describe the subjects' early history and family conditions. The descriptions, made by one of three clinical psychologists, were based on the subjects' retrospective recall, as expressed during intensive interviews, of both parents and childhood environment. These ratings were independent of the early family ratings, the mother ratings, and the California Q-Set personality descriptions.

In addition to the above data sources, a number of other variables such as intelligence, personality integration, and socioeconomic status of parents and of the subjects were included in the analyses. Finally, it is important to note that the environmental data are entirely independent of the CPI protocols on the basis of which the subjects were placed into sex role/socialization categories.

Relating the various sex role/socialization patterns, as defined by the CPI, to other and independent manifestations of adult personality—that is, the California Q-Set character formulations—serves to clarify the meaning of the groupings and addresses the question of their heuristic value. The antecedent data collected when the subjects were children (the early family ratings and the ratings of mothers) and those achieved retrospectively (the environmental Q descriptions) provide a developmental basis for our understanding of sex role definition and socialization. The results are presented, separately by sex, for each of the four subgroups that have been identified.

The analysis of several sets of data, each containing numerous variables and with respect to several groups of subjects, involves statistical and reportorial problems not commonly faced by psychologists. Many issues remain unresolved; meanwhile, various analytical approaches are conceivable. The considerations we deemed important, and our consequent decisions, follow.

Only the statistically differentiating variables are presented. Because sample sizes for certain data sets are frequently small, the power of the statistical tests is often rather low. In our judgment, the usual statistical threshold of significance (the .05 level) would have been excessively stringent because of the exploratory intent of the study and because of the unprecedented nature of some of the longitudinal data. Accordingly, all variables or Q items significant at or beyond the .10 level are reported.

Each "target" subgroup was compared with the complement group, consisting of all the remaining subjects of the same sex—that is, the three remaining subgroups combined. This comparison tactic loses some analytical sensitivity by neglecting the differences among the three groups merged to form the complement; however, the results issued by the "target"-versus-complement comparisons are likely to be more dependable in conveying the unique nature of the "target" group in the particular analysis.

The t test was used throughout for all comparisons. Though recognizing the statistical problem of evaluating multiple comparisons, we could find no coherent, defensible, and information-sensitive set of rules in the statistical literature for evaluating multiple comparisons with diverse subject groups and numerous variables in each of several data sets. In view of this statistical insufficiency, we relied on three jointly applied criteria to support the substantiality of the findings: First, the various data sets being analyzed are *methodologically independent* of one another. Second, within each data source, the quadrant analyses reach *generally acceptable levels of significance,* particularly for a frankly exploratory study. Third, and perhaps most important, the nonchance relationships issued by the various totally independent data sources and subject groups are clearly *psychologically convergent.* These three simultaneously applied criteria—one logical, one statistical, and one psychological—we deemed adequate for establishing the meaningfulness of the relationships observed.

Personality Characteristics and Antecedent Data
Associated with Different Sex Role/Socialization Patterns
in the Male Sample

High-Masculine/High-Socialized Male. The independently achieved Q data describing the adult personalities of the male subjects in this subgroup, and the various differentiating antecedent data, are presented in Table 5.2.

The high-masculine/high-socialized males were characterized by California Q-Set descriptions of their middle adulthood as self-confident, competent, optimistic men with buoyant affect. In looking at the developmental concomitants of this essentially healthy world outlook, the results, though somewhat sparse, suggest that the father was the more salient figure for the sex role acquisition of this group of men. A consistent picture of the father emerges as a somewhat introverted and undemonstrative man who guarded his own autonomy and granted his son the same prerogative. But also, the father was available to and accepting of his son. A similar factor of self-containment and lack of overinvolvement characterized the mother, joined with an absence of guilt- or dependency-inducing childrearing methods. Altogether, a friendly, somewhat neutral, atmosphere in the home is suggested wherein the son could develop free of intruding and compelling parental needs.

High-Masculine/Low-Socialized Males. Table 5.3 presents the relevant comparisons for the high-masculine/low-socialized males.

In contrast to the high-masculine/high-socialized males, the masculine, relatively nonsocialized men present an adult picture in which machismo, egotism, and undercontrol of impulse are salient features. These men appear, on the basis of their California Q-Set descriptions, as self-centered, impulsive, irresponsible, exploitative, independent men chafing at constraint and demand. That their hypermasculinity and bravado reflect a compensatory mechanism is suggested by the salient items indicating insecurity and vulnerability. The inability of these men to participate in a mutual interpersonal relationship appears to have alienated and isolated them from others. Available actuarial data reveals that men in this group were significantly lower in both educational attainment ($p < .05$) and socioeconomic status ($p < .05$).

The available antecedent data characterizing men in the high-masculine/low-socialization group are impressively uniform in implication. The results suggest that these men had weak, neurotic, somewhat rejecting fathers who provided poor identification models for their sons. The mothers were seen as resentful and dissatisfied about their social, maternal, and marital situations. They were dissatisfied with their husbands, both as companions and as sexual partners. Reacting to unsatisfied social and sexual needs, these mothers may have turned to their sons in a symbolically seductive bid for masculine attentions. In an environment that provided relatively little emotional satisfaction and acceptance, the sons may well have responded to their mothers with increased masculine self-awareness. This sense of masculine self, however, did not develop in the context of socialization practices that foster empathy or impulse restraint.

Low-Masculine/High-Socialized Males. The data differentiating the males in this subgroup are presented in Table 5.4.

The men in this group were, with respect to both ethical responsibility and impulse control, the reverse image of the high-masculine/low-socialized group described above. This group of relatively less masculine but socialized men were seen as overcontrolled, conventional, consistent, productive, and conscientious—traits generally encompassed by the Protestant ethic. In their interpersonal relationships, these men are perhaps unexciting, but they offer nurturance and fulfill duty. The constellation of Q items characterizing this "low masculine" group by no means suggests a feminine or passive orientation. Rather, the items appear to describe a pattern of benign and responsible masculinity in which aggressive components are relatively lacking.

The data obtained from ratings made during childhood and the retrospective environmental Q descriptions converge in their characterizations of the parents of men in the low-masculine/high-socialized group. The father provided a model for the son of success, ambition, adjustment, and mutuality in his interpersonal relationships. The mother possessed traits more worthy of emulation, perhaps, than any other group of mothers with sons. Although the son's comparatively low masculinity raises the question of a feminine identification with the mother, there was little in the nature of his adult personality configuration to support this view. Rather, it is the father's capacity for delay of gratification and commitment to long-range goals that seems to characterize the son. This interpretation is buttressed by actuarial data indicating that the low-masculine/high-socialized males were, as adults, significantly better educated ($p < .10$) and economically more secure ($p < .05$). It appears that the son had identified with the future orientation of the father and with the traits valued by the educated "gentle"-man. This identification, conjoined with the admirable personal qualities of the mothers and the harmonious nature of the home characteristic of men in this group, appeared to foster the assumption of personal responsibility, a manifest concern for other people, and the development of a benign, but relatively unspontaneous, adult personality—traits that only in an actuarially normative sense could be termed feminine. In this context, it is interesting to note that the men in this group were distinguished in adulthood by having larger families ($p < .05$) than the complement men.

Low-Masculine/Low-Socialized Males. The personality descriptions and antecedent data characterizing men in the low-masculine/low-socialized group are presented in Table 5.5.

The men low on the dimensions of masculinity and socialization were differentiated from the complement by a pattern of items conveying a picture of vulnerability and self-doubt. The causes of inadequacy and insecurity appear to be projected onto the external world, as indicated in the conjoined salient items of projection, extrapunitiveness, feelings of victimization, and sensitivity to criticism. These men placed little value on independence and autonomy and tended to be submissive and accommodating in their interpersonal relationships. Paralleling this pattern of interpersonal dependence was a lack of cognitive autonomy and an affective despondency.

The personal despair depicted by the California Q-Set descriptions of the low-masculine/low-socialized men seems consistent with the characterizations of the parents of the men. According to the antecedent data, both parents of men in this group seemed to have provided their sons with inadequate adult models. The fathers were distant from their sons and conflict-inducing, while the mothers were neurotic, energyless, and disaffected with their maternal roles. The parents had both experienced significantly more marriages ($p < .01$ for fathers; $p < .10$ for mothers), reflecting, perhaps, their respective inabilities to maintain close relationships with others. The homes these parents created seem to have isolated the sons in two ways: in a psychological isolation from the parents themselves (lack of discussion of problems, deemphasis on togetherness, absence of child-centeredness) and in a physical isolation of the sons from peer groups (lack of peer relations, deemphasis on values of peer acceptance, and social isolation of the home). These children seemed, therefore, to have been afforded less opportunity to develop a social, personal, or sexual identity.

Personality Characteristics and Antecedent Data Associated with Different Sex Role/Socialization Patterns in the Female Sample

High-Feminine/High-Socialized Females. The data distinguishing the contemporaneous personalities and antecedent experiences of women in the high-feminine/high-socialized group are presented in Table 5.6.

The personality descriptions of the feminine, socialized

women typify, in many respects, the culturally prescribed feminine sex role. They are conservative, controlling of impulse,
dependable, feminine but not yet sensuous, docile, and conventional. Despite these role-exemplary characteristics, however, a
note of anxiety is suggested by items reflecting vulnerability,
indecision, and personal dissatisfaction. The available antecedent data obtained during childhood were sparse but suggest a
home-and-family-centered environment. The environmental
Q-set descriptions reveal that the mother was the more salient
parent, and a close, warm, sharing mother/daughter relationship was portrayed. The mothers of women in this group appeared to be especially adequate feminine models, both preach-
ing and practicing central values of the role. The homes created
by these mothers were estimable, and it appears that a model
of what home can be is necessary if a girl is to be able to fulfill
effectively the future role of homemaker.

  High-Feminine/Low-Socialized Females. Table 5.7 reports the relationships distinguishing the group of high-feminine/
low-socialized women.

  A dynamic picture, surprisingly similar to but sparser
than that of the parallel male group, the high-masculine/low-
socialized men, is evident. Women in this group appear somewhat hedonistic, rejecting both conventional and achievement-
oriented values and manifesting narcissistic concerns. Available
actuarial data reveal women in this group to have been married
a greater number of times ($p < .01$), and the same trend was
seen in the marriage histories of their mothers ($p < .05$). Extrapolating from the antecedent information, it appears that these
women were provided an inadequate maternal role model; their
own mothers were described as rejecting both of their daughters
and of the maternal role. Further, these mothers were seen as
vulnerable and unable to establish homes for their families that
were satisfying and growth-inducing. The father/daughter relationship appeared to be the more salient one in the lives of the
high-feminine/low-socialized women; indeed, the father introduced a seductive element into the relationship that may have
precociously heightened the sexual self-awareness of these physically attractive girls.

Low-Feminine/High-Socialized Females. The data distinguishing the group of low-feminine/high-socialized women are presented in Table 5.8.

Women in this group appear to be relaxed, poised, outgoing, consciously comfortable and contented, but not at all introspective. They hold conservative, conventional values that are continuous with the value orientations of their parents. The actuarial data reveals that women in this group tended to marry somewhat later ($p < .10$), enjoyed a financially more advantaged position at the time of adolescence ($p < .05$), and, as adults, were more religious ($p < .05$). As children, these women were reared in stable, affectionate, comfortable, relatively unconflicted homes that in many ways appear to exemplify prevailing cultural values communicated to the children jointly by the parents. They diverge from the high-feminine/high-socialized women in that these less feminine but socialized women were presented with a more complex maternal role model than that of the stereotypic "American housewife," the role model for the high-feminine/high-socialized women. Although the mothers of these low-feminine/high-socialized women still represented classical Protestant virtues, the mothers joined these emphases with an orientation toward rationality, intellectual values, and considerable pressure toward achievement, which, in our culture, coincides with the masculine allocentric position (Gutmann, 1965). Although the finding was not significant, mothers in this group had the highest average placement for the Q item reflecting constructive engagement in activities outside the home. The fathers of women in the low-feminine/high-socialized group appear to have been accepting and affectionate.

Low-Feminine/Low-Socialized Females. Table 5.9 lists the relationships characterizing the group of low-feminine/low-socialized women.

In adulthood, women in the low-feminine/low-socialized group were described as assertive, critical, rebellious, and staunchly insistent on autonomy and independence. A constellation of Q items suggests superior intellect, but this is not reflected in a significantly higher measured intellectual level. Personal style and expressiveness, as well as decisiveness and competence, are evident. Actuarial data distinguished this group only by their smaller number of children ($p < .05$) and their disavowal of religious commitment as adults ($p < .10$). This group of women came from backgrounds in many ways similar to those of the comparable male grouping, the low-masculine/low-socialized men. The mothers of these women were depicted as neurotic, vulnerable, and martyred. They were uninvolved in both their marital and maternal roles, and their interpersonal relationships were characterized by conflict, hostility, and dissatisfaction. The fathers were described as active, authoritarian men who emphasized status and power and were not involved with their families. They tended to reject their daughters, and the father/ daughter relationship, like the mother/daughter dyad, was conflicted. The homes of the low-feminine/low-socialized women were described as beset by misfortune, marked by conflict, and exuding constriction and cheerlessness. Neither emotional support nor stabilizing value structures were provided to these women by the parents of either sex, preventing compensatory possibilities within the family.

Conclusions

The relationships issued by this study have been numerous and inundating. It is useful now to try to impose some organization on these findings with the intention of educing principles that can bring order and a wider frame of understanding to this welter of relationships. In what follows, our efforts to perceive system and symmetry sometimes involve evidence not as strong as we would like. The reader is encouraged to generate alternative integrations of our findings. Time and subsequent empirical data should tell which recognitions are helpful or misleading.

1. Considering the familial antecedents of the equivalent sex role/socialization groups for the two sexes, some interesting parallels can be seen.

The sex-appropriate, socialized individuals (high masculine/high socialized and high feminine/high socialized) seem to derive from family contexts in which there is clear and conventional role differentiation between the parents, where both parents appear to be psychologically healthy, where both parents were available both physically and psychologically—throughout adolescence, and where the like-sex parent is the more salient figure for identification than the opposite-sex parent. From this context men eventuate who are relaxedly competent and comfortable with themselves, but women who, though feminine and dependable, are somewhat tense and lacking in spontaneity. It is suggested that these individuals internalized parental values —with respect to both sex role and the nature of personal responsibility—through the process of *identification with the same-sex parent* in a context of familial harmony and traditional parental role definitions.

The sex-inappropriate/socialized individuals (low masculine/high socialized and low feminine/high socialized) have their origins in families where the parents offered more complex, androgynous role differentiations as a model for their children. Parents of the subjects in this group tended to be less stereotyped in their own definitions of masculinity and femininity, thus offering a wider range of behavioral and attitudinal possibilities to their offspring. Mothers of individuals in this group were characterized as relatively achievement-oriented, although simultaneously they fulfilled and achieved satisfaction from both maternal and marital roles. The fathers were respected and successful men but were able to share decision making and financial management with their wives. The parental relationship was characterized as satisfying and relatively conflict-free. Both parents appeared to be psychologically healthy and to have established emotionally satisfying, financially comfortable, and value-inculcating homes. Men and women in this group may be said to have manifested *androgynous identification.* Androgynous identification is the modeling of a parental pair in which neither father nor mother exemplifies the typical cultural sex role stereotypes but, rather, where both parents provide models for their children of competence, tolerance, consideration of others, and sharing of responsibilities. Rossi (1964) has suggested that sex roles should be culturally redefined to be more "androgynous" so that each sex cultivates the highly valued characteristics traditionally associated with the other sex. We have extended the use of the term *androgynous* to describe parental role models that depart from current sex role stereotypes in this way.

The sex-appropriate/unsocialized individuals (high masculine/low socialized and high feminine/low socialized) derive from families in which the same-sex parent was neurotic, was rejecting of the child, and provided a poor model for identification. The opposite-sex parent, however, was characterized as seductive. The home that these parents established for their children were transient in character, with the parents assuming little responsibility for the socialization of the child. Young people growing up in this familial context appeared to have achieved their sex role definition, not through identification, but via a process we term *reactivity*. According to this formulation, the child learns how to behave in sex-appropriate ways not by motivated modeling of the same-sex parent but rather by the reactions shaped in him or her by the behaviors of the opposite-sex parent. By selective reinforcement of complementary reactions, by responding to the child in sexually implicative ways, the opposite-sex parent molds the child's behaviors to fit a version of the traditionally defined sex role.

The final group—sex-inappropriate, unsocialized individuals (low masculine/low socialized and low feminine/low socialized)—have their roots in families characterized by conflict and psychopathology. The same-sex parent of both males and females was emotionally uninvolved, in relation both to the child and to the spouse. The opposite-sex parent, however, was conflict-inducing and salient. The mothers of the low-masculine males were described as having low energy level, as lacking in confidence, as neurotic, brittle, and depressed—characteristics also seen in their sons. The fathers of the low-feminine females were described as active, energetic, assertive men who were both power- and status-oriented. Again, the traits characterizing the fathers can be seen as well in the psychological descriptions of their daughters.

The homes in which the less socialized low-masculine and low-feminine individuals grew up were marked by conflict because of disparate values, and the children were somewhat isolated, reducing the possibility of compensatory positive experiences from the wider social environment. Besides the failure of the same-sex parents to provide adequate role models for the children in this group, the marriage of these parents also failed to provide a model of a healthy interpersonal relationship—a model that could facilitate subsequently the establishment of mutually respecting interpersonal relationships in adulthood. In the absence of adequate same-sex models, and buffeted by conflict and recrimination, women in the low-feminine/low-socialized group rejected the traditional feminine values presented by their mothers in the unattractive context of martyrdom and zealously assert their independence and competence. In the low-masculine/low-socialized group, men rejected the traditional masculine values presented by their uninvolved, neurotic fathers and express their dependency and inadequacy. It appears that the sex-role orientations of individuals in this group have been achieved by *emulation of the opposite-sex parent.*

The data issuing from these analyses, both for men and for women, suggest that a more articulated usage of the over-extended concept of identification is required. Important differences in developmental patterning are obscured when the term *identification* is applied grossly, as it has often been in the past. In the present study, we have seen the achievement of culturally appropriate sex typing via two quite different routes: through identification with or motivated modeling of the same-sex parent and reactively, in the sense of sex role tutoring by the opposite-sex parent. Similarly, the data for the low-masculine and low-feminine groups reveal that culturally deviant sex role definitions also can eventuate in two ways: by the process of androgynous identification—a pattern of identification that includes positive aspects of both parents who themselves are not prototypical sex role exemplifiers—and by emulation of the opposite-sex parent. In this last instance, the corollary rejection of the same-sex parent that was manifested by the low-masculine/low-socialized and low-feminine/low-socialized groups suggests that the sex role definitions and value orientations of these individuals were influenced not only by the cross-sex parent but also by a *counteractive* process as well—the determination to define oneself as *different from* the parent of the like sex. In the present study, it was impossible to distinguish between opposite-sex emulation and same-sex counteraction; perhaps they can never be clearly separated because they represent two facets of the same phenomenon.

2. Levels of masculinity and femininity show markedly different personality correlates when moderated by different levels of socialization. This is a most important recognition.

Each sex role, as defined by Western culture, has both positive and negative characteristics associated with it. Central to the female role are the positive functions of conservation and nurturance. However, empirical studies have regularly shown that associated with the female sex, in addition, are the negatively toned traits of inhibition of impulse, submission, anxiety, and the experience of guilt (Maccoby, 1966a). At the nexus of the male role in the larger contemporary culture are the functions of initiation and instrumentality (Gough, 1966). But coexisting with these positive functions are the negatively imbued traits of domination, aggression, impulsivity, and egocentrism.

In the male sample, men who were highly socialized (high masculine/high socialized and low masculine/high socialized) appear to have incorporated the *positive* sides of both masculine and feminine roles, respectively, with a consequent tempering of unmodulated masculine aggression. Thus, the socialized masculine men displayed such positive aspects of the male sex role as a free and relaxed playfulness, while the socialized, less masculine men exhibited such normatively "feminine" traits as nurturance, overcontrol of impulse, conventionality, and moral and personal consistency.

In contrast, men who were less socialized (high masculine/low socialized and low masculine/low socialized) showed a differential internalization of the *negative* aspects of the corresponding sex roles. The less socialized but masculine men displayed such undesirable "masculine" qualities as egocentric impulsivity, an absence of guiding values, instability in interpersonal relationships, and self-indulgence. The less socialized, less masculine men evidenced the full scale of vulnerabilities adversely coloring the female sex role; emotional dependence, anxiety, hypersensitivity, and gullibility.

For men, socialization appears to expand the personal options available; the "masculine" emphasis on competence and instrumentality becomes joined to a "feminine" emphasis on the interdependence of individuals. They have achieved an integration or balance of masculinity and femininity, of "agency" and "communion" (Bakan, 1966). This interpretation is buttressed by reference to the occupational commitments of the subjects. The socialized males were found primarily in the professions—the humanities and social welfare fields (for example, psychiatrist, welfare foundation executive, sociologist, city planner, teacher) for the low-masculine/high-socialized males, the technical professions for the high-masculine/high-socialized males (engineer, professor of a physical science, vice-president of an accounting firm, and other technical fields). The occupations of the low-socialized males were generally nonprofessional and, in the case of high-masculine/low-socialized men, machismo-emphasizing (for example, law enforcement). The occupations of the low-masculine/low-socialized group are difficult to summarize (included, for example, are a theater owner, a draftsman, a government executive, several managers, and a partner in a business enterprise).

The effects of socialization on women, however, are less salubrious. Characteristics that are essential for individuation and self-expression happen to have been defined by the culture as "masculine," and so, progressively, they must be relinquished in the case of female socialization. Socialization for women, therefore, regardless of level of femininity, becomes associated with control of impulse and expression and the renunciation of achievement and autonomy. Within this framework, the high-feminine/high-socialized women were found to be overcontrolled and somewhat constricted, while the low-feminine/high-socialized women, though still controlled, expressed their initiative by channeling impulse into skillful interpersonal functioning.

At the low end of the socialization continuum, we find undercontrol of impulse and rejection of the positive feminine values. However, there is a differential emphasis on achievement as a function of level of femininity. For high-feminine/low-socialized women, impulse was channeled into dependency, passivity, fantasy, and unconventionality. Low-feminine/low-socialized women, in contrast, have achieved an active adjustment, channeling impulse into cognitive pursuits and assertive autonomy. These women manifest a pattern of personal adaptation that agrees well with Keniston's (1971) portrayal of successful professional young women as comfortable with their assertiveness and competence but rejecting of their needs for relatedness.

The occupational histories of the women in the four groups are revealing. When the number of women in each of the groups who have been relatively continuously employed over the years, and who were employed in full-time positions at the time of interview, is recorded, chi-square analysis reveals significant differences among the four groups ($p < .05$). These differences are associated with socialization ($p < .01$) but are relatively independent of positioning on the femininity dimension.

The occupational choices of the women appear to be reasonably consistent with their sex role/socialization groupings in that the controlled high-feminine/high-socialized women who were employed were more often in technical, less interdependent job assignments (bookkeeping, commercial design, printing, bookbinding), while the high-feminine/low-socialized women were more likely to be employed in traditionally feminine fields (stylist, receptionist, teacher). The occupational commitments of the low-feminine/high-socialized group are more difficult to classify but are of somewhat higher occupational status (included are, for example, a writer, a store manager, and an administrator). The positions of women in the low-feminine/low-socialized group also were distinguished by their higher occupational status and, further, by their departure from "typical feminine interests" (Tyler, 1965). These women were functioning as managers, buyers, craftspersons, insurance agents, and statistical analysts.

When the employment histories of the women over their years of employment were examined, another interesting pattern emerges: an inverse relationship between occupational advancement and femininity. Of those employed, 75 percent of the low-feminine/high-socialized women and 75 percent of the low-feminine/low-socialized women were found to have shown a pattern of upward occupational mobility, while the comparable figure for the high-feminine/high-socialized women is 28 percent and, for the high-feminine/low-socialized women, 33 percent.

The socialization process, then, apparently has differential effects on the personality development of men and women. For males, socialization encourages more androgynous sex role identities, since some traditionally feminine concerns (conscientiousness, conservation, interdependency) are emphasized along with the press to renounce negative aspects of the masculine role (opportunism, restlessness, impulsivity). For women, the socialization process fosters the nurturant, submissive, conservative aspects of the female role and does not move them toward concerns or personal qualities conventionally defined as masculine—assertiveness, achievement orientation, independence. Indeed, such masculine tendencies are explicitly discouraged in the socialization of females. The sex role definitions of women, therefore, are narrowed by the socialization process, whereas for men the sex role definition is broadened by socialization.

The view that socialization for women in this society tends to inhibit their individuation, discourage their achievement, and restrict their autonomy has been expressed before. For example, Horner (1968) attributed a "fear of success" to women, based on her finding that women significantly more often than men (65 percent to 8 percent) expressed anxiety about academic success and also showed a significantly greater decrement in test performance under conditions of competition as compared with individual test administration. Extrapolating from her results, Horner suggests that women anticipate negative reactions and challenges to their femininity as a consequence of high levels of achievement. Keniston (1971) has commented that individuation requires women to come into conflict with their social environment, whereas for men, social expectations tend to facilitate, rather than inhibit, individuation. The interpretation offered here, that traditional socialization patterns tend to multiply and encourage utilization of environmental options for men while diminishing and discouraging invocation of environmental options for women, accords with the many empirical studies of sex differences in the attainment of both personal and professional autonomy (Hoffman, 1972).

The implications of these asymmetrical effects of socialization clearly have been significant. The larger question now is their requiredness.

Rossi (1964) has proposed that appropriate sex role behaviors be redefined by the society to permit each sex to cultivate positively valued characteristics that in the past have been traditionally linked with the other sex. The findings issuing from the present analyses suggest that her proposal would have salutary consequences. Such changes in societal constructions of appropriate sex role behaviors undoubtedly can be expected in the light of other trends already existing within the society. For example, access to higher education has expanded for large segments of young adults, and education appears to be associated with more androgynous sex role definitions (Dahlstrom and Welsh, 1960; Gough, 1968a; Murray, 1963). Larger numbers of women are now employed and in positions of higher status, and Vogel and others (1970) have shown that maternal employment is associated with less polarization in sex role definition. Finally, the experimentation with different sex role patterns that characterizes a numerically small but culturally influential group of contemporary young adults seeking alternative lifestyles may also facilitate societal change not only in sex role definitions but in the broader value emphases conveyed to our male and female children in the process of socialization.

Table 5.1. Characteristics of the Several Sex Role/
Socialization Subgroups.

Male sample (N = 66)[a]	
Low masculinity/high socialization (N = 26)	High masculinity/high socialization (N = 11)

$\overline{X}$		
Fe	18.3	12.7
So	43.4	39.8
IQ	121.8	117.4

Low masculinity/low socialization (N = 12)	High masculinity/low socialization (N = 17)

$\overline{X}$		
Fe	17.4	12.5
So	31.1	30.2
IQ	118.7	122.6

Female sample (N = 68)[b]	
High femininity/high socialization (N = 21)	Low femininity/high socialization (N = 19)

$\overline{X}$		
Fe	27.9	22.2
So	43.3	41.4
IQ	119.0	117.3

High femininity/low socialization (N = 11)	Low femininity/low socialization (N = 17)

$\overline{X}$		
Fe	26.8	21.1
So	34.7	32.6
IQ	111.6	120.9

Note: CPI = California Psychological Inventory.
[a]For CPI Femininity, $\overline{X}$ = 15.69, SD = 3.20. For CPI Socialization, $\overline{X}$ = 36.00, SD = 5.66.
[b]For CPI Femininity, $\overline{X}$ = 24.44, SD = 3.46. For CPI Socialization, $\overline{X}$ = 38.66, SD = 5.26

Table 5.2. Variables Distinguishing High-Masculine/High-Socialized Males from the Complement Group.

Adult personality characteristics, contemporaneously rated: California Q-Set (N = 11)

Items significantly higher than complement	*Items significantly lower than complement*
Has light touch***	Is self-dramatizing and histrionic***
Initiates humor**	Is self-pitying**
Is cheerful**	Feels victimized**
Responds to humor*	Is intospective**
Is calm and relaxed*	Creates and exploits dependency**
Feels satisfied with self*	Is self-defeating*
	Tends to ruminate*
	Feels a lack of personal meaning in life*

Antecedent family characteristics, based on ratings gathered when subjects were children: Early family ratings (N = 3); Mother ratings (N = 11)

Ratings of mothers	*Ratings of fathers*
Shares experiences with others**	Is socially shy and detached**
Feels satisfied with the home*	Is undemonstrative**
Has a close relationship with child*	Has a need for privacy*
	Withdraws in face of conflict*
	Is relaxed about educational goals*

Ratings of marital relationship	
Little conflict over income management*	

Mother ratings	
Is less anxious about making a good impression**	
Tends to be less frank and open in discussions*	

Antecedent family characteristics, retrospectively rated from case histories: Environmental Q-Set (N = 11)

Items significantly higher than complement	*Items significantly lower than complement*
Father available to S through adolescence**	Father tended to reject S**
Father encouraged Ss steps toward independence**	Mother emphasized cultural and artistic values*
Parents encouraged S to discuss problems*	Parents socialized or controlled S by conditional love*

*p < .10.   **p < .05.   ***p < .01.

Table 5.3. Variables Distinguishing High-Masculine/Low-Socialized Males from the Complement Group.

Adult personality characteristics, contemporaneously rated: California Q-Set (N = 11)

Items significantly higher than complement	Items significantly lower than complement
Is self-indulgent***	Is dependable, responsible***
Is self-dramatizing***	Judges self and others in
Tends to eroticize situations***	conventional terms***
Tends toward undercontrol	Has high aspiration level***
of impulse***	Is ethically consistent***
Characteristically pushes limits***	Has a clear-cut personality
Is rebellious, nonconforming**	structure***
Is sensitive to demands made	Is productive**
on him**	Is fastidious**
Is concerned with own adequacy	Tends toward overcontrol
as a person**	of impulse**
Feels a lack of personal meaning	Tends to arouse liking in others**
in life**	Behaves in a giving way**
Is interesting, arresting*	Feels satisfied with self**
Is extrapunitive, transfers blame*	Is emotionally bland*
Thinks unconventionally*	Is moralistic*
Is overreactive to frustrations,	Is cheerful*
irritable*	Is physically attractive*
	Is turned to for advice*
	Tends to give advice*

Antecedent family characteristics, based on ratings gathered when subjects were children:
Early family ratings (N = 4)
Mother ratings (N = 17)

Ratings of mothers	Ratings of fathers
Dissatisfied with leisure time	Withdraws in face of conflict***
activities of husband**	Is in poor health***
Is socially outgoing**	Has a low energy level**
Tends to resent not working**	Dissatisfied with leisure time
Worries about child's health**	activities of wife**
Lacks self-confidence*	Lacks physical stamina*
Feels need of advice*	Lacks self-confidence*
Is in poor health*	Feels need of advice*
Is hostile toward child*	Tends to worry, is tense*

Table 5.3. Variables Distinguishing High-Masculine/Low-Socialized Males from the Complement Group, Cont'd.

Antecedent family characteristics, based on ratings gathered when subjects were children

Ratings of marital relationship	
Sexual adjustment of parents is poor**	
Parents disagree over finances**	
Parents disagree about leisure time activities**	
Parents have discrepant educational values**	
Parents do not share management of finances*	
Parents judged nervous and unstable*	
Mother ratings	
Is critical of her child***	
Is open-minded*	
Appears tired and worn*	

Antecedent family characteristics, retrospectively rated from case histories: Environmental Q-set (N = 17)

Items significantly higher than complement	*Items significantly lower than complement*
Sexual interests of parents apparent to S**	Parents were philosophically conservative**
Mother was seductive toward S**	Parents emphasized values of fairness, equity, responsibility to others**
Father tended to reject S*	
Mother was constructively active outside of home*	Home environment was structured and predictable**
	S competed with siblings for attention of parents**

*p < .01.   **p < .05.   ***p < .01.

Table 5.4. Variables Distinguishing Low-Masculine/High-Socialized Males
from the Complement Group.

Adult personality characteristics, contemporaneously rated: California Q-Set (N = 25)

Items significantly higher than complement	Items significantly lower than complement
Tends toward overcontrol of impulse***	Is self-indulgent***
Does not vary roles**	Tends toward undercontrol of impulse***
Is emotionally bland**	Is unpredictable***
Has a clear-cut personality structure**	Is rebellious, nonconforming**
Is moralistic**	Tends to eroticize situations**
Judges self and others in conventional terms**	Tends to project feelings onto others*
Behaves in a giving way**	Is concerned about adequacy of body functioning*
Is dependable, responsible**	Is expressive*
Is concerned with philosophical problems**	
Is ethically consistent*	
Is productive*	
Compares self with others*	

Antecedent family characteristics, based on ratings gathered when subjects were children:
Early family ratings (N = 10)
Mother ratings (N = 23)

Ratings of mothers	Ratings of fathers
Is relaxed**	Worries about child's health***
Is physically healthy**	Tends to favor hereditarian (over environmental) explanations**
Is emotionally stable*	
Feels satisfied with husband's occupation*	

Ratings of marital relationship	
Parents have good marital adjustment*	
Parents tend to agree about discipline*	

Antecedent family characteristics, based on ratings gathered when subjects were children:
Early family ratings: (N = 10)

Ratings of marital relationship	
Parents share management of finances*	
Family is financially comfortable*	

Table 5.4. Variables Distinguishing Low-Masculine/High-Socialized Males from the Complement Group, Cont'd.

Mother ratings	
Has a pleasant voice***	Feels satisfied with her lot*
Has a pleasant facial expression**	Is interested in child*
Is emotionally reserved**	Is cooperative with study*
Is self-assured*	Is open-minded*
Is cheerful*	

Antecedent family characteristics, retrospectively rated from case histories: Environmental Q-Set (N = 26)

Items significantly higher *than complement*	*Items significantly* lower *than complement*
Parents emphasized value of fairness, equity, responsibility to others***	Sexual interests of parents were apparent to S***
Parents used rational explanations in socializing S**	Home atmosphere was marked by conflict and recrimination**
Father was a respected and successful member of the community**	Father's limitations and vulnerabilities were apparent*
Father was career oriented*	Father's interpersonal modes were conflict inducing*
Parents shared similar values*	Mother was neurotic, anxiety laden*
	Mother was long-suffering, defeated woman*

$*p < .10.$
$**p < .05.$
$***p < .01.$

Table 5.5. Variables Distinguishing Low-Masculine/Low-Socialized Males from the Complement Group.

Adult personality characteristics, contemporaneously rated: California Q-Set (N = 12)

Items significantly higher than complement	Items significantly lower than complement
Tends to feel guilty***	Values independence and autonomy***
Seeks reassurance from others***	Feels satisfied with self***
Is self-pitying***	Is condescending toward others**
Is vulnerable, fearful**	Does not vary roles**
Is concerned with adequacy of body functioning**	Sees the heart of important problems**
Tends to ruminate**	Is critical, skeptical**
Feels victimized**	Is calm and relaxed**
Is thin-skinned, sensitive to criticism**	Responds to humor**
Is self-defeating*	Is self-assertive*
Tends to project feelings onto others*	Is cheerful*
Is extrapunitive, transfers blame*	Is emotionally bland*

Antecedent family characteristics, based on ratings gathered when subjects were children:
Early family ratings (N = 3)
Mother ratings (N = 11)

Ratings of mothers	Ratings of fathers
Has a low energy level***	Is emotionally uninvolved in relationship with wife***
Feels a lack of self-confidence**	Is emotionally uninvolved in relationship with S***
Lacks physical stamina*	Is relaxed*
Worries over child's health*	

Ratings of marital relationship	
Relationship between parents characterized by hostility**	
Parents have poor marital adjustment**	

Table 5.5. Variables Distinguishing Low-Masculine/Low-Socialized Males from the Complement Group, Cont'd.

Antecedent family characteristics, based on ratings gathered when subjects were children

Ratings of marital relationship	
Sexual adjustment of parents is poor**	
Parents have discrepant religious attitudes**	
Marital adjustment index score low**	
Parents have discrepant standards of neatness*	
Mother ratings	
Is talkative**	
Is less cheerful**	
Feels less satisfied with her lot*	

Antecedent family characteristics, retrospectively rated from case histories: Environmental Q-Set (N = 11)

Items significantly higher than complement	Items significantly lower than complement
Home atmosphere was constricted suppressive, cheerless***	Home was child oriented**
Home atmosphere marked by conflict and recrimination***	Home was a center of activities for peers**
Mother was neurotic, anxiety laden***	Parents emphasized family "togetherness"**
Mother's interpersonal modes were conflict inducing**	Parents encouraged S to discuss problems**
Father's interpersonal modes were conflict inducing**	Parents shared similar values*
	Parents emphasized conformity, peer acceptance*
	S had contact with peers in childhood*
	Mother enjoyed her maternal role*

*p < .10.   **p < .05.   ***p < .01.

Table 5.6. Variables Distinguishing High-Feminine/High-Socialized
Females from the Complement Group.

Adult personality characteristics, contemporaneously rated: California Q-Set (N = 21)

Items significantly higher than complement	Items significantly lower than complement
Is fastidious***	Tends toward undercontrol of impulse***
Tends toward overcontrol of impulse***	Tends to be rebellious and nonconforming***
Is dependable, responsible**	Characteristically pushes limits***
Is vulnerable, fearful**	Expresses hostility directly**
Has high aspiration level**	Is satisfied with appearance*
Is moralistic*	Thinks unconventionally*
Is indecisive*	Is unpredictable*
Behaves in a feminine manner*	Enjoys sensuous experiences*
Favors conservative values*	Tends to eroticize situations*

Antecedent family characteristics, based on ratings gathered when subjects were children:
Early family ratings (N = 7)
Mother ratings (N = 10)

Ratings of mothers	Ratings of fathers
Feels satisfied with home**	Has affectionate relationship with wife*
Ratings of marital relationship	
Parents share similar interests***	
Parents have comfortable relationship with relatives**	
Mother ratings	
Has a pleasant facial expression**	

Antecedent family characteristics, based on ratings gathered when subjects were children:
Early family ratings

Mother ratings	
Has a pleasant voice	
Is mentally alert	

Table 5.6. Variables Distinguishing High-Feminine/High-Socialized Females from the Complement Group, Cont'd.

Antecedent family characteristics, retrospectively rated from case histories: Environmental Q-Set (N = 19)

Items significantly higher *than complement*	*Items significantly* lower *than complement*
S was reared in a stable setting**	Family experienced many tragedies and misfortunes***
Parents emphasized family "togetherness"***	Atmosphere of home was constricted, suppressive, cheerless***
Mother was available to S through adolescence***	Mother was neurotic, anxiety laden***
Mother emphasized values of tenderness and love in relationships***	Mother rejected S**
Mother enjoyed maternal role***	Mother's interpersonal modes were conflict inducing*
Mother and S interacted with each other**	Mother's limitations and vulnerabilities were apparent**
Mother was respected and admired member of the community**	Father's limitations and vulnerabilities were apparent**
Parents encouraged S to discuss problems*	Father was neurotic, anxiety laden**
Home environment was structured and predictable**	Home atmosphere marked by conflict and recrimination**
Parents emphasized values of fairness, equity, and responsibility to others**	
Home atmosphere was warm and feeling oriented**	
Parents shared similar values*	

$*p < .10.$
$**p < .05.$
$***p < .01.$

Table 5.7. Variables Distinguishing High-Feminine/Low-Socialized Females from the Complement Group.

Adult personality characteristics, contemporaneously rated: California Q-Set (N = 11)

Items significantly higher than complement	Items significantly lower than complement
Thinks in unconventional ways**	Is productive**
Enjoys fantasy and daydreaming**	Has high aspiration level*
Tends to eroticize situations**	Favors conservative values*

Antecedent family characteristics, based on ratings gathered when subjects were children: Early family ratings (N = 4); Mother ratings (N = 9)

Ratings of mothers	Ratings of fathers
None	None
Ratings of marital relationship	
Parents have discrepant educational values**	
Mother ratings	
Has a pleasant voice**	
Is curious and interested in study*	

Antecedent family characteristics, retrospectively rated from case histories: Environmental Q-Set (N = 10)

Items significantly higher than complement	Items significantly lower than complement
S was physically attractive**	Mother and S interacted with each other**
Mother tended to reject S**	Mother emphasized values of
Mother was neurotic, anxiety laden*	tenderness and love in relationships**
Mother's limitations and vulnerabilities apparent*	Home atmosphere was complex and sophisticated**
Father was seductive toward S*	Mother was well educated*
Home atmosphere was constricted, suppressive, cheerless*	Mother enjoyed her maternal role*
	S was reared in a stable family setting*
	Parents emphasized values of fairness, equity, responsibility to others*

*p < .10.   **p < .05.   ***p < .01.

Table 5.8. Variables Distinguishing Low-Feminine/High-Socialized
Females from the Complement Group.

Adult personality characteristics, contemporaneously rated: California Q-Set (N = 19)

Items significantly higher than complement	Items significantly lower than complement
Judges self and others in conventional terms***	Feels victimized**
Is calm, relaxed**	Tends to ruminate*
Feels satisfied with self**	Is moody**
Is satisfied with appearance*	Is sensitive to criticism*
Is gregarious*	Is rebellious, nonconforming*
Is socially poised*	Evaluates motivations of others in interpreting situations*
Favors conservative values*	

Antecedent family characteristics, based on ratings gathered when subjects were children: Early family ratings (N = 7); Mother ratings (N = 17)

Ratings of mothers	Ratings of fathers
Relationship with husband is affectionate***	Relationship with wife is affectionate***
Relationship with child is affectionate*	Relationship with child is affectionate**
Has close relationship with child**	Is even-tempered*
Is emotionally stable**	
Has close relationship with husband*	
Is socially outgoing*	

Ratings of marital relationship	
Parents have a good marital adjustment***	
Marital adjustment index score high***	
Parents tend to agree about discipline**	
Family is financially comfortable**	

Antecedent family characteristics, based on ratings gathered when subjects were children:

Mother ratings	
Has a high intellectual level***	Is interested in child**
Is verbally fluent***	Is cooperative with study**
Comprehends the study***	Seeks to make a good impression**
Feels satisfied with her lot***	Has high self-esteem**
Is mentally alert**	Is open-minded**
Is logical, precise in thinking**	Is curious about the study*
	Is self-assured*

Table 5.8. Variables Distinguishing Low-Feminine/High-Socialized
Females from the Complement Group, Cont'd.

Antecedent family characteristics, retrospectively rated from case histories:
Environmental Q-Set (N = 17)

Items significantly higher than complement	*Items significantly* lower than complement
Parents emphasized values of fairness, equity, and responsibility to others***	Sexual interests of parents apparent to S***
Parents emphasized conformity and peer acceptance***	S was subjected to some form of discrimination**
S was given household responsibilities as a child**	Home atmosphere characterized by conflict and recrimination**
Mother was overcontrolled**	Mother emphasized physical activity, being outdoors**
Mother pressured S to achieve**	Father's interpersonal modes were conflict inducing**
Financial condition of family was comfortable**	
Parents emphasized manners, propriety*	
Mother emphasized value of intellectual orientation, rationality*	
Mother was well educated*	
Father was a respected and successful member of the community*	

*p< .10.
**p< .05.
***p< .01.

Table 5.9. Variables Distinguishing Low-Feminine/Low-Socialized Females from the Complement Group.

Adult personality characteristics, contemporaneously rated: California Q-Set (N = 17)

Items significantly higher than complement	Items significantly lower than complement
Is assertive***	Gives up and withdraws when frustrated***
Is rebellious, nonconforming***	Is vulnerable, fearful**
Values independence and autonomy**	Is indecisive**
Is critical, skeptical**	Judges self and others in conventional terms**
Has wide interests**	Tends to project feelings onto others**
Is intelligent**	Is emotionally bland**
Is expressive**	Creates and exploits dependency**
Is interesting, arresting**	Is submissive*
Has insight**	Tends toward overcontrol of impulse*
Expresses hostility directly**	Tends to repress anxiety*
Able to see the heart of important problems*	Behaves in a feminine manner*
Has a rapid personal tempo*	
Evaluates motivations of others in interpreting situations*	

Antecedent family characteristics, based on ratings gathered when subjects were children: Early family ratings (N = 17) Mother ratings (N = 16)

Ratings of mothers	Ratings of fathers
Has help with housework**	Is dissatisfied with leisure time activities of wife***
Is emotionally uninvolved in relationship with husband**	Is comfortable about issue of sex instruction***
Is emotionally uninvolved in relationship with S**	Has a high energy level*
Relationship with husband characterized by hostility*	
Does not want more children*	
Dissatisfied with leisure time activities of husband*	

Ratings of marital relationship	
Parents in conflict over financial expenditures**	
Marital relationship is conflicted**	
Marital adjustment index score low**	

Table 5.9. Variables Distinguishing Low-Feminine/Low-Socialized Females
from the Complement Group, Cont'd.

Antecedent family characteristics, based on ratings gathered when subjects were children

Ratings of marital relationship	
Parents in conflict over management of finances*	
Mother ratings	
Feels less satisfied with her lot** Is anxious, worries*	

*Antecedent family characteristics, retrospectively rated from case histories:
Environmental Q Set (N = 17)*

Items significantly higher than complement	Items significantly lower than complement
Mother was neurotic, anxiety laden***	Parents emphasized conformity, peer acceptance***
Father's interpersonal modes were conflict inducing***	Home was well structured, predictable***
Father was neurotic, anxiety laden**	Home atmosphere reflected a genuine religious component***
Mother emphasized cultural and artistic values*	Family emphasized values of fairness, equity, and responsibility to others***
Mother was a long suffering, defeated woman**	Home was child oriented***
Mother's interpersonal modes were conflict inducing**	Parents emphasized family "togetherness"***
Mother's limitations and vulnerabilities were apparent**	Parents shared similar values**
Home atmosphere marked by conflict and recrimination*	S reared in a stable family setting**
Family experienced tragedies and misfortunes*	Home atmosphere was warm and feeling oriented**
S experienced cultural conflict in adolescence*	Father emphasized value of tenderness and love in relationships**
Home atmosphere was constricted, suppressive, cheerless*	Mother emphasized value of tenderness and love in relationships*
Father was authoritarian*	Parents used rational explanations in socializing S*
Father emphasized status and power*	
Father tended to reject S*	
Father's limitations and vulnerabilities were apparent*	

*p < .10.   **p < .05.   ***p < .01.

Chapter Six

✣

How Gender Differences Affect Children's Orientations to the World

The literature on gender differences is an agglomeration of inconsistent, often conflicting findings, based on research largely unguided by theory. Empirical assessments of psychological differences between males and females have been essentially undirected, and findings frequently have emerged *en passant* because the investigator's primary interest was focused on other questions. As Fairweather (1976, p. 267) concluded after reviewing the evidence for sex differences in cognition: "It must be stressed, finally, that the majority of studies reviewed here and elsewhere are both ill thought and ill performed. Whilst in other circumstances this may be regarded as the occupational hazard of the scientific enterprise, here such complacency is compounded by the social loadings placed upon these kinds of results. It is clearly very easy to include sex as a bonus factor in experiments which have little sci-

Originally published in E. K. Shapiro and E. Weber (Eds.), *Cognitive and Affective Growth: Developmental Interaction*. Hillsdale, N.J.: Erlbaum, 1981, with the title "Gender Differences in the Nature of Orientations Developed About the World."

entific merit. We cannot pretend that we are testing a theory of sex differences, since at present none can exist. *Legitimate studies of sex differences can only grow out of observations of clear individual differences in the investigation of salient psychological processes*" (italics added). These "salient psychological processes" must be identified, however, embedded in a conceptual framework, and used to inform empiricism on sex-related differences.

A second, related problem contributing to the inconsistent findings surrounding research on gender differences is that the variables studied are often conceptualized and operationalized in different ways by different investigators. Consider, for one instance, ways used to operationalize the construct of suggestibility (for example, the Asch group conformity experiment, yielding to group consensus in discussion situations, responses to questionnaires, observations of targeted behaviors following presentation of information designed to modify opinion) and the confusing, often inconsistent results eventuating from studies using these very different methods to investigate presumably the same psychological phenomenon. Also complicating the problem of achieving a more coherent literature surrounding specific constructs is that particular operational transformations may not be supportable as indicators of the construct supposedly the focus of investigation. Consider, for example, the ways in which prosocial behaviors have been assessed. The correlates of prosocial behavior when operationalized as the sharing of redeemable tokens with an unseen, anonymous, nonexistent peer are different from those found when prosocial behavior is assessed using observations of a child's actual "helping" behaviors in situations where providing help is appropriate. Also contributing to untidiness in the empirical realm is the tendency to define psychological variables in global, insufficiently articulated ways, a practice which tends to obscure relationships that might be discerned if more differentiated measures of the construct under consideration were used.

A third problem characterizing the data base on which our conclusions about gender differences depend is that in many areas this base is neither sufficiently comprehensive nor

robust with regard to statistical power to support generalization. In research on sex-related differences, there is need for
more focused studies that respect conventional methodological
principles, utilize samples that are large, salient, and relatively
free of selective bias, and employ instruments meeting conventional psychometric standards.

Fourth, as fully discussed in Chapter Two of the present
volume, the aggregated data pertaining to sex-related differences are biased in a number of ways. Young children have been
overrepresented. In Maccoby and Jacklin (1974), conclusions
about sex differences are based on studies conducted predominantly with children. Seventy-five percent of the researches included in their tables used subject samples twelve years of age
and younger. To the extent that gender differences increase
with age (Block, 1976a, 1976b, 1979a; Terman and Tyler,
1954), this data base cannot be considered representative or
pertinent. Another source of bias is the unfortunate tendency
of psychologists to use "samples of convenience," samples selected for reasons of ready availability (for example, university
nursery school children, college students enrolled in introduc-
tory psychology courses). It is unlikely that such samples are
representative of the population of preschoolers or of young
adults. Bias in sampling strategies can affect the results of gender comparisons and, if present, must qualify conclusions.

In summary, operations used to evaluate particular constructs are often conceptually insensitive and lacking in reliability and/or construct validity. In view of these problems (and
others uncited), it is clear that we need to chart some new directions in gender-related research that are guided by explicit
conceptual models and implemented with finely tuned instruments.

What follows is a still inchoate, tentative formulation that
seeks to provide a coherent organizing structure for interpreting
some of the gender differences that have been reliably identified. This conceptual interpretation of gender differences is
then related to the cognitive processing proclivities of the two
sexes, specifically to modes of processing new experiential inputs, both cognitive and affective. Finally, a link is forged be-

tween the differential socialization experiences of males and females and the development of personality structures. The formulation being offered does not derive from a set of critical experiments. Rather, it represents an aggregation and integration of a number of discrete, isolated, but implicative results obtained by other investigators in an attempt to provide links in the evidential chain being constructed.

Before embarking on this conjectural voyage, it is important to note that the emphasis on sex differentiated socialization practices accorded here does not imply that gender differences are viewed solely as a function of sociocultural/psychological forces. Rather, gender differences are viewed as manifestations of genetic, biological, historical/cultural, and psychological factors complexly interacting in an open system in which particular factors assume differential salience at different developmental periods. It is assumed that a fundamental life task for individuals is that of mediating between coexisting internal biological impulses and external socializing forces. Manifestations of gender, then, represent a synthesis of biological and cultural factors and forces as these are mediated by the individual's cognitive and ego structures.

A Conceptual Organization of Sex-Related Psychological Differences

I propose that the gender differences established with some degree of reliability can be organized and viewed as representing the different ways that males and females process experience. On the basis of evaluation of research on sex differences offered by Maccoby and Jacklin (1974), my reinterpretation of their conclusions (Block, 1976a, 1976b), and earlier assessments of sex differences by Maccoby (1966a), Tyler (1965), and Terman and Tyler (1954), females appear, on the average, to excel relative to males in areas of cognitive processing that involve verbal ability—such as memory for narrative and verbal fluency. Females also appear, on the average, to differ from males in the personality realm in manifesting lesser curiosity and exploratory behavior, lesser confidence in performance, greater timidity, greater tendency to be influenced, and more susceptibility to anxiety. In their social behaviors, females also differ from males. Accordingly, females, when contrasted with males, are more empathic when empathy is defined as manifesting more vicarious, veridical responses to another's distress (M. L. Hoffman, 1977) and engage in more prosocial behaviors (Smith, Haan, and Block, 1970). They also maintain closer proximity to friends, demonstrate greater compliance with authority, and are more concerned about behaving in ways that are socially approved. Underlying this set of phenotypically dissimilar intellectual and personological characteristics is, I suggest, a common theme. In processing experiences that deviate from previously established expectations, females, more than males, appear to be more conserving and to rely more—and longer—on the utilization of existing cognitive and personality structures, responding to new experiences in ways that are consistent with prior understandings. Attempts are made to fit new, discrepant information or experience into existing structures, and these structures, or schemata, are extended or revised only when required and then by a series of incremental steps, parsimoniously taken. This mode of processing experience— more frequently used by females than males, as proposed here— may have important advantages for the species. Females' greater emphasis on the conservation of existing structures ensures greater continuity across time and generations and may well serve a sociobiological function in preserving those cultural traditions and historical values having special survival utility.

Turning now to reliably identified characteristics distinguishing males, it is suggested that males differ from females in their characteristic modes of processing new experiences. With regard to cognitive processing, males appear to excel in problems that involve restructuring, breaking set, and developing new strategies for generating solutions. Males also score higher, on the average, on measures of spatial and quantitative abilities, measures that require extrapolation in the perceptual/spatial domain. Males differ from females, on the average, in personality characteristics that include exploratory behavior and curiosity, activity, and self-confidence in problem-solving situations.

In their interpersonal relationships, males, relative to females, tend to be more aggressive, dominant, and competitive. A common thread underlying this phenotypically disparate set of behaviors is the greater tendency of males to deal with new experiences deviating from previous understandings in ways that involve active attempts to transform or to restructure earlier premises. Males more readily initiate efforts to construct new cognitive structures capable of encompassing the information that has stressed existing structures. This mode of processing information—more frequently used by males than by females, as proposed here—also has advantages for the species. The greater tendency of males to respond to disequilibrating experiences by restructuring, by devising alternative premises, and by creating new psychological structures provides a source of innovation for society and may serve a sociobiological function in giving impetus to social and cultural change.

There is a risk that the conceptualization being offered only provides yet another bipolar dimension for differentiating males and females. To be sure, there is some overlap with other conceptions: the agency/communion distinction of Bakan (1966), the allocentric/autocentric concepts of Gutmann (1965), the instrumental/expressive orientation discussed by Parsons and Bales (1955), and the conservation/initiation dimension as elaborated by Gough (1968a). The present conceptualization would represent only a trivial rephrasing of the works of these theorists were it to stop at this point. However, the differences in ways of processing experience postulated here are implicative for the quality of psychological (and human) functioning and are importantly affected by differences in the early socialization of males and females, differences that help to create the diverging environmental contexts in which they develop. If this conjecture proves correct, then we may be in a position to suggest modifications of a socialization process that perhaps derives more than is now required from a cultural past no longer relevant. Modes of socializing children and differentiating gender roles that were once useful may no longer have functional significance in contemporary technological societies and may serve to constrain the possibilities of both males and females as they attempt to forge identities, formulate life goals, and realize their potentials (Block, 1973; L. W. Hoffman, 1977a).

Before going on to discuss early experiences influencing the ways in which individuals manage new experiential inputs, a few caveats and qualifications are required. For purposes of exposition, the distinction between two modes of processing experience is being emphasized. Of course, all individuals use both modes of processing experience at different times and under different circumstances. However, it may prove useful to consider the *preferred* or *dominant* mode characterizing a person. In reacting to new experiences that fail to conform to expectation, some persons, and females more than males, tend to be oriented more toward fitting new observational data into existing psychological structures. They tend to persist longer than males in efforts to fit (to assimilate, in Piagetian terms) new information before shifting their efforts to create new structures (to accommodate, in Piagetian terms).* Processing of new experiential inputs by other persons, and males more than females, tends to be characterized by a greater readiness to abandon psychological schemata not articulating readily with new experiences, in favor of restructuring or transforming existing structures or formulating new schemata that will encompass refractory information. All persons use both modes of processing experience at different times, ideally invoking each in context-responsive ways. Overreliance on any one strategy for processing information may be dysfunctional. The use of procrustean methods to fit or mold new perceptions into existing schemata results in a selective, distorted, oversimplified view of the world (Perry, 1968b), whereas premature jettisoning of established structures and zealously sought redefinition of premises may result in an ahistorical, overarticulated, compartmentalized view of the world.

*My recognition that the use of the assimilative and accommodative modes of processing new experiences may be sex-differentiated derived from discussions with Jack Block, who has discussed Piaget's concepts of assimilation and accommodation in the context of personality as well as cognitive functioning (Block, 1982).

Socialization Influences on Sex-Differentiated Modes
of Processing Experience

Modes of processing experience and the psychological structures resulting therefrom are influenced by the child's very early experiences in interaction with primary caretakers. Caretakers affect in many ways—both implicit and explicit—the child's interests, play, opportunities for manipulation and exploration, and expectations that inform his or her constructions about the world. Parental choices of toys and play materials, channeling of play, encouragement of the child's "experiments in nature" (Piaget, 1952), tolerance for active exploration, and even assignment of household chores not only influence the child's developing conceptions of gender roles but help to determine, within the limits set by genetic inheritance, the course of psychological development as well.

In attempting to elucidate the development of sex-related differences from the psychological perspective that is the focus of this chapter, I propose that sex-differentiated parenting, socialization, and shaping behaviors influence boys and girls in ways that differentially modify their cognitive and affective development. To show how the different experiences of boys and girls and the different environmental contexts in which they live, learn, and grow shape the nature and development of their cognitive and ego structures, four principal areas of influence will be discussed.

1. The child's cognitive constructions about the world, that is, the nature of the premise system developed by the child.
2. The extent and quality of exploratory behavior manifested by the child.
3. The frequency with which the child encounters conflict or disequilibrating experiences that challenge previously established understandings.
4. The strategies developed by the child to deal with new experimental inputs.

Influences on the Child's Developing Premise System

Although many experiences in early childhood influence the child's developing conceptions of the world, for the present purposes, only those socialization experiences that are sex-differentiated are considered. Three such sex-differentiated parenting behaviors are discussed: (1) the differential experience of boys and girls in receiving contingent responding, (2) the differential opportunity accorded boys and girls for independent exploration, and (3) the differential exposure of boys and girls to disequilibrating experiences. With regard to the nature of the premise system that the young child begins to establish very early in life, I contend that the differential exposure of boys and girls to contingency relationships affects the nature of the premises about the world and about the self that are being evolved. Among the sources of this differential experience with contingency relationships are parental and teacher responses to the behaviors of the young child and the characteristics of the toys made available to boys and to girls.

Contingency Responding of Caretakers. Observations in the literature suggest that males experience more contingent responding than females from both mothers and fathers. Murphy and Moriarty (1976), for example, note that mothers of males are more responsive in the feeding situation to the child's signals of wanting to stop feeding than are mothers of females. Walraven (1974) also observed mothers and infants during feeding and found that, following a loud auditory stimulus, mothers were more attentive to their male infants' reactions than to those of their female infants. Both mothers and fathers have been observed to respond more frequently to vocalizations initiated by their sons while more frequently initiating vocalization with their daughters (Lewis and Freedle, 1973; Parke and Sawin, 1976; Yarrow, 1975). Mothers have also been found to be more responsive to movements and playlike activities initiated by male infants than by female infants (Lewis, 1972a).

Turning to data on somewhat older children, the results of studies of sex differences in positive and negative reinforcements given children are consistent over a broad age range and indicate that boys receive more physical punishment and negative reinforcement from parents when they behave in ways that violate parental standards (Maccoby and Jacklin, 1974). In an elegant study specifically designed to assess differences in the contingent responding of mothers and fathers to their sons and daughters, Margolin and Patterson (1975), using sequential analysis, found that boys receive significantly more positive responses than girls from both their mothers and fathers. Observing parental behaviors that immediately followed either deviant or prosocial behaviors, these investigators found that fathers responded positively to their sons almost *twice* as often as to their daughters. These results accord with data summarized by Maccoby and Jacklin (1974), who concluded that boys received more negative contingent responding and that when sex differences in positive reinforcement are found, the results tend to favor boys. Thus, the data from numerous studies, using different methods and assessing parental behaviors with children of various ages, suggest that boys experience more contingent responding from their parents than girls.

Contingent Responding of Teachers. Not only does the literature yield evidence of more frequent contingent responding to the behaviors of the child by parents of males than of females, but this pattern of response is characteristic of teachers as well. Serbin and others (1973) investigated sex-differentiated contingent responding to specific child behaviors on the part of nursery school teachers. The rate of teacher response to disruptive behavior in boys was significantly higher than it was to girls. Their analyses controlled for difference in the frequencies of such behaviors by boys and by girls. Teachers also showed higher rates of response to boys' solicitation behaviors than to girls' and, additionally, solicitation of attention on the part of boys evoked significantly more instructional behavior on the part of the teachers. Specifically, in response to boys' requests, teachers held more extended conversations, gave more brief instructions, and provided more extended directions than they did in response to solicitation behaviors from girls. Other studies of nursery school teachers' behaviors (Felsenthal, 1970; Meyer and Thompson, 1956) support these findings, demonstrating that the behaviors of boys in the classroom are more likely to evoke attention and response, both positive and negative, than the behaviors of girls.

Together, these several findings suggest greater adult contingent responding to the behaviors of boys than to those of girls. Because few studies have looked explicitly at sequential contingency behaviors of parents and teachers, it is difficult to provide vigorous documentation for my assertion about sex differences in contingency experiences. The available evidence is supporting, however, and it is to be hoped that these conjectures will stimulate additional systematic research efforts in this area.

Differential Experience with Feedback from Toys. Another source of differential experience with contingency relations on the part of boys and girls derives from the nature of the toys that are provided and considered sex-appropriate for boys and for girls. The literature on toy preference is replete with lists indicating the preferred toys of boys and girls (Fagot, 1977; Fein and others, 1975; Goldberg and Lewis, 1969; Rheingold and Cook, 1975). However, it is necessary to go beyond simple cataloguing of preferred toys and examine the characteristics of toys preferred by males and females with regard to their potential influence on the psychological development of children. Yarrow and his colleagues (1972) have demonstrated the incisive results that can be obtained when a conceptual approach is used to classify toys. These investigators categorized inanimate objects in the infant's environment according to their *responsiveness, complexity,* and *variety.* These three dimensions were then found to relate to a variety of infant behaviors in several domains, including motor development, exploratory behaviors, and goal-directed behaviors. Rheingold and Cook (1975) also developed "higher-order" categorizations of toys on the basis of "world orientations" and concluded, from their analysis of toys found in the rooms of girls and the rooms of boys, that "boys were provided objects that encourage activities directed away from home . . . and girls [were provided] objects that encourage activities directed toward the home—keeping house and caring for children" (p. 463).

Reflecting on the aggregated data surrounding the nature of the toys provided to and preferred by boys and by girls suggests that the toys differ in six important ways: (1) Boys' toys, more than girls' toys, provide contingent feedback. (2) Boys' toys encourage more active manipulation. (3) Boys' toys encourage more engagement of the *physical* world. (4) Boys' toys afford more inventive possibilities. (5) Girls' toys, more than boys' toys, encourage imitative play. (6) Girls' toys encourage more engagement of the *social* world.

I propose that these differences in the formal characteristics of toys provide boys and girls with different experiences during their early formative years, experiences that affect the development of the premise systems that underlie their self- (and world-) orientations.

The nature of the preferred toys of boys (blocks, vehicles, tools) encourages manipulative play and provides more feedback. Yarrow and others (1972) found that toy responsiveness (feedback potential) was related to the developmental level of the infant, exploratory behavior, goal orientation, reaching and grasping behaviors, and secondary circular reactions that reflect "the infant's repeated efforts to evoke feedback from objects" (p. 27). These results emphasize the importance of considering the higher-order effects of toys on the development of cognitive schemata in boys and in girls.

Girls' toys, in contrast to boys', encourage imitative play, particularly in the context of household and nurturing activities (Rheingold and Cook, 1975). The toys made available to girls are less amenable to inventive changes, and their uses are more prescribed (Rosenfeld, 1975). The toys typically provided to girls encourage interaction in the social world rather than the physical one. The inherent characteristics of girls' toys provide less informative feedback than boys' toys, which encourage play in the physical world. Inadequately balanced block constructions, for example, will topple. Haphazard arrangements of doll furniture, however, are unlikely to evoke *physical* consequences; such arrangements are more apt to elicit *social* consequences in the form of critical comments or corrective suggestions from mother, siblings, or peers. I suggest that differences exist in the quality of feedback from the physical and social worlds. Feedback from the physical world is more likely to be immediate, consistent, and unambiguous. The clarity of this feedback benefits the eduction of principles about the workings of the physical world. Feedback from the physical world is also impersonal and is likely to encourage self-generated problem-solving attempts to test the nature of the physical reality and/or to rectify mistakes. Feedback from the social world, however, is less consistent, less clear, and often delayed. Given these conditions, the principles guiding social interactions are difficult to discern. Further, feedback from the social world is more often personal than impersonal, and comments may imply criticism, criticism that may disrupt play, have a disheartening effect, and deprive the child of feelings of efficacy and competence.

Importance of Contingent Responding. Contingent responding appears to have consequential implications for cognitive development. Contingent responding by mothers has been found to relate to the early development of object relationships (Sander, 1976), the infant's general developmental level, social responsiveness, and goal-directed behaviors (Yarrow and others, 1972), the quality of attachment as shown by one-year-olds' responses to a strange situation (Ainsworth and Bell, 1969), and later coping behaviors (Murphy and Moriarty, 1976).

Contingent responding to the infant's signals and behaviors facilitates the infant's developing awareness of his or her evocative role in eliciting responses and effects from both the social and the physical worlds, thereby influencing the premises the young child develops about the nature of his or her relationship with the larger world. These early experiences of efficacy are the precursors of later instrumental competence. The construction of a premise system that suggests "My actions can produce effects in the world" increases the child's motivation to explore, to experiment, and to master. These observations about contingent experiences and their influence on cognitive development and the acquisition of particular personological characteristics have been noted and emphasized by numerous investigators. Characteristics of the inanimate and/or social environment have been related to infant motivation (Yarrow and others, 1972), to effectance motive (White, 1959), to the concept of "intrinsic motivation" (Hunt, 1965), to a "generalized expectancy model" (Lewis and Goldberg, 1969), to "contingency awareness" (Watson and Ramey, 1972), to "learned helplessness" (Dweck and others, 1978; Seligman, 1975), and to Piaget's (1952) characterization of the child as an active, information-processing organism. These writings converge in emphasizing the relation among activity, feedback, effectance, and/or developing competence.

The recognition advanced here is that an active, experimental approach to the environment is facilitated to a greater extent in males by their more frequent experiences with feedback and contingent responding. By virtue of these sex-differentiated experiences with feedback and contingent responding, males are more likely than females to develop a premise system about the world that posits "Actions have effects" and to develop a premise system about the self that posits efficacy and instrumentality. Data demonstrating the greater instrumentality of boys in barrier situations (Block, Block, and Harrington, 1975; Goldberg and Lewis, 1969) and in goal-directed situations (Yarrow, 1975) and their lesser "learned helplessness" (Dweck and others, 1978) reflect a premise system—an expectancy— that includes instrumental competence.

These expectations of orderly effects resulting from effective actions serve to increase the salience of stimulus control differentially for males and females. As documented in two studies by Gunnar-vonGnechten (1977, 1978), males appear to attach greater importance to the ability to control events originating in the environment. A potentially frightening toy was more distressing to boys who could not control its onset than it was to boys who had been taught to operate the toy themselves and thus to control the onset of a somewhat noxious, noisy stimulus. The relation between fear and inability to control onset of an aversive event was found *only* in the sample of boys; in the sample of girls, fear was unrelated to the ability to control. The results of the first study were replicated in the second study, and Gunnar-vonGnechten concluded that having control over external events is a more salient concern for four-year-old boys than for girls. Bronson (1971) also demonstrated boys' greater interest in feedback in a study where, in each of three observed episodes, boys, more frequently than girls, acted on stimuli in ways that produced contingent effects.

Although data on sex-differentiated parental contingency behaviors are suggestive, the studies are too few to permit strong conclusions. Few researchers have examined sex differences in maternal contingent responding, and even fewer have assessed contingent responding by the fathers. Because differences in the child's contingency experiences with parents and with toys appear to influence the psychological structures developed to process experience, more systematic, focused research on these questions is clearly required.

Sex-Related Differences in Imitative Play

In discussing differences between boys' and girls' toys with respect to their feedback potential, it has also been noted that the toys more typically provided to girls than to boys encourage more imitative play, play in which the child models maternal nurturing and caretaking behaviors and housekeeping tasks. Whereas many toys preferred by boys also elicit imitative play (vehicles, soldiers, arms), other toys preferred by boys (blocks, tools) elicit structural and manipulative play. The effects of providing girls with toys that predispose them toward imitative play at an early age may be reflected in their greater tendency toward imitation in other contexts as well.

Observations of children's play in nursery school settings indicate that girls engage more often in doll play, dance, and dressing up like adults significantly more often than boys (Fagot, 1974, 1977). They have been observed to imitate and help the teacher more often in the nursery school setting (Etaugh, Collins, and Gerson, 1975) and to imitate primary human relationships in their group play activities (Lever, 1976). They also appear to be more prone to imitate the behaviors of an adult model (Bell, Weller, and Waldrop, 1971; Pedersen and Bell, 1970; Portuges and Feshbach, 1972). This general conclusion about imitation must be qualified by considerations of setting and the nature of the behaviors being modeled. Although imitation provides the child with a behavioral formula that can be applied in specific situations, imitation does not encourage active problem-solving attempts, nor does it facilitate deuterolearning —"learning how to learn"—of the sort discussed by Bateson (1942).

Additional perspective and implication accrue to the findings surrounding sex differences in the toys and play activities of males and females when the results of a study by Carpenter (1979) are considered. Carpenter analyzed the play activities of nursery school children with respect to their degree of structure, which was defined as the availability of a model performing given activities and by the amount of direction or instruction given. On the basis of composite measures of structuredness, Carpenter found that girls played significantly more often in high-structure activities, whereas boys played in low-structure activities. Independent measures of compliance of innovative play in the activity settings revealed that compliance was significantly and positively associated with high-structure activities and that innovative play was significantly and positively associated with activity characterized as low in structure. Carpenter's results are consistent with observations of differences in the formal characteristics of the games played by older boys and girls (Lever, 1976). On the playground, the games in which boys and girls spontaneously participate were found to differ on several dimensions. Of particular interest in the present context is Lever's observation that girls participated in highly structured, turn-taking games that are regulated by invariable procedural rules and do not involve contingent rules of strategy. Boys' games, though rule-governed, rewarded initiative, improvisation, and extemporaneity. Lever's observations affirmed Carpenter's findings with an older age group and suggest that more structured games, preferred by girls, demand prescriptive behaviors and discourage experimentation and innovation.

Although it is widely acknowledged that play is an important vehicle for children's learning about themselves and the world, the ways in which the *formal* characteristics of particular toys, play activities, and games differentially affect the developing psychological structures of males and females have been largely ignored until very recently. The specific qualities of child/object interactions elicited by particular toys or play situations and their implications for personality development and cognitive functioning are only now beginning to be explored systematically.

Sex-Related Differences in Exploratory Behaviors

We turn now to the second set of psychological behaviors supported by sex-differentiated parental socialization practices and shaping behaviors that exert influence on organism/environment interactions and affect the child's developing psychological structures—namely, exploratory behaviors. Exploratory behaviors have been shown to relate to the child's perceived ability to control or to elicit response from the environment (Piaget, 1952; Watson and Ramey, 1972; White, 1959), sustaining the secondary circular reactions of the early sensorimotor period and ramifying at later ages to influence other cognitive strategies and problem-solving orientations.

Boys have been described by a number of investigators as engaging in more manipulation of objects than girls (Bell, Weller, and Waldrop, 1971; Clarke-Stewart, 1973; Fagot, 1974, 1977; Pedersen and Bell, 1970), as more curious (Daehler, 1970; Hutt, 1970; Smock and Holt, 1962), as engaging in more exploratory behavior (Goldberg and Lewis, 1969; Maccoby, 1966a; Maccoby and Jacklin, 1974; Starr, 1969), and as participating more often in play activities characterized by the low structure that fosters innovative, independent play (Carpenter, 1979). The further finding that the play of girls is more sedentary (Bell, Weller, and Waldrop, 1971; Goldberg and Lewis, 1969; Pedersen and Bell, 1970) again emphasizes the diverging characteristics of the play of boys and girls.

In seeking to identify parental behaviors that might promote more exploratory behavior on the part of males, the literature reveals a rather consistent pattern of male infants being given more physical stimulation by parents than female infants (Lewis, 1972a; Moss, 1967, 1974; Parke and O'Leary, 1976;

Yarrow, 1975). Male infants are held, aroused, and provided stimulation for gross motor behaviors more than female infants (Parke and Sawin, 1976). Yarrow (1975) found that mothers interacted more frequently with male infants, at higher levels of intensity, and with richer, more varied interactions than did mothers of female infants. Such stimulation is seen as encouraging greater responsiveness to the environment on the part of males. Boys also were found to be given greater freedom to explore the neighborhood (Saegert and Hart, 1976).

In contrast to their male peers, girls were observed to play in greater proximity to their mothers both at home and in the laboratory (Fagot, 1977; Goldberg and Lewis, 1969; Lewis and Weintraub, 1974; Messer and Lewis, 1972), to be subjected to closer supervision of their activities (Block, 1979a; Newson and Newson, 1968), and to play closer to home (Saegert and Hart, 1976). These sex-differentiated socialization emphases may discourage girls from venturing far from home or the primary caretaker and may contribute to the greater timidity and lesser confidence noted in females at later ages.

In evaluating the specific features of sex-differentiated toys that may relate to greater exploratory behaviors on the part of males, boys' toys, according to the criteria used by Rheingold and Cook (1975) to classify toys, were found to direct them more into activities oriented away from home. As noted earlier, boys' toys afford more inventive possibilities (Rosenfeld, 1975) and elicit less stereotyped play (Carpenter, 1979). In addition to the particular characteristics of masculine toys, males are given a greater variety of toys than are females, thus promoting play engagement with a broader range of stimulus objects. Rheingold and Cook (1975) found twice as many *categories* of toys in the rooms of boys as in the rooms of girls, a finding consistent with the trend toward greater variety of toys for male infants found by Yarrow and others (1972).

The differential assignment of household chores to boys and girls also supports the proximal/distal observations previously noted in that boys more often are given chores taking them out of the house and/or farther away from the home, whereas girls are assigned homebound chores such as cleaning and helping to babysit (Duncan, Schuman, and Duncan, 1973; Whiting and Edwards, 1975). When we examine these seemingly inconsequential differences in chore assignments, it will be seen that they have rather substantial developmental implications. Not only do their chores permit boys the opportunity for more independent exploration of and commerce with the larger world, but Whiting and Edwards (1975) note that differential chore assignments affect the interpersonal interactions of boys and girls as well. Because girls are more often assigned household chores, they interact more with adults and younger siblings than with peers. Boys, in contrast, are given more errands and in some cultures are charged with the responsibility for taking animals to pasture and herding, chore assignments that permit more interaction with peers. Within the perspective being developed here, these different interactional contexts defined in part by chore assignment have diverging implications for the psychological development of the sexes. The context for girls encourages social interactions focused on home and family, emphasizes imitation of adult behaviors and activities, fosters sensitivity to the needs of others, and often involves compromising one's own wishes for the welfare of the larger family or social group. In contrast, the chore assignments given boys encourage exploratory forays into the larger world, thereby increasing their familiarity with the world outside the home, providing opportunities for experimentation, and promoting independent problem solving. The exploration permitted males at an early age may have long-term cognitive effects because improvisation, trial and error, and experimentation extend the behavioral repertoire and facilitate the development of alternative and flexibly sequenced cognitive strategies.

Thus, the nature of the toys, the sex-differentiated encouragement of proximity to the mother, and the kinds of chores assigned to males and to females function to shape different "world orientations" and environmental contexts for boys and for girls. Together, these several sex-differentiated parental emphases and behaviors serve to define the home and family as the appropriate sphere of activity for girls and to define the world outside the home as the more salient sphere for boys.

Differential Exposure to Disequilibrating Experiences

Another area in which sex-differentiated parental behaviors and socialization practices influence the child's cognitive and personality development is the timing, frequency, and nature of the child's encounters with disequilibrating experiences. As proposed by Hunt (1961, 1964), Piaget (1952), Loevinger (1976), Perry (1968b), Riegel (1976), and Sigel and Cocking (1976), the development and elaboration of cognitive and ego structures are mediated by a dialectical process that is catalyzed by confronting new inputs or experiences that cannot be incorporated into existing understandings or extant psychological structures. Exposure to such experiences forces reconsideration of previously established premises and, under optimal conditions, results in the restructuring of understanding and revision of one's premises. Within the average expectable environment, there appear to be important gender differences in the timing, intensity, and frequency with which disequilibrium is experienced by the two sexes.

The infant begins life in a psychologically undifferentiated and helpless state, depending on someone else to perform the many functions necessary for survival. Over the first several months of life, and through a gradual process of learning to delay gratification and to tolerate minor frustrations, the infant begins to differentiate self from nonself and to develop attachment to the caring adult, an attachment that is similar for children of both sexes. Sometime during the second half of the first year of life, however, the male toddler in the average expectable environment experiences a massive discontinuity, one not shared by female toddlers. It is at this time that the mother, in the service of encouraging appropriate gender role definition, begins actively to distance herself from her son. The distancing of the son is achieved by different stratagems. Male infants, more than female infants, receive proximal stimulation from their mothers in the first few months of life, but the pattern appears to change at around six months of age, with proximal stimulation of males decreasing (Lewis, 1972a; Lewis and Weintraub, 1974). Mothers also report that boys are weaned earlier than girls (Block, 1979a; Sears, Maccoby, and Levin, 1957). The intriguing, but as yet empirically unverified, suggestion by pediatricians that mothers tend to hold their female infants *en face* while holding their male infants facing outward toward the external world also may be a manifestation of distancing behavior. In response to their child's distress, fear, or frustration, mothers appear to use different stratagems with males and females. Mothers are more likely to pick up a distressed female toddler, whereas they are more likely to dismiss signs of distress in male toddlers, encouraging them to resume play (Lewis, 1972a). The earlier and greater emphasis on the development of sex-appropriate behaviors on the part of males may serve also to encourage mother/son disengagement (Lansky, 1967; Parke, 1978). Mother/son distancing behavior is a widely recognized phenomenon among primates, where it has been observed that male infants are "peripheralized" at an earlier age than females, the mother rejecting the male infant sooner and forcing him into earlier contact with peers (Nash and Ransom, 1971).

I suggest that males experience a discontinuity in the nature of the relationship with their mothers that is achieved by a set of distancing behaviors of the sort described. No such shift in maternal behavior is experienced by female toddlers, whose relationship with their mothers remains close and continuous over the childhood years. Although this discontinuity in the attachment relationship with the mother has been discussed by many theorists and developmentalists (Fenichel, 1945; Freud, 1943; Lynn, 1975; Maccoby and Jacklin, 1974), the discussion has been cast almost exclusively in terms of identification and achievement of appropriate sex typing. However, this early experience with discontinuity may have a consequential impact on cognitive development as well. The male child is forced to develop new schemata capable of encompassing the perception that mother is failing to respond in ways consistent with expectation. Not only does the male toddler's early experience with change in the nature of his mother's behaviors toward him challenge his developing premise system about the constancy of objects, but it is likely to affect his perceptions about the dependability of the social world as well. The early distancing by the mother may be instrumental in directing the interactions of males more toward the physical world; it may, as demonstrated in primary studies (Nash and Ransom, 1971), encourage their pattern of extended peer relationships and may contribute also to caution and/or anxiety at later ages about investing themselves in intimate, sharing relationships.

For female toddlers, the nature of the relationship with both parents in the average expectable environment tends to remain relatively constant over the childhood period. Girls are not subjected to the disequilibrating experience of disruption in the relationship with their primary attachment figure. Unlike boys, girls at an early age are spared the task of revising understandings and restructuring their behaviors vis-à-vis their parents. Greater consistency in the quality of primary relationships, encouragement of proximity, and emphasis on imitative behaviors, particularly maternal, nurturing behaviors, combine to ensure a more predictable, constant world for girls than for boys.

Not only does the male child encounter major experiential discrepancies at an earlier age, but I suggest that he encounters them more frequently over the years as well. Childrearing orientations that encourage curiosity, independence, and exploration of the larger environment—more frequent among the parents of boys—increase the probability that the child will encounter new experiences challenging existing premises. Childrearing orientations that encourage physical proximity as well as psychological closeness, emphasize supervision of the child's activities, discourage independence (Hoffman, 1972, 1977a), encourage "ladylike" behaviors, and provide help, sometimes gratuitously, in problem-solving situations (Block, 1976b; Rothbart, 1971) serve to lessen the opportunities for girls to engage in active, independent exploration of the environment, protect them against frequent encounters with discrepancy, and diminish their need to improvise alternative problem-solving strategies.

A series of research studies attest to the detrimental effects of excessive maternal helpfulness and overprotectiveness on achievement, self-confidence, and specific skill acquisition (Bing, 1963; Gunnar-vonGnechten, 1977; Harrington, Block, and Block, 1978; Hermans, ter Laak, and Maes, 1972; Hoffman, 1972; Kagan and Moss, 1962; Lynn, 1969; Sigel and Cocking,

1976). Indeed, this tendency toward overhelp appears to be a hazard of the mother/daughter relationship.

These parental protective behaviors, more frequent among parents of girls, motivated initially by a concern for the child's safety and well-being, have the unintended consequence of protecting the child from experiencing the discrepancies that encourage cognitive differentiation, facilitate alternative modes of problem solving, and contribute to feelings of efficacy (Sigel and Cocking, 1976).

Differential Strategies for Coping with New Experiences

Sex-differentiated parental socialization practices, many of which are reinforced by other socializing agents, contribute to the divergent strategies developed by boys and by girls to cope with discrepant experiences. The data from several sources agree in suggesting that socialization behaviors manifested more frequently by parents of females tend to foster proximity, discourage independent problem solving, restrict exploration, minimize contingency experiences, and discourage active play and experimentation in the physical world. Because females are provided fewer opportunities for independent exploration and experimentation, because their toys encourage imitative play, because their play activities are more structured, and because proximity to mothers facilitates imitative behaviors, females are more likely to rely on existing structures in processing new inputs, finding it more difficult to modify premises, restructure experience, and forge new psychological structures.

In contrast, the socialization experiences of males appear to be less constraining of activity and more encouraging of exploration. Because boys are given greater freedom to venture into the outside world, they are more often in a position to encounter situations that must be dealt with independently and improvisationally. Reliance on existing psychological structures may prove insufficient, and new alternatives must be generated and tested. By virtue of the greater opportunity of males to encounter discrepancies, existing structures are, of necessity, more often subject to a disequilibration that may provide the occasion for structure modification. These early experiences of males, which demand reexamination of premises, restructuring of understandings, and the construction of new schemata, may serve to prepare males for the less predictable, less structured world they will inhabit in their adult lives.

Conclusions

As we move toward a new era in which equality of opportunity for the sexes is being stressed, it is important that we closely examine existing socialization processes, noting their potential effects on the premise systems generated, the cognitive heuristics evolved, and the ego structures developed by males and females. According to the conceptualization offered here, the differential socialization experiences of males and females consequentially influence the nature of the child's interactions with the environment. I suggest that the greater experience of males with contingency relationships promotes the development, in them, of a premise system that warrants feelings of efficacy. Further, it is proposed that differences in the developmental contexts of males and females differentially affect their emerging psychological structures. The nature of the toys given males engages them, to a greater extent than females, in the physical world of objects, where feedback is more certain and consistent and emphasizes the qualities of the *object*. In addition, the greater opportunity accorded males to explore independently the larger environment outside the home places more demands on them for independent problem solving. The developmental context of females, in contrast, is more interpersonal. In the social world, feedback is less consistent and more often emphasizes qualities of the *subject*. The greater proximity of females to family members, as well as the greater chaperonage given them over the childhood and adolescent years, reduces the demand for independent problem solving. The greater exposure of males to disequilibrating, disconfirming experiences as a probabilistic function of the larger space of free movement granted them provides males more opportunity than females to generate hypotheses, develop new premises, and restructure achieved understandings.

The characteristics of the environments experienced by

males and females begin to diverge early in life, and it seems clear that external socializing forces, in conjunction with internal biological processes, encourage boys and girls to begin to select for themselves different activities, games, and milieus. I suggest, and empirical evidence is admittedly sparse, that the environmental contexts experienced by males and females differ along dimensions such as structure, predictability, and the need for improvisation. Differences in these environmental parameters are seen as affecting the nature of the premise systems developed by males and females and as predisposing the two sexes toward the use of different cognitive heuristics—a greater tendency toward the use of conserving, fitting, assimilative strategies on the part of females (strategies consistent with Bakan's, 1966, concept of communion) and a greater tendency toward the use of innovative, structure-creating, accommodative strategies on the part of males (strategies consistent with Bakan's concept of agency). The conceptualization and integration of the data presented in Chapter One led to the conclusion that socialization experiences that encourage the integration of communion and agency benefit ego development. Here I draw the further conclusion that socialization practices that encourage the development of both assimilative and accommodative modes of problem solving and their application in context-responsive ways would benefit the problem-solving competencies of males and females alike.

Chapter Seven

Gender Differences and Implications for Educational Policy

In little more than a decade, the number of universities and colleges dedicated to single-sex education has declined precipitously. During this period more than 50 percent of the 300 women's colleges in this country either became coeducational institutions or closed their doors (Carnegie Commission on Higher Education, 1973b; "Coeducation and Women's Colleges," 1973). Many of the remaining women's colleges are currently reexamining their commitment to single-sex education and debating their future enrollment policies. The shift to coeducation among men's colleges has been even more rapid, with more than 70 percent of former all-male institutions becoming coeducational ("Coeducation and Women's Colleges," 1973). However, data on the undergraduate origins of men and women who subsequently obtained doctoral degrees and, in the

Preparation of this essay was supported by a National Institute of Mental Health Research Scientist Award and by Smith, Mount Holyoke, and Wellesley Colleges. I wish to express my appreciation to Jill Conway, president of Smith College, for her encouragement, patience, and always-affirming feedback.

207

case of women, were recognized for their professional contributions have raised some questions about the long-range consequences of this shift to coeducation at the college and university level (Astin, 1974; Newcomer, 1959; Oates and Williamson, 1978; Tidball, 1973; Tidball and Kistiakowsky, 1976). The findings of these investigators suggest that women's colleges are overrepresented in terms of the number of their graduates who attain distinction; there appears to be an asymmetry in the effects of single-sex education whereby academic achievement in women, as defined by obtaining a doctoral degree, is associated with single-sex undergraduate education to a greater extent than for men (Oates and Williamson, 1978; Tidball and Kistiakowsky, 1976); and the "Seven Sisters" women's colleges have contributed a disproportionately larger number of distinguished women than other single-sex and coeducational institutions (Oates and Williamson, 1978). Among the twenty-five undergraduate institutions ranked highest over four decades in the percentage of graduates of each sex who obtained doctorates, ten women's colleges, but only five men's colleges, are represented. Tidball and Kistiakowsky (1976) summarize their findings by noting: "In particular, nine institutions, seven private women's colleges, and two private universities stand out as major contributors [to the advanced education] of women. . . . The majority of institutions ranked high for men, either in total output (principally large universities) or in percentage output (principally small, private, coeducational colleges), do not appear on the comparable lists for women. It may therefore be concluded that there are distinct differences in the baccalaureate origins of women and men who have earned doctorates" (pp. 651–652).

     If the data over a period of four decades can be used for extrapolation, these several surveys suggest that the recent shift toward coeducation may be disadvantageous for women, particularly for those with strong intellectual orientations. This apparent sex-related difference in academic achievement as a function of educational context, if true, carries great educational and social implications. But closer and more rigorous evaluation of these trends and discussion of their significance for educational policies have been delayed and complicated by the on-rush of cultural changes that imperil extrapolations based on data obtained earlier. Changes in enrollment policies over the past decade have introduced new and different selective factors associated with the choice of an undergraduate institution. The opportunity for intellectually gifted women to enroll in prestigious universities formerly accessible only to men has introduced a new educational option for women that has changed the composition of student bodies in many institutions. The recent efforts to redefine traditional conceptions of gender roles and to extend opportunities for women, the effects of affirmative action programs on admission policies of graduate and professional schools, and the changes in the number of women faculty members in both women's colleges and coeducational institutions (Healey, 1963; Tidball, 1973) are additional factors that now must be taken into account when conducting research to replicate and unconfound the results of earlier studies. Decisions regarding future undergraduate education must be informed by systematic, broadly based, contemporary studies incorporating analyses of the effects of different educational environments on men and on women. And these studies have not yet been done.

Nevertheless, it is possible to draw both on the findings of past research on comparisons of educational institutions and on the field of developmental psychology and to formulate, with some theory and conjecture, an outlook and some recommendations regarding educational policies that would recognize and respect gender differences in requirements and possibilities. The present chapter attempts this task. First, the relevant literature concerned with the psychological impact of single-sex compared with coeducational colleges is surveyed and integrated. Second, the recent literature on psychological sex differences and on the evidence for sex-differentiated socialization is summarized and placed in the larger context of personality and cognitive development. Understanding the psychological differences known to characterize males and females offers insights about the qualities of educational environments that would tend to foster, for male and female students alike, the realization of intellectual and personal potentials. Finally, drawing on the implications of these recognitions, I try to specify the kinds of college experience that can be expected to encourage personal and intellectual maturity, and I develop some implications of the findings with regard to future educational planning.

Research Evaluating Single-Sex Versus Coeducational Colleges

Large-scale studies comparing single-sex education and coeducational institutions have been conducted in other countries (for example, Bridgeland, 1971; Dale, 1969; Jones, Shallcrass, and Dennis, 1972; Wood and Ferguson, 1974), particularly in England. These researches will not be discussed here, because important differences characterize the educational systems of other countries and the predominant focus of these studies has been on secondary schools. Studies of colleges and universities done in this country that lack a specific comparative component (for example, Katz and Associates, 1968; Perry, 1968a, 1968b; Sanford, 1956) also are not included despite the insights they have provided about the impact of the college experience. (For an in-depth review and integration of this body of literature, see Feldman and Newcomb, 1969.)

Effects on Students' Academic Involvement and Perceptions of the College Experience

One of the most ambitious comparative studies evaluating the contemporaneous as well as long-term effects of different educational environments is the Cooperative Institutional Research Program (Astin, 1963, 1968a, 1968b, 1977; Astin and Panos, 1969; Astin, King, and Richardson, 1975). This longitudinal research investigation of approximately 200,000 students enrolled in more than 300 colleges and universities of diverse types includes wide-ranging data on student attitudes, values, and outcomes, as well as information about the characteristics of participating institutions (Astin, 1968a). In this ongoing study, entering freshmen are given a battery of tests, and selected samples of students are retested at graduation and in early adulthood. The most recent published data were obtained from follow-up studies conducted in 1974. In summarizing the comparisons involving single-sex colleges, Astin (1977, p. 252) concluded: "Some of the most dramatic effects were associated with attending men's or women's colleges. . . . Both types of single-sex colleges facilitate student involvement in several areas: academic, interaction with faculty, and verbal aggressiveness. The latter is stronger at women's than at men's colleges. Men's and women's colleges also have a positive effect on intellectual self-esteem. Students at single-sex colleges are much more satisfied than students at coeducational colleges with virtually all aspects of college life: student-faculty relations, quality of instruction, curricular variety, student friendships, and quality of science programs. The only area where students are less satisfied is social life. This negative effect is much stronger for men than for women."

From Astin's analyses of student responses to questionnaires and tests, it appears that single-sex colleges have highly beneficial effects on both males and females. Astin also notes some sex-differentiated effects with regard to verbal assertiveness, participation in student government, satisfaction with college social life, political liberalism, college grades, and later attainments. From the data presented, however, it is impossible to assess the likely replicability of the diverging patterns of findings for males and for females.

Effects on Academic and Professional Achievement. A series of survey studies evaluating the baccalaureate origins of women who attained academic or professional distinction show that women's colleges are overrepresented (Astin, 1974; Carnegie Commission on Higher Education, 1973b; Newcomer, 1959; Oates and Williamson, 1978; Tidball, 1973; Tidball and Kistiakowsky, 1976). The results of Tidball and Kistiakowsky's study show that more female graduates, both in absolute number and in percentage, who obtained doctoral degrees during the period between 1920 and 1973 had their undergraduate origins in women's colleges. Newcomer (1959) surveyed all women scholars listed in *American Men* [!] *of Science* and the *Dictionary of*

American Biography and reported that 34 percent of all women scholars listed in these two works had attended women's colleges whose enrollments accounted for only 16 percent of all women students. A similar overrepresentation of women's colleges was found by Tidball (1973), who randomly sampled 500 women in each of three volumes of *Who's Who of American Women* and found that a significantly greater number of women recognized for their achievements had been undergraduates in women's colleges. Oates and Williamson (1978) used the 1974–75 edition of *Who's Who in America* to compile a list of 3,000 women achievers and indexed their baccalaureate origins. Their results demonstrate again a strong relationship between attendance in a single-sex college and achievement in women. Oates and Williamson's study is unusual in that it controlled for institutional size. Significantly higher rates of achievement still were found among women who had attended women's colleges than among women who had attended coeducational institutions of comparable size. The findings of Astin's research (1977) support these survey results in demonstrating that attendance at a women's college is associated with higher career aspirations and with greater likelihood of entering graduate or professional schools after completion of the undergraduate degree.

Effects on Choice of College Major. In addition to producing more graduates who achieved some degree of academic and/or professional distinction, women's colleges have had a higher percentage of students majoring in mathematics and science (Astin and Panos, 1969; Carnegie Commission on Higher Education, 1973b; Newcomer, 1959; Tidball and Kistiakowsky, 1976; Mattfeld, 1980). Newcomer placed this finding in a larger context by noting the greater tendency for both men and women in single-sex colleges and universities to choose less traditionally sex-typed majors than students in coeducational institutions. While only 7 percent of the men in coeducational colleges majored in the arts and humanities, the comparable figure was 19 percent in all-male colleges. Newcomer also reported that approximately twice as many women in women's colleges majored in mathematics and the sciences as in coeducational colleges (19 percent versus 10 percent, respectively). The Newcomer findings were corroborated by the survey of Tidball and Kistiakow-sky (1976), who found that twelve of the twenty-five institutions with the highest percentages of men who subsequently obtained their doctorates in the arts and humanities were, despite their smaller numbers, men's colleges. Among the twenty-four highest-ranked institutions with respect to the percentages of women who subsequently obtained their doctorates in the physical sciences and engineering were nine women's colleges. And Mattfeld (1980) found that during the five-year period from 1973 to 1978, Barnard, Mount Holyoke, and Wellesley *each* graduated more women in chemistry than Harvard, Yale, Cornell, and Princeton *combined*. This tendency toward less sex-typing in single-sex schools was also found at the secondary level by Wood and Ferguson (1974) and by Finn, who has reported his findings of a cross-national study in an unpublished paper. Boys in single-sex secondary schools were found to achieve significantly higher grades in art than did boys in co-educational schools, while girls in single-sex schools obtained significantly higher grades in the sciences than their peers in coeducational institutions.

Effects on Attrition Rates in College. Not only have studies comparing single-sex and coeducational institutions found differences in academic and/or professional achievement and in choice of major, but lower dropout rates have been reported for students in single-sex colleges as well (Astin, 1974, 1977; Astin and Panos, 1969). These findings may be a function of the greater educational commitment on the part of students in single-sex colleges and/or the greater ability of such schools to meet the psychological and educational needs of their students. This latter interpretation is supported by the greater satisfactions found by Astin (1977) to characterize the undergraduate experiences of men and women enrolled in single-sex colleges. The greater commitment on the part of students enrolled in men's and women's colleges, in contrast to those enrolled in coeducational institutions, is reflected in their greater degree of academic involvement, in their more frequent interactions with faculty, and in their more active participation in seminars and class discussions (Astin, 1977). With regard to intellectual development, single-sex colleges appear to have served students' needs well.

Effects on Participation in Extracurricular Activities. In terms of extracurricular activities, differences also have been reported between single-sex and coeducational institutions. Greater opportunity to engage in the school governance structure and to assume positions of leadership accrue to women attending women's colleges (Astin, 1977; Carnegie Commission on Higher Education, 1973b). In 1970, women constituted only 5 percent of the student body presidents in coeducational institutions and, except for editorial posts, were underrepresented in other positions as well (Group for the Advancement of Psychiatry, 1975). The greater opportunity for female students in women's colleges to gain experience in leadership roles in campus organizations and activities not only increases self-confidence but also provides experiences that would be expected to benefit their later professional and personal lives.

Effects on Personality and Attitudinal Characteristics. A final set of studies concerned with single-sex education addressed nonintellective factors, evaluating differences in self-confidence and fear of failure as well as differences in values, political/social attitudes, marital status, and life satisfaction in adulthood.

In an attempt to explain the differential findings in the psychological literature surrounding achievement motivation in males and in females, Horner (1968, 1970, 1972) hypothesized that the performance of women in achievement-relevant situations is impeded to a greater extent than is the performance of men by anxiety of a sort that she labeled "fear of success." Horner's thesis rests on the assumption that achievement in women conflicts with the traditional societal definition of the appropriate feminine role. For women, the possibility of success, particularly in areas conventionally considered nonfeminine, arouses conflict and creates an anticipation of negative consequences in the form of social rejection or of being perceived as less feminine. Because achievement historically has been a principal component of the masculine gender role, the attainment of success for women, according to Horner's argument, is neither ego- nor socially syntonic.

Horner found a higher percentage of negative consequences in the projective stories told by women in response to a success cue involving a woman at the top of her class in medical school ("Anne") than were found either in the comparable stories by men or in the stories by both males and females when the successful figure was male ("John"). Horner reciprocally validated both her measure and her conceptual formulation in an experiment comparing performance under competitive and noncompetitive conditions. Her findings on fear of success and the poorer performance of women in a competitive situation led Horner (1972) to question the wisdom of the contemporary emphasis on coeducation. Horner has suggested that the trend toward coeducation, which increases the salience of cross-sex competition as well as exacerbating the conflict between achievement and affiliation (Hoffman, 1972), may be disadvantageous for women, particularly for women of ability. This suggestion gains pertinence when it is recognized that both Horner (1968) and Hoffman (1974, 1977a) have found that academically superior females, in contrast to their less gifted classmates, manifest greater fear of success.

Some recent studies have failed to replicate Horner's original results on fear of success, finding no evidence of sex differences (see Spence and Helmreich, 1978, for a summary of these studies). Other investigators have emphasized the role of situational factors in response tendencies (for example, Condry and Dyer, 1976). Although findings surrounding fear of success have been challenged, a study by Hoffman (1977b) provides further evidence for the validity of Horner's measure and the consistency of scores for women over time while failing to find evidence of validity in a sample of men. Hoffman concluded in another study that fear of success appears to be a reliable behavioral predisposition in women and that "both the concept and the measure cannot be disregarded despite the difficulties that have arisen in their use" (1977a, p. 321).

Winchel, Fenner, and Shaver (1974), in an unusually well-controlled study, evaluated fear-of-success imagery among 252 high school seniors attending Jewish private schools—either single-sex or coeducational—in a middle- to upper-middle-class community in Brooklyn. In this relatively homogeneous sample,

Winchel and associates replicated Horner's original finding of greater frequency of negative consequences projected by both sexes in response to the story when the successful person was female (the Anne cue) than when the story had a male success figure (the John cue). These investigators also found a significant difference between the proportions of fear-of-success stories evoked by the Anne cue in females attending coeducational schools (40.9 percent) and those attending single-sex schools (15.8 percent). The corresponding percentages of fear-of-success responses for the sample of males were not significantly different. In another analysis, Winchel and associates found a significantly higher percentage of fear of success among girls who had attended coeducational elementary *and* secondary schools than among girls who attended noncoeducational elementary and high schools. These investigators note that their findings are compatible with Horner's suggestion that increased cross-sex competition increases fear of success in females. They also observe that the tendency to become anxious in the face of cross-sex competition appears to be established early. They conclude that their results "indicate that developmental studies of fear of success should include preadolescent groups and should treat school environment as an important variable. On the practical side, the results seem to argue for noncoed school" (p. 729).

Although the foregoing findings derive from a highly selected and unrepresentative sample of high school seniors, the results fit well with the findings obtained by Horner and Hoffman with college-age females. Because of the controls for socioeconomic and cultural backgrounds, geographical area, and quality of schools that were included in the research design of Winchel and associates, the results of the comparisons of single-sex and coeducational schools are compelling. Consistent with these results, a constellation of findings that includes higher educational ambitions, increased intellectual self-esteem, and greater assertiveness in interactions with faculty and peers appears to distinguish women enrolled in women's colleges from those in coeducational institutions (Astin, 1977). It may be that women are less ambivalent about pursuing their intellectual interests in an environment that deemphasizes traditional gender role stereotyping, minimizes direct intellectual competition with males, and provides a supporting social and collegial network (Conway, 1977). This generalization is provided some empirical support by the results of an experiment evaluating the effects of sex composition of four-person groups on the participation rates in the play of a complex game (Lockheed, 1976). The research was designed to compare participation rates in four-person single-sex and mixed-sex groups and the effects of group composition on order of participation. Two important findings emerge from the study. Lockheed reports that no differences were found in the rates of participation at either the individual or the group level between males and females in single-sex groups. Significant *order* effects were found, however. Males initially assigned to mixed-sex groups showed significantly higher participation rates and manifested a pattern of emergent male leadership. However, when the game was entered into first in single-sex groups and subsequently played in mixed-sex groups, the participation rates of males and females did not differ. In a carefully controlled analysis, it was found that the rates of participation for females (but not for males) *increased significantly as a function of prior experience in the single-sex condition.* Learning the task in the single-sex group provided participants the opportunity to determine for themselves their specific task competencies, which, for the females, resulted in significantly increased initiative in the mixed-sex group. The importance of performance-specific competence for degree of participation in mixed-sex groups is suggested also by the results of a study by Stake and Stake (1979). The findings that task-specific experience influences the behavior of females to a greater extent suggest that the opportunity to develop realistic estimates of their own abilities in situations without cross-sex competition or traditional gender role stereotyping benefits the performance of women. Results from these laboratory-based studies may help to explain the facilitative effects of women's colleges on female performance.

In the area of attitudes, values, and political/social orientations, Astin (1977) reports that women's colleges, more than coeducational institutions, tend to encourage increasingly liberal political/social attitudes, a greater interest in esthetic values, and a declining interest in business-oriented values. For males, however, attending men's colleges was not found to be associated with significant increases in political liberalism (perhaps because of males' greater liberalism as entering freshmen) or with a significant decline of interest in the business world. Such results suggest that the effects of single-sex education on the attitudes of male and female students diverge. It is probable that more incisive studies would point to other areas in which the reactions of male and female students to the college experience differ.

Effects on Marital Status. Bayer (1969) reported that enrollment in a coeducational institution, rather than in a women's college, increased the chances of marriage for women. However, a study by Bayer (1972) and the analyses of Astin (1977) failed to replicate this earlier finding. According to Astin, students attending single-sex institutions are less likely to *plan* marriage during their undergraduate years and, in fact, were less likely to marry during college. Because of the failure to control for differences in intentions about marriage at the time of entry into college, the erroneous conclusion was drawn that attendance at a coeducational institution enhanced the student's chance of marriage. Astin's reanalysis of the data, controlling for differences in initial marriage plans, found no differences in the marriage rates between students in single-sex colleges and those in coeducational institutions (Astin, 1977).

A study of the long-term effects of different undergraduate experiences investigated the marital status and happiness of approximately 2,500 men and women who had attended either single-sex or coeducational undergraduate institutions (Atherton, 1973). Not unexpectedly, in both the samples of men and women, there was a higher percentage of professionals among those who had attended single-sex colleges than those who had attended coeducational institutions. There were no differences in the rates of divorce or separation for either men or women, nor were there significant differences in the results of an overall "happiness index" devised by the investigator.

Taken together, the findings from the available studies suggest that single-sex education appears to benefit the academic achievement of women, to be associated with subsequent recognition for professional contributions, to provide an environment in which non-sex-typed interests may be pursued more readily, to enhance self-esteem, to provide more opportunities for leadership, to neither advantage nor disadvantage marital status, and—if one can extrapolate from the study of high school seniors—to be associated with lesser fear of success in the domain of achievement. Coeducational colleges appear to maintain to a greater degree stereotypic differences between males and females in behavior, personality, aspiration, and achievement (Astin, 1977).

The Data Base Providing Comparisons of Single-Sex
and Coeducational Institutions: An Evaluation

In reviewing the foregoing investigations of different educational environments, a number of methodological deficiencies become evident, deficiencies that must qualify conclusions.

The majority of studies relied on survey information and secondary sources (that is, citation indexes), whereas intensive, longitudinal investigations are required. Many of the studies report on data from earlier generations of students, and the extent to which these findings continue to apply in the present, quite different era is problematical. There also is frequent failure to control for selective factors characterizing different educational institutions. The superior achievement of alumnae from women's colleges reported in survey studies may reflect little beyond selective factors associated with admission to a prestigious women's college. Young women electing to attend a women's college often have a long family tradition of achievement, come from families with higher socioeconomic status, may be intellectually more competent, and may have more clearly defined educational or professional goals that they wish to pursue in an atmosphere that minimizes conflicts surrounding achievement and intellectual competence. Such selective factors operating at college entry require control or evaluation if subsequent outcome measures are to be interpreted appropriately.

There has been little effort to incorporate assessments of institutional characteristics—both objective indexes and student perceptions—which may mediate different educational outcomes. Astin's research (1968a, 1968b, 1977) took a giant stride in this direction, and future researchers would do well to emulate his model, extending it to include other salient features of institutional environments (for example, the quality of "support systems" available to students, the political/social climate, distribution of faculty time among teaching, research, and student advising, the adequacy of student counseling services). The importance of this approach is underscored by the results of a study by Chickering (1974), who developed criteria for evaluating the institutional characteristics of colleges and examined the degree and nature of personality change in students (as indexed by the Omnibus Personality Inventory) over the college years as a function of institutional characteristics. His data indicate that the qualities of educational environments interact with student characteristics in determining personality change in college. Although Chickering's data do not permit assessment of relative changes in single-sex versus coeducational institutions or of the differential influences of institutional characteristics on males and females, they do demonstrate the importance of considering personality and institutional interactions. Certainly, evaluation of the nature and quality of educational contexts is a difficult task. People will differ in their choice of criteria, and many factors contributing to the quality of an institution tend to be ephemeral. But the effort is required if Astin's (1977, p. 3) forced and regretful conclusion, "There is surprisingly little one can say with confidence about the impact of college," is to be revised.

A final problem in the designs of most studies of educational outcomes is their failure to conduct sex-differentiated comparisons and to examine the *relative* effectiveness of different environmental contexts for men and for women. Institutional characteristics may not affect the two sexes equally, and indeed there is some evidence, albeit tentative, supporting this possibility. The findings of Tidball and Kistiakowsky (1976) suggest that the range of institutions supportive of predoctoral training for women (primarily women's colleges) is narrower than is true for men. Asymmetrical results for male and female achievement patterns have been found when the sex ratios of faculties are compared (Tidball, 1973). Tidball reports a direct and significant relationship between the number of women faculty members at a college and the number of women from that college who were high achievers after their undergraduate years, a relationship that held for women in both single-sex and coeducational institutions. No relationship was found, however, between the subsequent academic achievement of males and the proportion of male faculty members they had experienced as undergraduates. Astin (1977) points out some additional contrasting effects of men's and women's colleges. Men attending men's colleges, in contrast to those attending coeducational institutions, are more likely to participate and achieve in athletics, to participate more frequently in honors programs, and to obtain better grades. None of these factors significantly distinguishes between females in single-sex and in coeducational institutions. Women attending women's colleges, in contrast to those attending coeducational institutions, are more likely to be politically liberal, to have esthetic interests, to have been in positions of leadership, to have higher academic aspirations, and to not drop out of college. None of these factors significantly distinguishes between males in single-sex and in coeducational institutions. These sex differentiated results require closer study than they yet have been given.

Taken together, the several methodological problems afflicting demonstrations of the divergent effects of single-sex and coeducational institutions on men and women suggest the need for research studies designed to permit systematic and controlled comparisons of different types of academic environment. Further, studies are needed that would compare the specific effects of different educational environments on the intellectual and personal development of male and female students. These conclusions accord with those of Barber (1977), who has been urging research to investigate "the ways in which and the extent to which similar education may lead to different post-educational outcomes for men and women" (p. 25). The studies and findings reviewed in preceding pages, though consistent in suggesting that single-sex and coeducational institutions may not have parallel effects on males and females, are not sufficiently robust yet to suggest implementation of specific curricular and extracurricular changes. Rather, they identify a necessary direction for further research effort in order to clarify findings and to establish dependable generalizations that can properly inform future decision making. It is pertinent to note that results demonstrating the differential effects of particular qualities of educational environments on males and on females are consistent with findings emerging from comparative studies of males and females in other contexts. The literature on psychological sex differences can provide an interesting and ample basis for explaining the different influences of similar educational environments on the sexes.

Research Evaluating Sex Differences in
Behavior and Performance

The literature concerned with psychological sex differences has been surveyed and summarized by Maccoby and Jacklin (1974), who concluded that there were a number of "unfounded beliefs about sex differences" (p. 349). After surveying the results of approximately 1,600 studies published, for the most part, between 1966 and 1973, they concluded, from their interpretation of the literature, that there is well-established evidence for the superior verbal ability of females, the superiority of males with respect to mathematics and visual/spatial ability, and the greater aggressivity of males. Maccoby and Jacklin concluded that the evidence was equivocal with respect to seven additional areas: (1) tactile sensitivity, (2) fear, timidity, and anxiety, (3) anxiety level, (4) competitiveness, (5) dominance, (6) compliance, and (7) nurturance and "maternal" behaviors. Finally, in evaluating the evidence concerning differential socialization of the two sexes, Maccoby and Jacklin found "surprisingly little differentiation in parent behavior according to the sex of the child" (p. 338). Although conceding that there are some areas (for example, sex typing as narrowly defined; toy preference) where differential "shaping" appears to occur, they concluded that "the reinforcement contingencies for the two sexes appear to be remarkably similar" (p. 342). This work and its debatable conclusions are discussed and evaluated fully in Chapters Two and Three of the present volume.

Because social and educational policy decisions will be influenced by the nature and the extent of differences understood to exist between the sexes, it is important that the conclusions drawn from studies involving comparisons of males and females be closely evaluated. In the years since the appearance of the Maccoby and Jacklin volume and my critique of that volume (Block, 1976a, 1976b), additional critiques of their work and reanalyses of the data underlying some of their conclusions have been offered (Cooper, 1979; Eagly, 1978; M. L. Hoffman, 1977).

After reviewing the literature on empathy, Hoffman concluded that clear sex differences exist favoring females. Eagly reexamined research studies evaluating sex related differences in influenceability and concluded that females, more oriented to interpersonal goals in group settings than males, tend to yield to group pressures for conformity more than males. This conclusion is buttressed by Cooper's reanalysis of the data on con formity evaluated by Maccoby and Jacklin. In experiments on field dependence/independence, the performance of both adolescent and adult females is generally found to be more field-dependent than that of males, indicating that females are more influenced by the surrounding field or context than males (Witkin and others, 1962), a finding with obvious implications for research on educational environments. With regard to social behaviors, Wheeler and Nezlek (1977) examined daily records of the social interactions of entering university students for two weeks in a fall semester and two weeks in a spring semester and found evidence of a different patterning for males and females. Entering college women socialized more intensely in the new environment than males and, to a greater extent than males, made use of their same-sex best friends to deal with the stimulation (and anxiety) experienced in the new, unfamiliar situation. This latter finding, together with data from Waldrop and Halverson (1975) indicating that girls develop more intensive peer relationships in contrast to the more extensive friendship networks of boys, provide evidence for sex-related differences in friendship patterns.

In a reanalysis of studies contributing to Maccoby and Jacklin's conclusions with respect to achievement, Caplan (1979) finds a sex-differentiated pattern of achievement according to the presence or absence of an adult. The achievement behaviors of males remain relatively constant with or without adult presence; females, however, appear to demonstrate higher levels of achievement in the presence of an adult than when no adult is present. Caplan's observations are congruent with those of Hoffman (1972) in suggesting that social (adult) approval may motivate achievement in females to a greater extent than in males. These results imply that reorganization of intellectual potential for females, more than for males, may depend on contextual factors and the availability of faculty support.

These several reanalyses of the data presented by Maccoby and Jacklin, and the results of additional studies evaluating sex-related differences in cognitive functioning and personality characteristics, have consequential implications for educational policy. See, for example, Graham (1978) for differences in performance anxiety in male and female science majors; Gunnar-vonGnechten (1978) for evidence of differential salience of control over external events in males and females; Lever (1976) for findings suggesting that females have greater difficulty than males conducting negotiations in conflict situations arising during playground games; Helson (1968) and Hetherington and McIntyre (1975) for a discussion of different patterns of personality characteristics surrounding creativity in males and females; Lockheed (1976) and Stake and Stake (1979) for evidence that specific task-related competence affects group participation to a greater extent in females than in males.

Before pursuing the implications of these many sex-related differences, it is important to briefly discuss my perspective on the biological bases of gender differences and the possible plasticities in human behavior that necessarily underlie future social and educational planning. One's position with regard to the question of biological determinism versus behavioral plasticity will influence the implications—societal, economic, and educational—to be drawn from the sex-related socialization differences to be brought forward shortly.

Biological Constraints on Psychological Sex Differences

Virtually all contemporary psychologists express themselves as viewing behavior as complexly determined by the interaction of genetic and experiential factors. Though formally committed to an interactive position, many scientists still view biological constraints as paramount (and therefore, in effect, as experientially noninteractive) in shaping behavior and in specifying capacities. When broadly enough stated, such a view is undeniable; one cannot disavow the biological matrix from which humans derive and ascribe gender differences in behavior solely to environmental conditions or to the individual's learning history. However, biological factors have been shown to function with such enormous complexity, and to be so often dependent in amplifying or dampening ways on the experiences encountered by the individual, as to make the broad statement of the importance of biology often no more than a vague assertion of an ideological position.

As a case in point, consider the straightforward endocrinological hypothesis that has been advanced ascribing the greater aggressivity of males to their higher androgen levels. Experiments have shown androgen administration to increase aggressivity in female vertebrates (Money and Ehrhardt, 1972; Svare and Gandelman, 1975). But also, the female hormone estrogen administered to newborn female rats has been shown to increase their adulthood aggressivity (Goy and Resko, 1972), a finding embarrassing to the simple androgen hypothesis. And, to further complicate the issue, Beach (1975) has reported that the behavioral effects of hormonal stimulation depend on the timing of their administration. The complexity of the androgen/ aggression relationship is illustrated also in the studies of Olweus and others (1980), who found that in each of two samples the testosterone levels in males related most clearly to only one type of aggression—aggression in response to provocation—and showed only negligible relationships to other clearly separable forms of aggressive behavior, such as aggressive attitudes, aggressive impulses, and unprovoked physical and verbal aggression.

Introducing further subtleties that must be taken into account in understanding endocrine functioning is the series of studies by Rose, Gordon, and Bernstein (1972) demonstrating that the testosterone levels of male rhesus monkeys are affected by the animal's social environment. These investigators found that the testosterone levels of monkeys previously low in the social dominance hierarchy showed a significant rise when the subjects were given access to sexually receptive females whom they could dominate and engage in sex; subsequently, the testosterone levels fell significantly when the male was exposed briefly to a large group of males and decisively defeated in a fight. In a final manipulation of the social environment, the testosterone levels rose again, significantly, when the nondominant males were once again given access to receptive females. These and other results manifesting the exquisite responsivity of the hormonal system to social and sexual experience are relatively recent; the field continues to burgeon. The implications of these developments have been well summarized by Rossi (1976, p. 18): "Recent endocrinological research findings pertinent to the interpretation of sex differences will suggest how inadequate any simple model is of sex hormones and their effects upon the behavior of men and women." Equivalent complexities and empirical insufficiencies beset efforts to explain gender differences biologically in terms of hemispheric dominance, or in terms of the differential timing of myelination, or the genes carried by the X- and Y-chromosomes, or other such proffered conjectures. Scientific advance may in time make some or even all of these hypotheses empirically persuasive; currently none is compelling.

For the present, it may be wise for psychology to borrow a concept and a recognition that has proved useful in ethology in recent years—the concept of *modal action patterns* (Barlow,

1977). The concept of a modal action pattern specifies that an action or action sequence may be said, in a statistical sense, to characterize a species or subspecies while allowing for variation, perhaps great variation, about the statistical mode as a function of genetic variation and of the demand quality of the particular ecosystem confronting individual members of the species. The concept recognizes the existence of biologically grounded behavioral propensities but does not insist on the existence of uniform, almost reflexive behaviors as evidence of genetic influence. Most important, it recognizes that biological propensities may be manifest in behavior in diverse and complex ways, as organisms are shaped by or selected by the (often changing) environment in which they must function.

Applied to the question of gender differences, the idea of modal action patterns suggests that although biology does lay down certain modal behavioral dispositions for males and for females, biology also allows for great variation about these behavioral modes. Moreover, and most important, the ways in which such behavioral propensities as exist issue into behavior is a complex (and *largely unexplored*) function of the structure of the environment impinging on the individual males and females seeking to construct for themselves modes of living.

Given the present state of scientific knowledge regarding gender differences, it seems clear that the nature and extent of the relationships between human sexual dimorphism and human psychological functioning require considerable and careful explorations. While recognizing some unfortunate ways in which current cultural prescriptions for sex roles attenuate human possibilities, close exploration of human sex differences and plasticity is both scientifically conservative (in not prejudging outcome) and a necessary scientific research strategy for the future. Only by systematic and safeguarded research exploring the changeability of psychological sex differences will we be able to establish the possibilities provided and the limits set by our genetic propensities.

From this perspective, it now becomes relevant to examine the sociocultural context and the socialization emphases typically experienced by contemporary males and females.

Sex-Differentiated Socialization

Summarizing briefly from Block (1979a) and Chapter Three of the present volume and looking first at socialization values, the results of six studies converge in finding the self-described childrearing orientations of mothers and fathers to be differentiating. The overall conclusions provide evidence for (1) sex-differentiated parental socialization behaviors, (2) specific, consistent sex-of-parent and sex-of-child interaction effects, (3) increasing sex differentiation in socialization emphases with age of the child, and (4) consistency across socioeconomic levels, educational levels, and cultural origins of the parents in the sex-related socialization emphases of mothers and fathers.

With respect to the socialization of sons, the self-described childrearing emphases of both mothers and fathers in several independent samples press achievement and competition more on their sons than on their daughters. In addition, both parents encourage their sons, more than their daughters, to control the expression of affect, to be independent, and to assume personal responsibility. They employ punishment more with their sons than with their daughters. In addition, fathers appear more authoritarian in their rearing of sons than of daughters: They are more strict, more firm, more endorsing of physical punishment, less tolerant of aggression directed toward themselves by their sons, and less accepting of behaviors deviating from the traditional masculine stereotypes.

The self-described childrearing emphases of parents of daughters indicate the parent/daughter relationship, in contrast to the parent/son relationship, is characterized by greater warmth and physical closeness, greater confidence in the trust-worthiness and truthfulness of their daughters, greater expectation by mothers and fathers alike of "ladylike" behavior, greater reluctance to punish daughters, and greater encouragement to "contemplate" life. Additionally, mothers of daughters tend to be more restrictive of their daughters and to engage in closer supervision of their activities.

The findings of the empirical investigation of sex-differentiated socialization emphases are congruent with the results of Barry, Bacon, and Child (1957), who reported significant and consistent sex-related socialization emphases in a variety of cultures, girls receiving more pressure to be nurturant, obedient, and responsible and boys receiving more pressure from parents and the larger culture to achieve and to be self-reliant. The results fit also with Hoffman's (1977b) findings from a large-scale survey study showing that parents expected their sons, more frequently than their daughters, to be independent, self-reliant, highly educated, ambitious, hardworking, career-oriented, intelligent, and strong-willed. In contrast, parents more often expected their daughters to be kind, unselfish, attractive, loving, and well-mannered and to have a good marriage and be a good parent.

Studies of the *actual* behaviors directed toward the child by mother (typically) and by fathers (occasionally) also provide evidence for sex-differentiated parental behaviors. An implicative area in which parents of boys and parents of girls have been observed to differ is in the frequency of their contingent responding to behaviors initiated by their infant. In the feeding situation, mothers were observed to be more responsive and attentive to signals from their male infants than from their female infants (Murphy and Moriarty, 1976; Walraven, 1974). Both mothers and fathers have been observed to react more contingently to the vocalizations of boys than to the vocalizations of girls (Lewis and Freedle, 1973; Parke and Sawin, 1976; Yarrow, 1975). These apparent differences in contingent responding noted in infancy appear to continue through the childhood years; it has been shown in numerous studies at different age levels that boys receive both more positive and more negative feedback, including physical punishment, from parents (Maccoby and Jacklin, 1974; Margolin and Patterson, 1975). The well-designed study of sequential interactions conducted by Margolin and Patterson, for example, revealed that *both* parents responded contingently to males more than females; fathers of boys responded positively to the child more than twice as often as fathers of girls.

Differences in contingency experiences in the interpersonal realm are augmented by differences in the contingent possibilities afforded by the toys typically provided to boys and girls. Boys are given a greater variety of toys than girls, and there are important differences in the kinds of toys parents provide for boys and girls (Rheingold and Cook, 1975; Yarrow and others, 1972). Boys' toys, more than girls' toys, afford inventive possibilities (Rosenfeld, 1975), encourage manipulation, and provide more explicit feedback from the physical world. Girls' toys, in contrast, tend to encourage imitation, are more often used in proximity to the caretaker, and provide less opportunity for variation and innovation. Differences in toy preferences of boys and girls have been documented in numerous studies (Fagot, 1977; Goldberg and Lewis, 1969; Fein and others, 1975). It seems likely that differential exposure to toys with dissimilar characteristics provides different kinds of experiences for boys and girls that importantly influence cognitive development, a recognition also advanced by Hoffman (1977b) and Carpenter (1979).

In addition to being more contingently responsive to actions initiated by males than by females, parents have been observed also to provide more physical stimulation for boys than for girls. Male infants are held and aroused more, and they are also given more stimulation for gross motor activity (Moss, 1967, 1974; Lewis, 1972a; Parke and O'Leary, 1976; Yarrow, 1975). In Yarrow's study of mother/infant interactions, mothers of males were observed to interact more frequently with their infants, at higher intensity levels, and with richer, more varied behaviors. These observational studies, demonstrating that infant boys are given more physical stimulation than girls, are consistent with the sex-related socialization differences in the encouragement of exploratory behaviors found later in childhood.

Studies of sex-differentiated parental socialization behaviors generally report that boys are given more freedom to explore than girls. Girls have been observed to play more proximally to their mothers (Lewis and Weintraub, 1974; Messer and Lewis, 1972), to be allowed fewer excursions from home (Saegert and Hart, 1976), to be encouraged by their mothers to follow them around the house (Fagot, 1977), and to be more closely supervised in their activities (Newson and Newson, 1968). The differential assignment of household chores to boys and to girls also reflects proximity differences, since boys are given chores that take them out of the house more often and/ or farther away from home, while girls are assigned homebound chores of cleaning, "helping," babysitting—chores that are done in proximity to other family members. Such sex-differentiated chore assignments encourage the greater embeddedness of girls in the social milieu of the family (Duncan, Schuman, and Duncan, 1973; Whiting and Edwards, 1975). Chodorow (1974) argues that the different social contexts experienced by boys and by girls over the childhood years account for the development of many psychological sex differences, particularly those reflecting the greater embeddedness of women in social networks in contrast to the more individualistic, mastery-emphasizing contexts of men. Chodorow's observation is consistent with Gutmann's (1965) distinction between the "allocentric" milieu and the "autocentric" milieu in which males and females, respectively, are socialized and also with the "agentic"/"communal" distinction proposed by Bakan (1966), for which Carlson (1971a) has provided empirical evidence.

When the separate teaching behaviors of fathers and mothers were videotaped, observed, and independently rated, greater sex differentiation in the teaching behaviors of fathers than of mothers was found (Block, Block, and Harrington, 1975). Fathers set higher standards and placed greater emphasis on cognitive achievement for their sons than for their daughters in the teaching/learning situation. With their daughters, fathers focused more on the interpersonal aspects of the teaching situation, encouraging, supporting, joking and playing, and protecting. Day (1975) found a similar sex-differentiated pattern in adults' teaching behaviors in an experiment where the investigator manipulated the presumption of the sex of her two-year-old subjects. Adults, particularly males, provided more goal-directed reinforcements to presumed boys and expected them to do significantly better on the tasks than presumed girls. Presumed girls were given more compliments and encouragement. Together, these results indicate that adults, particularly fathers, act in more instrumental, task-oriented, mastery-emphasizing ways with their sons and in more expressive, less intellectually rigorous ways with their daughters (see also Radin, 1976). Lamb, Owen, and Chase-Lansdale (1979) summarize the results of observational studies of the father/daughter relationship by noting that the message conveyed to young girls appears to be that success is to be attained via affective relationships rather than through their independent achievements, a conclusion consistent with Hoffman's earlier thesis (1972).

The lesser paternal emphasis on achievement and mastery in girls is reflected also, but differently, in maternal behaviors. Mothers of girls have been observed to provide help in problem-solving situations more than mothers of boys, but this help is offered when it is not required (Gunnar-vonGnechten, 1977, 1978; Rothbart, 1971; Rothbart and Rothbart, 1976). Mothers respond with more positive affect to bids for help from girls than from boys (Fagot, 1978b) and provide girls more immediate physical comfort after a frustrating experience (Lewis, 1972a). Not only do parents appear to deemphasize independent achievement with their daughters, but the results of a recent study by Greif (1979) suggest that parents may devalue their daughters' efforts as well. Studying communication patterns within families, Greif (1979) found that parents interrupt their daughters more than their sons, thus conveying a metamessage that the ideas of their daughters are considered less important, less worthy of respect. Interestingly, Greif's results also indicate that mothers were interrupted more frequently than fathers, a finding reported also by Steinberg and Hill (1978) in their studies of family communication patterns. It is likely that such metamessages importantly influence the development of self-esteem in young girls and women.

As the preceding studies indicated, evidence has been accruing suggesting that parents do treat their sons differently than their daughters. Several factors may contribute to the discrepancy between this clear trend in the several kinds of data reported here and the null conclusions that Maccoby and Jacklin reached in 1974. First, the increase in the number of researches that include fathers as well as mothers is undoubtedly involved, since fathers have been found to be more sex-differentiating in their behaviors than mothers. While the influential role of the father in socialization has been emphasized by many (Biller, 1971; Hetherington and Deu, 1971; Lamb, 1976; Lynn, 1974; Osofsky and O'Connell, 1972; Stein and Bailey, 1973), it is highlighted and given added import by the results of recent observational studies of father/child interactions. Second, recent observational investigations have employed more sophisticated research methods and have included larger subject panels, thus enhancing the statistical power of many studies. Third, dependent variables are now more often defined in differentiated, conceptually coherent ways, permitting relationships to emerge that formerly were obscured when parenting dimensions such as warmth or hostility or authoritarianism were defined in global, conceptually hodgepodge ways. Fourth, the socialization process itself has been subjected to scrutiny, and new dimensions of parenting have suggested themselves, dimensions of consequence not assessed earlier.

Although the researches cited suggest differences in parent behaviors in a number of domains as a function of the sex of the child, more empirical efforts are required to evaluate the robustness of these effects, to define the limits of generalization, to identify factors influencing sex-differentiated parental behaviors, and to evaluate stringently the specific impact, over time, of these sex-differentiated parenting emphases on personality and cognitive development.

To the extent that sex-related differences in family socialization patterns are echoed in the behaviors of teachers at the elementary and secondary school levels and faculty in colleges and universities, the sex-typed behaviors of males and females are continually reinforced. Considerable evidence for such reinforcement in the classroom exists. Observations of nursery school teachers' behaviors demonstrate, in several studies, that boys are given more attention, both positive and negative, than girls (for example, Meyer and Thompson, 1956; Felsenthal, 1970; Serbin and others, 1973). Serbin and others (1973) also found differences in the responses given to boys and girls in reaction to solicitation behaviors: Teachers were not only more likely to respond to boys, but they responded in ways which were more helpful and which provided more specific information, a finding consistent with comparisons of maternal behaviors reported by Golden and Birns (1975). But it is a recent study of teaching behavior with fifth-grade children who were solving concept evaluation problems that is most distressing in its implications for intellectually advantaged girls (Frey, 1979). In this investigation, teaching behaviors of men and women tutors were recorded as they taught boys and girls of two ability levels (high and moderate achievement). Of the four groups of pupils, *high-achieving girls received the lowest levels of supportive, ego-enhancing feedback*; they also received significantly fewer laudatory attributional statements. The findings from this laboratory study agree with the findings regarding sex-differentiated classroom teacher behavior reported by Sears and Feldman (1966), in which fourth- and fifth-grade teachers interacted more with boys, gave boys more positive feedback, and directed more criticism toward girls.

At the university level, survey studies of student attitudes find female students more often report that their professors do not take their intellectual aspirations seriously (Hochschild, 1975) and that they failed to socialize women in professional roles (Heyman, 1977). The attrition of women in higher education may reflect, among other factors, the pernicious effects of this pattern of discouragement and negative reinforcement on achievement motivation. In 1975 Hochschild reported that at the University of California, Berkeley, for example, women composed 41 percent of the entering class, 37 percent of the graduating seniors, 31 percent of the applicants for admission to graduate school, 28 percent of the graduates admitted, 24 percent of the doctoral students, 21 percent of the advanced doctoral students, and 12 percent of those receiving doctoral degrees. These results from the home, laboratory, and classroom settings consistently suggest that girls, even high-achieving girls, are given less encouragement for their efforts than their male peers. The gender differences in confidence, self-concept, and problem-solving behaviors noted by Hoffman (1977b), Tyler (1965), and others may well derive from the home and early classroom experiences, which often discourage and denigrate the efforts of girls.

In addition to specific teacher behaviors, the larger elementary and secondary school environments reinforce gender differences and traditional sex role behaviors as well. Males hold the more prestigious positions in the school systems; female teachers are less professionally identified and committed; schoolyards tend to be sex-segregated as a function of the different activity preferences of boys and girls; and classroom chores tend to be allocated in a sex-differentiated way (Guttentag and Bray, 1977). Further, on the playground, the games in which boys and girls spontaneously participate are sex-differentiated and deviate in their formal characteristics. Boys' games typically involve teams made up of a number of peers, and both within-team cooperation and between-team competition are stressed. Boys' games involve more gross motor activity and, though rule-governed, they reward initiative, improvisation, and extemporaneity. The games spontaneously chosen by girls typically involve fewer players, make fewer demands for coordination of activities with other players, emphasize a more restricted range of motor skills, and are rule-governed in ways that discourage improvisation.

These differences in teacher behaviors, institutional arrangements, and peer activities (all discussed in earlier chapters) accentuate differences between males and females and reinforce the sex-differentiating socialization behaviors of parents by extending the network of sex-differentiating socializing agents beyond the family while still providing continuity of experience for the child.

In summary, there appears to be appreciable differential socialization at home and at school that allows boys greater freedom to explore and encourages curiosity, independence, and the testing of oneself, both in achievement and in competitive settings. This socialization pattern tends to extend the experiential options for males. For females, the socialization process tends to discourage exploration, circumscribes spheres of activity, emphasizes proprieties, and provides close supervision, thus narrowing their experiential options. Access to experience and the opportunity to engage the world have been shown by numerous investigators to relate to cognitive development (Dennis, 1973; Hunt, 1961, 1964, 1976; Piaget, 1930, 1952; Sigel and Cocking, 1976). I turn now to a more conceptual and developmental effort to understand the differential opportunities afforded boys and girls to explore the larger world.

Implications of Sex-Differentiated Socialization

Building on the evidence cited in earlier sections, my focus shifts now to the implications of sex-related differences in socialization for cognitive development.

Applying a developmental perspective to the gender differences observed, I propose that the sex-differentiated socialization and parental "shaping" behaviors empirically observed can affect boys and girls in ways that importantly influence the deep structure of their cognitive development. Three fundamental early bases for later cognitive development will be identified and related to the socialization patterns noted as differentially characterizing the sexes. The three *Anlagen* on which so much of subsequent cognitive development hinges are (1) the individual's premises about the responsivity of the world to his or her actions, (2) the extent of the individual's "experimentation with nature," and (3) the individual's cognitive strategies for responding to discrepant experiences.

Premises About the Responsivity of the World to One's Actions. Experience with contingency relations has important cognitive consequences, as demonstrated by Yarrow and others (1972), who found contingency understandings to be related to general developmental level, goal direction, and the exploratory behaviors of infants. To the extent that modes of processing information and the enduring cognitive structures resulting therefrom derive from the child's very early experiences with contingency relations during the sensorimotor period (Piaget, 1954), parent/child interactions and "shaping" behaviors that are sex-differentiating with respect to contingency experiences and contingency successes can assume appreciable significance.

Earlier, in summarizing the literature on sex-differentiated socialization, it was noted that boys, more than girls, receive contingent responding in the form of attention, responsivity, and both encouraging and critical feedback from parents and teachers and that they are also given toys with more feedback potential.

I suggest that these earlier and more frequent experiences of boys with contingency relations benefit motivation, goal orientation, and development of efficacy (and, as important, a sense of efficacy). The greater experience of boys with contingent responding, both in their interpersonal relationships and with toys, can be expected to foster a developing awareness of the evocative role they play in eliciting effects from the environment. These early experiences of efficacy help to build the personality and cognitive foundations on which later instrumental competence depends. Boys more than girls, then, as presently socialized in this culture, are helped to develop a premise system that presumes or anticipates the individual's mastery and instrumental competence.

Extent of "Experimentation with Nature." Sigel and Cocking (1976) have drawn attention to the effects of insufficient parental "distancing" on the development of children's representational thought. They found that adult distancing behaviors promote the child's active engagement in problem solving and increase the likelihood of the child's encountering discrepancies between experience and expectation that cannot be assimilated, thus placing demands on the child to alter approach, to reexamine earlier understandings, and to modify premises. Data from several sources converge in suggesting that socialization practices that foster proximity, discourage independent problem solving by premature or unnecessary intervention, restrict exploration, and discourage active play, even if these socialization emphases are motivated by concern for the child's safety and well-being, may impede the child in creating the cognitive recognitions and cognitive fluencies that represent cognitive development.

Earlier, in summarizing the literature on sex-differentiated socialization, it was noted that boys, more than girls, are reared in ways encouraging curiosity, independence, and exploration of the environment—behaviors requisite for the kind of experimentation deemed critical by Piaget for facilitating the development of cognitive structures. In contrast, the more restrictive childrearing practices characterizing parents of girls, such as emphasis on physical proximity, "ladylike" behaviors, supervision, and the provision of sometimes gratuitous help in problem-solving situations would appear to lessen the opportunities for girls to engage in active experimentation with the environment, to encounter discrepancies, and to resolve them. Boys, more than girls, then, as presently socialized in this culture, are afforded greater opportunities for "discovering," "inventing," and "understanding" the world in which they must live.

Cognitive Strategies for Responding to Discrepant Experiences. The notions of cognitive assimilation and cognitive accommodation, owing largely to Piaget (1954), are widely known in developmental psychology. The process of assimilation involves the fitting of new information or experience into preexisting cognitive schemata; the process of accommodation involves the formation or re-formation of cognitive schemata capable of encompassing new information or experience at variance with prior understandings. Whereas the adaptation to new experience, according to Piaget (1954, 1970), always and simultaneously requires both assimilation and accommodation as two sides of one coin, the usage of the concepts here departs from Piaget in separating these two cognitive strategies. Of course, all individuals use both modes of processing experience at different times, perhaps in rapid succession, and under different circumstances. Nevertheless, it is useful to consider the preferred or dominant mode, assimilation or accommodation, characterizing a person. Further, if the assimilative mode indeed has a built-in priority over the accommodative mode, it becomes of interest to ascertain the personal point at which an individual crosses over from continuing with attempts at assimilation to begin the task of creating a new and integrative accommodation. In reacting to new experiences that fail to conform to the expectations generated from existing schemata, some persons have an ability (and even an insistence) to see whether they can encompass the new information in ways that require little or no modification of previously established premises. Other persons encountering new experiential inputs have a greater readiness (and even preference) to leave cognitive schemata that do not mesh readily with the new information and to move on to the formulation of new and sufficient meaning-making structures.

Both assimilation and accommodation may be seen as serving an evolutionarily adaptive function. Assimilation conserves existing structures, sometimes in creative ways, and provides continuity with the past, thus helping to perpetuate cultural traditions and historical values. Accommodation results in the creation, sometimes unnecessarily, of new adaptive modes, thus fostering social innovation and cultural change. When both modes of processing experience are available to the individual, and when they can be invoked in context-responsive ways, problem-solving effectiveness is broadened. An overreliance on either strategy for processing disconfirming information will prove dysfunctional if it is out of phase with the real world. The use of procrustean and perseverative methods to fit, shape, or mold new perceptions into preexisting schemata can result in a projective, distorted, oversimplified, rigid approach to the world (Perry, 1968a), while premature jettisoning of established schemata and zealously sought or passively accepted redefinition of premises may result in an ahistorical, compartmentalized, overly situational, standardless, impulsive approach to the world.

The literature review presented earlier has suggested that females grow up in a more structured and directive world than males. Parental supervision, restrictions on exploration, household chore assignments, proximity emphases, and the more frequent—sometimes unnecessary—help provided girls in problem-solving situations combine to create a more canalized and more predictable environment for girls than for boys. Encounters with the world outside the home are both more extensive and less controlled in the case of boys. Contributing also to the more structured world of girls is the greater structure of their preferred play activities, which, more than the play of boys, involve model availability and the provision of instruction (Carpenter, 1979). At older ages, the games preferred by girls also

are more structured and make fewer demands for improvisation than the games of boys, which often require extemporaneity
and the ability to take advantage of a momentarily advantageous situation. Relatively structured environments, in contrast with those less structured, have been found to elicit less
creativity and more compliance in the play behaviors of children (Carpenter, 1979), to be associated with less task engagement (Fagot, 1973), and to be related to intolerance of ambiguity (Harrington, Block, and Block, 1978). These many and
repeated differences in the learning environments experienced
by girls and by boys can be expected to have powerful and general effects on the cognitive strategies invoked at times when
expectations fail.

Specifically, I suggest that girls, more than boys, are socialized in ways that encourage the use of assimilative strategies
for processing new information, while boys, more than girls, are
socialized in ways that encourage the use of accommodative
strategies when confronted with informational inputs discrepant
with prior understandings. Further, I suggest that girls, more
than boys, are slower to leave efforts to assimilate cognitively
for efforts to accommodate cognitively. The socialization practices that surround females with relatively structured environments would appear to emphasize the adaptive rewards of efforts
to be assimilative and to discourage the anxiety-inducing efforts
of innovative accommodation. Boys, in contrast, influenced by
their experiences in a less predictable world where ad hoc strategies are often demanded, become freer and more confident in
abandoning structures that no longer seem to work and freer to
assume the risk of seeking a restructure.

Admittedly, empirical evidence supporting the proposition that males and females differ in their preferred modes for
dealing with new informational inputs is sparse. There has not
yet been research directly evaluating preferences for assimilative
as compared with accommodative strategies. Nevertheless, and
until such research begins to be available and can be brought to
bear on the proposition, the heuristic conjecture that boys,
more than girls, as presently socialized in this culture, invoke
the process of cognitive accommodation would appear to assimi-

late many of the data and other, more informal observations on the different ways the sexes tend to resolve disconfirming experiences.

Overall, I propose that sex-differentiated socialization practices influence the cognitive development of males and females in several ways that separately and in summation provide more opportunity for males than for females to engage in independent problem solving in a variety of contexts. The differential provision for the two sexes to actively engage the larger world outside the familiar and protected home environment is seen as creating different premises about the world, as developing different competencies, and as reinforcing the use of different cognitive heuristics for dealing with new experience. This discussion has focused primarily on early socialization patterns that, according to the argument being advanced here, differentially affect the cognitive development of males and females. However, experiences with contingently responsive environments, opportunities to explore new domains, and the encouragement of independent experimentation—in the physical, symbolic, and personal worlds—continue to determine importantly the course of development during the adolescent and adult years. The problems associated with premature closure of identity in adolescence and with the foreclosure of experience in late adulthood attest to the decisive role that exploration, active engagement, and a sense of efficacy play in supporting psychological growth at all age levels.

With the recognition of socialization as an ongoing process throughout the life cycle, we turn now to reconsider, in the light of earlier discussion, the qualities of the educational environments that may be expected to enhance the personal and intellectual development of male and female students alike.

Implications of Sex-Related Differences
for Educational Policy

In this final section, the educational implications of the sex-related socialization emphases and psychological sex differences identified will be explored. The relation between some institutional characteristics of women's colleges and the developmental needs of women students will be discussed to provide an understanding of the facilitative effects women's colleges appear to have for many women. Some implications of sex-differentiated socialization patterns will be drawn for educational institutions. And some recommendations concerning future educational policies will be advanced.

Characteristics of Women's Colleges and the Developmental Needs of Women Students. The comparative studies of educational environments suggest that women's colleges—particularly those in the northeastern United States—with their higher ratios of women faculty members, intellectually gifted students, greater freedom from sex role stereotyping, higher standards of excellence, and commitment to psychological growth of the student (Conway, 1977), are especially fostering of the intellectual development and professional achievements of the highly select group of young women forming their student bodies. It is likely that many of these students would flourish in other quality colleges as well. However, for some women—those conflicted about their achievement aspirations, fearing cross-sex competition, having nontraditional academic interests, needing supportive contacts with faculty, lacking successful same-sex role models in their own families—the availability of women's colleges may be crucial for the realization of their full intellectual and personal development.

For males, however, the results of comparative surveys indicate that attending a men's college is not uniquely associated with the achievement of academic or professional eminence. Both large coeducational universities with distinguished academic departments and small, prestigious coeducational colleges contribute their share of male graduates who later achieve distinction (Tidball and Kistiakowsky, 1976). This difference in the nature of the educational institutions associated with subsequent scholarly achievement and professional distinction in males and in females suggests that the relation between student needs and institutional characteristics may differ as a function of sex.

Although structural differences (for example, smaller enrollments, higher female faculty ratios, quality of counseling facilities, more alumni involvement) that distinguish women's colleges from coeducational institutions surely contribute to their advantage over many coeducational colleges for some women, a more complete and differentiated understanding requires consideration of the environmental qualities and press characterizing women's colleges as compared with coeducational colleges and the special ways in which these conditions relate to the needs of female students.

Several features differentiating the modal educational environment of women's colleges from the modal environment of coeducational institutions were identified in the comparative studies reviewed earlier. Women's colleges provide environments that, to a greater extent than coeducational institutions, (1) encourage the pursuit of academic interests regardless of traditional definitions of sex-appropriateness, (2) permit the unself-conscious development of competencies in an atmosphere free of cross-sex competition, (3) lessen the conflict between achievement and peer acceptance, (4) increase the availability of successful female role models, (5) provide a model of egalitarianism in the workplace, and (6) increase the opportunity to assume responsible positions of leadership in the college community. Each of these factors differentiating educational environments will be considered briefly in the context of the sex-related psychological and socialization differences identified earlier.

Pursuit of Nontraditional Academic Interests. Comparative studies of educational institutions find that greater numbers of students in single-sex colleges major in academic subjects deviating from conventional notions of sex-appropriateness. The problems for women of pursuing an academic course of study considered sex-inappropriate by conventional standards in coeducational institutions are reflected in the results of three separate studies, each conducted on a different university campus (Graham, 1978; Schwenn, 1971; Tangri, 1969). These investigators have reported significantly more shifts by women in designated majors over the college years from less sex-typed, academically demanding majors (for example, mathematics and science) to more traditional majors (for example, humanities and social science). This greater tendency of female students to gravitate toward more traditional majors has been interpreted as an expression of anxiety engendered by the failure to conform to conventional gender role stereotypes and as a reaction to perceived lack of support from predominantly male professors (Graham and Birns, 1979). Level of academic competence does not appear to explain the shift in major (Ernest, 1976; Graham, 1978) for women students. Graham's research (1978) demonstrated that female attrition from the first-year science course for majors was unrelated to a measure of ability (that is, the mathematics score on the Scholastic Aptitude Test) and measures of achievement (that is, course grades). It appears that the desire to be evaluated positively by others, particularly by cross-sex peers, the felt lack of support from faculty, and societal and parental pressures for conformity to traditional definitions of femininity (for example, Komarovsky, 1959) all concatenate to dissuade young women from pursuing nontraditional academic or career goals. In the single-sex college environment, however, nontraditional interests can be pursued with less ambivalence, since sex role stereotyping appears to be a less salient evaluative dimension for faculty and peers alike.

Development of Competencies in an Atmosphere That Minimizes Cross-Sex Competition. The sex-related differences surrounding confidence in problem-solving situations are among the most robust findings in the literature. Females, relative to males, underestimate their abilities, undervalue their performance, attribute failure to personal limitations, and are reluctant to assert themselves in task-oriented, mixed-sex groups. Lockheed's (1976) experiment, cited earlier, demonstrates the beneficial effects on females' self-confidence of learning particular task skills in a single-sex group situation before participating in a mixed-sex group. The opportunity to develop task competencies and confidence initially in a single-sex context appears to permit more active participation of women subsequently in a mixed-sex group engaged in a problem-solving task. The apparent anxiety experienced by women in situations involving cross-sex competition, particularly under conditions of lesser task familiarity and/or lesser sex-appropriateness of the task, may be a consequence of the socialization practices earlier noted as discouraging competition, providing less affirming feedback, and deemphasizing the achievements of women. It will be recalled that both parents and teachers held lower expectations for the performance levels of females than males. Furthermore, teachers criticized and denigrated the work and efforts of females more than that of males. Lockheed's systematic experiment may be viewed as reproducing in the laboratory some of the effects of the single-sex college environment. Her results demonstrate the importance for women of having the opportunity to develop skills and competencies in contexts free of cross-sex competition and evaluation. The asymmetrical effects of the experimental manipulation on males and on females suggest that the single-sex college environment may be more important for women than for men in facilitating the development of intellectual competencies and self-confidence.

Lessening the Conflict Between Achievement and Peer Acceptance. In addition to females' greater anxieties about performance-related competencies, their behavior in achievement-related contexts is affected also by their anticipation of rejection by male peers following on success. The Carnegie Commission (1973b) noted that women in coeducational institutions are more reluctant to participate actively in class discussion for fear of being perceived as unfeminine and, therefore, as unattractive. The conflict between achievement and affiliative needs has been widely discussed (for example, Hoffman, 1972; Horner, 1968, 1970, 1972; Mednick, Tangri, and Hoffman, 1975) and appears to be a sex-specific effect. Societal definitions of appropriate feminine behavior emphasize the nurturing, affiliative roles of women and discourage, even negatively reinforce, achievement-oriented behaviors. However, for males, even though the demands associated with occupational success may intrude on personal time or family life, the conflicts so engendered appear to center on the price of success *per se* rather than on the fear of social rejection resulting from success (Hoffman, 1974, 1977a; Winchel, Fenner, and Shaver, 1974). Women's colleges may reduce the conflict for some women between the need for achievement and the need for affiliation because achievement-related behaviors are not in the immediate purview of male peers and may be supported more positively by faculty.

Increasing the Availability of Same-Sex Role Models. The significant relationship, noted earlier, between the academic achievement of women and the number of women faculty members associated with their undergraduate institutions, a relationship that did not hold for males (Tidball, 1973), suggests the importance of faculty composition for women students. Women faculty members serve as role models for students, providing tangible evidence that women can achieve, conveying styles of interaction, scholarship, and argument associated with success, offering support for career aspirations and understanding of the conflicts and anxieties besetting women students, and creating a collegial atmosphere for women students that is often lacking in male-dominated institutions (Hochschild, 1975; White, 1970). In both family and educational contexts, the importance of having successful, competent role models has been demonstrated (Hetherington and Frankie, 1967; Lucas, Kelvin, and Ohja, 1965). However, it is a current fact of academic life that in coeducational institutions women typically occupy positions of lower academic rank than their male colleagues (Hochschild, 1975). Hence, female role models in this context have a blurred and contradictory image or influence because of the inferior status of women in such colleges and universities. Because male professors, in contrast to female professors, are more likely to be judged successful, a conflict may be generated for female students between identifying with a *same-sex* role model and identifying with a *successful* (that is, male) role model (Lucas, Kelvin, and Ohja, 1965). Such a conflict does not exist for male students, who have the opportunity to identify with role models who are both same-sex and successful. Because larger numbers of female faculty members typically occupy higher academic levels in women's colleges, this potential source of conflict surrounding academic role models is lessened.

Although the importance of women faculty members as role models, support providers, and mentors cannot be disputed (see, for example, Group for the Advancement of Psychiatry,

1975), the effects on women of predominantly *male* faculties have been little discussed. Surveys of students in coeducational institutions indicate that women more often than men complain that their academic aspirations are not taken seriously by male faculty members, that they are perceived as less dedicated to scholarly pursuits, that they have less opportunity to work collaboratively with faculty members, and that they are less frequently invited to participate in informal, collegial exchanges (Graham, 1978; Heyman, 1977; Hochschild, 1975). These perceived behaviors of male professors with their female students echo the leitmotif of fathers' socialization emphases and teaching behaviors described earlier with their daughters. It will be remembered that fathers of daughters, more than fathers of sons, deemphasize achievement, have lower standards of performance for their daughters, neglect the cognitive elements of teaching situations, and focus on the interpersonal aspects of the teaching/learning tasks. In short, fathers appear to emphasize less and to encourage less the intellectual development of their daughters. Male faculty members, by providing less encouragement for the intellectual aspirations of their female students, thus may be seen as reinforcing the messages earlier conveyed by fathers in the family context. To the extent that the socialization themes characteristic of the father/daughter relationship are reflected in the pattern of male-faculty/female-student interactions, female achievement will continue to be deemphasized, female contributions will continue to be devalued, and female professional aspirations will continue to be taken less seriously. The academic interest of women students in coeducational institutions, in contrast to women in single-sex colleges, will be less often affirmed because of the higher ratios of male faculty in the coeducational institutions. Although single-sex schools may offer more support for the intellectual development and professional preparation of their students than is provided by coeducational institutions, the recent trend toward greater male representation on the faculties and in the administration of women's colleges (Carnegie Commission, 1973b) requires close consideration, since an overrepresentation of males could well have unanticipated negative consequences for women students.

Women's colleges represent one of the few institutions of any type in this country where males and females work side by side in roughly equal numbers at all levels and ranks—as trustees, tenured faculty, nontenured faculty, and staff (Mattfeld, 1980). They therefore provide students with a model of equality in the workplace. Students observe collegial cross-sex interactions among faculty members where mutual respect is the norm. The opportunity to observe egalitarian relationships between male and female faculty members may stimulate women students to define career goals that would enable them to experience similar patterns of egalitarian interaction in their own professional lives.

Providing the Opportunity to Assume Positions of Leadership on Campus. The greater opportunity for women enrolled in women's colleges to assume positions of leadership on their campuses has been given clear documentation (Carnegie Commission, 1973b; Group for the Advancement of Psychiatry, 1975). In women's colleges, women can be "first-class citizens" (Bird, 1972), participating responsibly in their own governance. Given the greater parental supervision, lesser emphasis on independent problem solving, and the anxieties and self-doubts found to be more characteristic of females than of males, the opportunity provided women in single-sex colleges to assume responsible, decision-requiring, negotiating roles in the campus community may provide needed corrective and growth experiences. Such experiences may be expected to benefit the sense of efficacy and the self-confidence of women as they embark on their life courses.

In summary, several characteristics—psychological and structural—of the modal environments of women's colleges have been shown to relate importantly to certain personal and intellectual developmental needs of female students. This meshing of individual needs and institutional characteristics may explain some of the facilitative effects of women's colleges on their students.

Qualities of Educational Environments Expected to
Foster Effective Problem-Solving Strategies

In an earlier section of this chapter, some sex-differentiated socialization practices and emphases presumed to affect
the deep structure of cognitive development for males and for
females were identified and discussed. It was argued that particular parental "shaping" behaviors and childrearing orientations,
found more often to characterize parents of boys than of girls,
tend to encourage intellectual curiosity, promote feelings of
efficacy, and advance competence in independent problem solving. Extending these arguments to include institutions of higher
education, I suggest that the intellectual development of students during the college years will be in part determined by the
extent to which college or university policies and programs incorporate, in age-appropriate ways, some of the socialization
principles and practices that have been found to facilitate cognitive development in children.

Educational environments that provide the opportunity
for independent exploration and experimentation, encourage
active engagement of ideas, afford supportive contingent feedback, deemphasize conformity to sex role stereotypes, and discourage "template" solutions in the form of ideological prescriptions or rote recitations may be expected to foster intellectual curiosity and commitment in students. Such educational
environments also should enhance student feelings of efficacy
and assist the development of a repertoire of cognitive principles and strategies to be invoked flexibly in accordance with
contextual demands. The kind of self-motivated learning evolving from engagement, experimentation, and the self-eduction
of principles has been called "deuterolearning" by Gregory
Bateson (1972). Deuterolearning is distinguished from content-
oriented rote or technique-oriented template learning. Deuterolearning (learning to learn) is facilitated in contexts that encourage independent exploration and experimentation of the sort
advocated by Piaget and encouraged by some colleges and universities. Deuterolearning is not context-limited; the principles
educed can be generalized across time and across situations.

Therefore, it is particularly important, in a time of rapid social change, that educators provide the kinds of learning experiences for students facilitative of deuterolearning in order to equip them better for dealing with the changing world that is their future.

However, the kind of learning environment conducive to deuterolearning (an environment emphasizing self-motivated inquiry, experimentation, and discovery) is a newer and stranger experience for females than for males, given the more structured, supervised, prescribed, and proscribed world of girlhood as compared with boyhood. We should expect, therefore, that females would find less structured, less supportive educational environments more anxiety-arousing than males. The likelihood that encounters with the widening world and the engendered self-reorganization will be managed constructively will depend both on the existence and nature of environmental supports and on the tolerance of the particular individual for ambiguity and change when beset by fear of the new, anxiety occasioned by rejection of parent-derived values, concern about one's ability to negotiate change, defensiveness about admitting the inadequacies of one's previous constructions of self and society, fear of rejection by peers, and/or concern about parental reactions (Perry, 1968a, 1968b). The special qualities of women's colleges can be of crucial and constructive significance during this decisive characterological choice point in helping women to develop a sense of competence and to forge a sense of identity and commitment. The emphasis accorded faculty/student contacts and discussions, the presence of role models, the availability of counseling services, the surround of like-minded and discursive peer groups (Brown, 1977), and generalized institutional support foster an educational context encouraging analysis, experimentation with ideas, and opportunities that will ready women for the contemporary, unanticipated world for which their earlier socialization did not prepare them.

My review and evaluation of the literature concerned with comparative studies of single-sex and coeducational institutions has suggested that women's colleges, more than coeducational institutions, appear to encourage intellectual achievement and to prepare their graduates for careers of distinction. In reaching this conclusion, however, it must be recognized that not all entering college women aspire to academic or professional careers, that the role of alumnae in providing an effective "old girls' network" has not been evaluated, that many conclusions derive from an earlier sociopolitical era, that many women who have attained professional distinction had their baccalaureate origins in coeducational institutions, and that the effects on students, both male and female, of the relatively recent changes in enrollment policies of single-sex colleges that have become coeducational have not yet been assessed. These qualifications on conclusions pose important questions for future research.

A second conclusion suggested by the numerous sex-specific, asymmetrical effects found in the literature is that different educational contexts differentially influence, in many ways, the personality and intellectual development of male and female students over the college years. This conclusion also points to the need for more systematic and focused comparative studies designed to assess the factors involved in such sex-differentiated effects.

While both single-sex and coeducational colleges may broaden the intellectual perspectives and enlarge the horizons of students leaving the protective, structured world of their families for the first time, women's colleges, by virtue of their structural characteristics and value emphases, may be in a better position to compensate for the earlier, competence-circumscribing socialization experiences of girlhood. This compensatory competence-accelerating effect may prove increasingly important in an era of social change. The lesser reinforcement of competence and academic achievement given women by significant socializing agents not only interferes with their realization of their full personal potential but, given societal changes and societal needs, is unrealistic as well. Declining family sizes, increasing longevity, economic necessity, and the frequency of divorce are causing increasing numbers of women to spend greater numbers of years in the work force (Hoffman, 1977b) and to seek careers. Socializing institutions, including colleges and universities, have a responsibility to adapt to these changing social realities in order better to prepare women for their different roles in the immediately looming world.

The asymmetry in the effects of particular experiences on males and on females, the relationship among academic achievement, professional distinction, and graduation from a women's college (for example, Tidball, 1973), and the wide range of individual differences among students—differences in backgrounds, interests, aspirations, values, motivation, maturity, independence, and competences—all suggest that the needs of future student generations may be best served by an educational system emphasizing diversity in the educational options available. In order to improve the "fit" between the psychological characteristics of students and the qualities of the learning environment, institutions with different curricular programs, emphases, policies, student bodies, and structural characteristics are essential. Because single-sex colleges appear to play an important role in the personal and intellectual development of many students, they represent an important educational resource that should not unthinkingly be forfeited to achieve educational "homogeneity," integration of the sexes, or improved financial standing for colleges. The women's college evolved historically in response to certain important needs and aspirations unmet by alternatives. Despite contemporary societal shifts, for many women the special function and special contribution of such institutions remain.

Chapter Eight

Differential
Sex Role Socialization
and Psychological Functioning

Efforts to understand the psychological differences between the sexes and the extent to which these differences may be influenced by gender-differentiated socialization emphases have thus far been largely empirical and unguided by theory. A voluminous literature bearing on sex-related differences and parental socialization practices has accumulated, but this empiricism has not taken on or been provided with conceptual form. The present chapter offers, with some tremulousness, some interpretations and conjectures aspiring toward that theoretical goal. I begin with a necessarily selective, highly distilled review of gender differences in personality functioning, conclusions derived from the available literature and from some recent findings issuing from the longitudinal study being conducted by my husband, Jack Block, and

Previously published in *Child Development*, December 1983, with the title "Differential Premises Arising from Differential Socialization of the Sexes: Some Conjectures." Copyright © 1983 the Society for Research in Child Development, Inc. Research for this study was supported by a National Institute of Mental Health grant to Jeanne H. Block and Jack Block and a NIMH Research Scientist Award to Jeanne H. Block.

me. The evidence regarding sex-differentiated socialization practices experienced by males and by females is then summarized
and leads me to two recognitions: that males and females grow
up in psychological learning contexts that are importantly different and that these differing contexts have large implications
for their subsequent psychological functioning. Finally, a conceptual rubric for integrating some of the empirical findings surrounding sex differences is offered, and implications are drawn
from this conceptualization regarding the adaptational heuristics developed by males and by females. Necessarily, certain
portions of this final, gathering-together chapter overlap in coverage with earlier chapters.

My intentions and the necessary limits of my interest
here are as follows:

I am not concerned here with the role of biological factors, important though they are in laying down certain modal
behavioral dispositions for males and females. Biology allows
for great variation about these behavioral modes (Barlow,
1977) as a complex (and largely unexplored) function of the
environment as it impinges on the individual organism seeking
to construct a sufficient mode of living. For humans, the environment is largely a social one, and so my present focus cen-
ters on socialization influences.

I acknowledge that the developmental literature cannot
now tell us whether differential socialization precedes differentiation of the behavior of boys and girls or whether it follows
and augments such differentiation. In the interest of achieving
a better scientific understanding of development, one strategy
is to look at the relative timing of various experiences and various behaviors, to see which came first. However, the relevant
observations have not been made and, because of significant
conceptual and research difficulties, will be slow in coming. Another strategy for gaining developmental understanding is more
akin to the experimental method in that it involves changing
antecedent conditions in order to observe the eventual consequences. Obviously, if sexual differentiation of behavior precedes differential socialization, we are unable to manipulate this
biologically ordained antecedent condition. But if we presume

that differential socialization may precede sex-differentiated behaviors and orientations and seek to identify the nature and circumstances of this differential socialization, there then develops the opportunity to thoughtfully and ethically modify the conditions of socialization and observe the behavioral consequences. By this orientation, developmental understanding can be advanced and, with it, the possible release of presently constrained human potential. Accepting the likelihood of the importance of differential socialization, my concern here is to attempt to discern and specify the differences in the way boys and girls are reared.

I am aware that in many respects the empirical literature is ambiguous or inconsistent in implication, insufficient or unsystematic in coverage, and conceptually and methodologically deficient. Other psychologists might well read and evaluate differently the literature I am surveying. In my view, developmental psychology has been overly conservative, has deferred too much to null findings based on unreliable, poorly operationalized measures, and will not benefit appreciably by awaiting further accretion and subsequent meta-analysis of conceptually unguided and qualitatively unevaluated empiricism. In the early stages of the development of scientific knowledge—"the context of discovery" theoretical risk taking leads to possibilities. Conceptual suggestions that are false leads will be quickly recognized subsequently in "the context of justification" (Reichenbach, 1951) and cast aside. My intention here is to try for a conceptualization I know to be incomplete, insufficient, and perhaps even somewhat procrustean in the hope that the conjectures offered may be useful in organizing the welter of observations now available and fruitful in directing subsequent inquiry.

Attempts to distill the literature in any area are always difficult and contention-inducing, particularly when inconsistencies characterize many of the research findings. In the area of sex differences, the attempt to develop and convey conclusions is particularly hazardous not only because of problems characterizing the data base but also because the topic of sex differences has become politicized. The conclusions drawn may have a consequential effect on social policies and therefore on people; yet, conclusions represent only inferences. To properly evaluate such inferences, the auxiliary set of premises and prior assumptions on which these inferences depend should be made explicit, insofar as possible. These evaluative principles are delineated and discussed extensively in earlier chapters of the present volume; here I mention them again, if only briefly.

Unfortunately, there is still the tendency in developmental psychology and elsewhere to review the empirical literature passively, using the "box score" approach—simply totting up the number of differences and "nondifferences" found in a number of studies. Such an approach is almost assured of finding "inconsistencies," inconsistencies that additional equivalent empiricism will multiply rather than reconcile. In my view, the empiricism integrator should accept the difficult and controversial responsibility of evaluating the conceptual and methodological quality of the studies being reviewed. In addition, the research evaluator should be alert to considerations not yet attended to that may organize seemingly inconsistent findings. In reaching the conclusions that follow, I have sought converging empirical evidence for differences between the sexes across studies of different age levels, different kinds of samples, and different modes of assessment. Where inconsistencies existed, I tried to weight studies in terms of the reliabilities of the measures employed, the power of the research design, and what I deem to be the appropriateness of the operationalization of the construct being studied. I have also considered whether findings are age- or sample- or method-bound. For example, many experimental findings of a "nondifference" between the sexes are clearly attributable to the use of unreliable and invalid measures; certain kinds of "inconsistency" are resolved when it is observed that sex-related differences increase with age or that the inconsistency is inextricably confounded with the different reactive behaviors of blacks and whites in testing situations (Block, 1976a, 1976b).

Generally, the data available on sex differences and summarized here have emerged from studies comparing only *mean levels of response* for males and females. A focus on mean response levels is, of course, not uninteresting, but it tells us little about *the pattern or organization existing among variables within males and within females.* In our own longitudinal study, when looked for, reliable and large sex differences in the organization of variables abound. Understanding these sex-related differences in psychological organization remains a significant task for the future, but their presence should be recognized and thought about. Finally, for balance, I note that the present focus on sex differences should not diminish recognition of the large degree of overlap characterizing score distributions for the sexes and of the more general principle that a psychology of males and females will ultimately have to fit within and be a psychology of human beings.

Sex-Related Differences in Personality

The gender differences in personality considered here may be grouped into seven conceptual areas: aggression, activity, impulsivity, susceptibility to anxiety, achievement-related behaviors, self-concept, and social relationships. The conclusions to be offered about sex-related differences are informed by the evaluations of other psychologists who have surveyed the literature with regard to sex differences; several critiques and reanalyses (Cooper, 1979; Eagly, 1978; Hoffman, 1977a) of the data underlying the influential conclusions of Maccoby and Jacklin (1974) about the evidence for sex differences in psychological functioning; the findings from many recent empirical studies of psychological sex differences; and the results (generally as yet unpublished) of comparisons of boys and girls on psychological variables assessed in our longitudinal study of ego and cognitive development (Block and Block, 1980b; Harrington, Block, and Block, 1978).

Aggression. Research findings surrounding aggression are perhaps the most consistent in the literature and indicate that males are more aggressive than females, and from an early age (Bandura, Ross, and Ross, 1963; Buss, 1966; Eme, 1979; Maccoby and Jacklin, 1974; Moyer, 1974; Pedersen and Bell, 1970; Tyler, 1965). Males engage in more rough-and-tumble play (Di Pietro, 1979; Omark, Omark, and Edelman, 1973); attempt more often to dominate peers (Omark and Edelman, 1973; Omark, Omark, and Edelman, 1973); engage in more physical aggression (Fagot, 1978b; Omark, Omark, and Edelman, 1973); exhibit more antisocial behavior (Eme, 1979; Magnusson, Duner, and Zetterblom, 1975; Moyer, 1974; Wadsworth, 1979); prefer television programs with more aggressive content (Block and Block, 1980b; McLeod, Atkin, and Chaffee, 1972; and, depending on context, are more competitive than females (Kagan and Madsen, 1972; McManis, 1966; Martin, 1973; Spence and Helmreich, 1978). Results demonstrating the greater aggressivity of males have been obtained in the laboratory setting and in naturalistic settings and generalize to the animal kingdom as well (for example, Mitchell, 1979). Although Tieger (1980) has demurred regarding this conclusion, a further review (and rejoinder) by Maccoby and Jacklin (1980) has brought together many and strong lines of evidence for greater male aggressivity.

Activity Level. Research findings surrounding gender differences in activity level are less compelling than those found with respect to aggression. When significant results are found, boys typically score higher on activity indexes than girls (Block and Block, 1980b; Buss, Block, and Block, 1980; Eaton and Keats, 1982; Eme, 1979; Fagot, 1978b; Halverson and Waldrop, 1973; Maccoby, 1966a; Pedersen and Bell, 1970; Richman, Stevenson, and Graham, 1975; Smith and Daglish, 1977), and this directional pattern is also typically found in studies when comparisons fail to achieve conventional significance levels. Males have also been observed to be more curious and to engage in more exploration (Block and Block, 1980b; Hutt, 1970; Smock and Holt, 1962), behaviors that conceptually may reflect activity level (and also may reflect impulsivity and risk taking, as discussed below). Maccoby and Jacklin (1974, p. 144) note, "In the age range from three to six, there is a clear trend for boys to show more curiosity and exploratory behavior." In an elegant natural experiment conducted at a zoo, sex differences in curiosity and associated risk taking were observed in children age three to six and seven to eleven by Ginsburg and Miller (1982). Boys engage in more manipulation of objects (Clarke-Stewart, 1973; Fagot, 1974, 1978b; Pedersen and Bell,

1970), react more strongly to barriers to attractive goal objects (Brehm and Weinraub, 1977), and play outdoors more than girls (Fagot and Littman, 1975; Harper and Sanders, 1975). Studies of older boys and adult males show that they perceive and describe themselves as more daring and adventurous than females (Kenney and White, 1966; Longstreth, 1970). Consistent with males' greater adventurousness is the set of findings (Manheimer and others, 1966; Manheimer and Mellinger, 1967) demonstrating, perhaps definitively, in an enormous and representative sample ($N = 8,874$) that boys have significantly more accidents requiring emergency medical treatment at every age level between four and eighteen years, a finding confirmed by Willerman (1979) in studies of toddlers. While activity level and exploration have been shown to be sensitive to environmental and social contexts, the accrued findings also consistently suggest that males both are more active and engage in more exploratory behaviors than females.

Impulsivity. Although impulsivity is related conceptually both to the expression of aggression and to exploratory behavior, it encompasses other kinds of behaviors as well that have proved to be sex-discriminating. When impulsivity is defined broadly to include insufficient control of impulse, the inability to delay gratification, risk taking, and overreactivity to frustration, males have been found to be more impulsive than females (Block and Block, 1980b; Maccoby, 1966a; Tyler, 1965). According to Maccoby and Jacklin, males tend to be more mischievous (cited in Maccoby, 1980; Smith and Daglish, 1977) and are more likely to manifest more behavior problems related to undercontrol of impulse (temper tantrums, stealing, disruptive behaviors) than girls (Beller and Neubauer, 1963; Eme, 1979; Singer, Westphal, and Niswander, 1968; Werry and Quay, 1971). The assessment of impulse control in adults is complicated by the difficulty of designing controlled laboratory studies. Although some naturalistic studies have been done in which, for example, the driving behaviors of adult males and females have been observed systematically and found to reflect both greater impatience and impulsivity on the part of male drivers than of female drivers (Doob and Gross, 1968; Ebbesen and

Haney, 1973; Hagen, 1975; Leff and Gunn, 1973), the scientific data base surrounding impulsivity in adulthood is somewhat thin.

Susceptibility to Anxiety. A constellation of findings suggests that female adolescents are more fearful, manifest greater anxiety, and have less confidence in their abilities than males. On self-report measures, females acknowledge more anxiety. Further, they expect to do less well than males on problem-solving tasks, judge the adequacy of their performance less favorably than males, and blame lack of ability for their failures more often than males, who blame lack of motivation for theirs. Females also attribute their successes to luck more often than males, who attribute their successes to ability (Crandall, 1969; Dweck and others, 1978; Maccoby, 1966a; Spence and Helmreich, 1978; Tyler, 1965). The lesser sense of competence characteristic of female adolescents extends into adulthood as well. Over the crucial age period from eighteen to twenty-six years, females studied longitudinally demonstrated a decrease in ego sufficiency, while males during the corresponding period showed an increase in their perceived sense of competence (Nawas, 1971).

Related to the greater susceptibility to anxiety found among females is the finding that women score higher on measures of social desirability and, at least at the younger ages when compliance with adults is studied, females are found to be more compliant (Block and Block, 1980b; Maccoby and Jacklin, 1974; Stouwie, 1971, 1972; Whiting and Edwards, 1975). Behaving in socially approved ways represents both a cooperative orientation and an effective strategy for warding off anxiety engendered by anticipation of disapproval from peers or adults. Also related to the findings surrounding anxiety is the greater tendency of females to yield to group pressures in experiments designed to assess influenceability. Eagly (1978), in reviewing the literature on suggestibility and influenceability, concluded that females in group situations characterized by uncertainty are more influenced by peer pressures than males, a result extended by Cooper's (1979) reanalysis of the data cited by Maccoby and Jacklin pertaining to conformity in group situations. Even though situational factors such as the nature of the targeted task and the constitution of the group may affect results in studies on influenceability, the conclusions that females are more conforming still appear warranted. The results of two additional experiments suggest something about the dynamics underlying the less assertive behaviors of women in groups (Lockheed, 1976; Stake and Stake, 1979). These studies show that the confidence of women, as reflected by their participation rates in group situations, can be increased if they have been provided the opportunity to develop specific task-related competencies *prior* to experiencing the pressures attendant on participation in mixed-sex groups. These findings amplify Eagly's observation that task familiarity *per se* is an important moderator variable in experiments investigating the behaviors of females in mixed-sex groups.

Achievement. Studies in the achievement domain have often issued inconsistent sex-specific results. Accordingly, it is difficult to summarize this large and complex body of data with regard to gender differences. According to Crandall (1969) and Frieze (1973), females express less confidence in problem-solving situations than males and tend to underestimate their level of performance. They do not differ, however, by being less persistent or less motivated in achievement-relevant situations (Maccoby and Jacklin, 1974). Instead, it appears that females are *differently* motivated than males. The achievement of males is stimulated under challenging, ego-involving situations, whereas these same situational factors do not facilitate—and may even impair—the performance of females. In this connection, Hoffman (1972) has suggested that affiliative and achievement needs of females are often in conflict and that when achievement threatens interpersonal acceptance, anxiety is aroused to the detriment of performance. It also appears that, for children, the presence or absence of an adult in the achievement setting has a sex-differentiated effect, facilitating the performance of females and having little effect on the performance of males (Caplan, 1979). These observations accord with those of Hoffman (1972) and Crandall (1967) in suggesting that social (adult) approval may subserve achievement in females to a greater extent than males. Further evidence for sex-related motivational differences in the achievement domain is provided by Spence (1979) and Spence and Helmreich (1978), who distinguish four achievement areas—Work, Mastery, Competitiveness, and Personal Unconcern. They find significant sex differences on their Mastery and Competitiveness scales, with males scoring higher, while on the Work scale females scored higher. Finally, traditional socialization agents tend to indicate what are appropriate male domains of achievement and what are appropriate female domains (Fox, Tobin, and Brody, 1979). Because of these stereotypes, achievement in a "sex-inappropriate" domain is discouraged, and when ventured into, the effort is likely to be begun in and burdened by an absence of self-confidence. Thus, the results of numerous studies have suggested that the constellation of personality variables and situational factors associated with achievement in women is reliably different from the set of factors associated with achievement in men.

Potency of the Self-Concept. Not only do males appear to feel more confident in problem-solving situations, but their self-concept includes feelings of greater personal efficacy as well. Males show less evidence than females of "learned helplessness" in achievement situations (Dweck and others, 1978), and results of studies on young children indicate that the opportunity to exert control over external events is a more salient issue for boys than for girls (Gunnar-vonGnechten, 1978). Data indicating the greater tendency of males to score higher on the Lie and Defensiveness scales of psychological inventories also suggest that the self-images of males, in contrast to those of females, include stronger feelings of being able to control (or to manipulate) the external world—even if by occasional dissimulation. Males describe themselves as more powerful, ambitious, and energetic and as perceiving themselves as having more control over external events than females (Bem, 1974; Block, 1973; Spence and Helmreich, 1978). The self-descriptions of males, more than those of females, include concepts of agency (Bakan, 1966; Block, 1973), efficacy, initiative (Gough, 1968b), instrumentality (Parsons and Bales, 1955; Spence and Helmreich, 1978)—all reflections of a self-concept in which potency and mastery are important components. In contrast, females describe themselves as more generous, sensitive, nurturing, considerate, and concerned for others (for example, Bem, 1974; Block, 1973; Carlson, 1971a; Spence and Helmreich, 1978; Spence, Helmreich, and Stapp, 1975). The self-concepts of females emphasize interpersonal relations and communion (Bakan, 1966; Block, 1973), conservation of societal values and human relationships (Gough, 1968b), expressiveness (Parsons and Bales, 1955; Spence and Helmreich, 1978), and deemphasized competition and mastery.

Social Orientations. Social behaviors of the two sexes have been found to diverge in a number of areas. M. L. Hoffman (1977) reviewed psychological studies of empathy and concluded that clear sex differences exist, females being the more empathic sex. That is, on the average, females, more than males, tend to manifest more vicarious and veridical affective responses in reaction to another person's feelings. Reviewing the results of seventy-five studies of the interpretation of nonverbal cues, Hall (1978) concluded that females more accurately discern emotions from nonverbal cues than males. Among college students, females engage in significantly more prosocial extracurricular activities. Reanalyzing data on student activism obtained from three samples of university students on two university campuses reported in Smith, Haan, and Block (1970) and Block (1972), I found females involved themselves significantly more often than males in constructivist, prosocial activities, while significantly greater numbers of males actively involved themselves in political/social dissent and protest. Considering social groups and friendship patterns, females appear to be more affiliative (Lansky and others, 1961; Hoffman, 1977a), to be more cooperative (McClintock and Moskowitz, 1976), and to develop more intensive, more intimate social relationships in contrast to the more extensive and less intimate relationships developed by males (Caldwell and Peplau, 1982; Omark and Edelman, 1973; Waldrop and Halverson, 1975). Girls were observed to play more often in small groups, while boys tended to play in large groups (Lever, 1976). Females also, more than males, maintain greater proximity to other persons, as reflected in measures of eye contact, distance, and physical contact (Ashear and Snortum, 1971; Levine and Sutton-Smith, 1973; Omark, Omark, and Edelman, 1973; Russo, 1975; Tennis and Dabbs, 1975). Wheeler and Nezlek (1977) examined the daily records of social interactions of entering university students for two weeks at the beginning and at the end of the academic year and found evidence of a different patterning in the social interactions of males and females. Entering college women socialized more intensively in the new environment and also made greater use of their same-sex best friend to help them deal with the stimulation (and anxiety) experienced in the new situation. That friendship groups serve different needs in males and females is suggested by Rubin (1980), who notes that boys view the group as a collective entity, emphasizing solidarity, loyalty, and shared activities, while girls perceive the group as an intimate network, emphasizing the sharing of confidences and support. Females also, across cultures and across species, appear to express more interest in babies and to engage in more nurturing behaviors (Blakemore, 1979; Feldman and Nash, 1977; Frodi and Lamb, 1978; Goldberg, Blumberg, and Kriger, 1982; Jay, 1963; Whiting and Whiting, 1975). Both the data derived from self-reports and from observational studies provide considerable evidence that women are more interpersonally oriented than men (Block, 1973; Carlson, 1971a; Chodorow, 1974; Greever, Tseng, and Friedland, 1973; Mehrabian, 1971; Vinacke and others, 1974; Weller, Shlomi, and Zimot, 1976), who appear to have a more individualistic, instrumental orientation to the world.

Sex-Differentiated Socialization

I now consider the sociocultural contexts and the socialization emphases experienced over the childhood and adolescent years by contemporary males and females. The psychological milieus in which the development of boys and of girls takes place are examined because it seems likely that the particular sex-differentiated parental emphases and societal pressures that can be observed contribute to the psychological sex differences identified above, especially those based on differences in self-reflection and self-evaluation.

Parental Self-Reports of Childrearing Emphases. Looking at parental socialization values (see Chapter Three), I summarized the results of six studies in which the self-described childrearing orientations of mothers and fathers were compared. Overall, there is appreciable evidence for sex-differentiated parental socialization behaviors; specific, consistent sex-of-parent and sex-of-child interaction effects; sex differentiation in socialization emphases that appear to increase with the age of the child; and many sex-related socialization values of mothers and of fathers that appear relatively consistent across socioeconomic levels, educational levels, and cultural backgrounds.

With respect to the socialization of sons, the self-described childrearing emphases of both mothers and fathers in several independent samples indicate that both parents tend to press achievement and competition more on their sons than on their daughters. In addition, both parents encourage their sons, more than their daughters, to control the expression of affect, to be independent, and to assume personal responsibility. They employ punishment more with their sons than with their daughters. In addition, fathers appear more authoritarian than mothers in their rearing of their sons: They are more strict, more firm, more endorsing of physical punishment, less tolerant of aggression directed toward themselves by their sons, and less accepting of behaviors deviating from the traditional masculine stereotype.

The self-described childrearing emphases of parents of daughters indicate that the parent/daughter relationship, in contrast to the parent/son relationship, is characterized by greater warmth and physical closeness, greater confidence in the trustworthiness and truthfulness of their daughters, greater expectation by both mothers and fathers of "ladylike" behavior, greater reluctance to punish daughters, and greater encouragement of the daughter to reflect on life. Additionally, mothers of daughters tend to be more restrictive of their daughters and to engage in closer supervision of their activities.

These findings are consistent with Barry, Bacon, and Child's (1957) findings of significant and consistent sex-related socialization emphases in a variety of cultures. They observed that girls received more pressure to be nurturant, obedient, and responsible and boys received more pressure from parents and the larger culture to achieve and be self-reliant. Tudiver (1979) reports similar findings from a study using both observational and self-report methods to assess sex-differentiated parenting. These results also are consonant with Hoffman's (1977a) findings from a large-scale survey study showing that parents expect their sons, more frequently than their daughters, to be independent, self-reliant, highly educated, ambitious, hard-working, career-oriented, intelligent, and strong-willed. In contrast, parents more often expect their daughters to be kind, unselfish, attractive, loving, and well-mannered and to have a good marriage and to be a good parent.

Observational Studies of Parental Behaviors. Even in the first year of life, sex-differentiated parental interactions with infants have been observed (Lamb, 1977; Lewis, 1972a; Martin, Maccoby, and Jacklin, 1981; Moss, 1967; Parke and Sawin, 1976). One implicative area in which parents of boys and parents of girls have been observed to differ is in the frequency of their contingent responding to behaviors initiated by their child. In the feeding situation, mothers were observed to be more responsive and attentive to signals from their male infants than their female infants (Murphy and Moriarty, 1976; Walraven, 1974). Indeed, Moss (1967) found, after controlling for the state of the infant with respect to irritability and sleepiness, that mothers were significantly more stimulating and arousing of their male infants than their female infants. Both mothers and fathers have been observed to react more contingently to the vocalizations of boys than to the vocalizations of girls (for example, Lewis and Freedle, 1973; Parke and Sawin, 1976; Yarrow, 1975; but not Moss, 1967). These apparent differences in parental contingent responding noted in infancy appear to continue through the childhood years. It has been shown in numerous studies at different age levels that boys not only receive more negative feedback, including physical punishment, from parents but also receive more positive feedback as well (for example, Maccoby and Jacklin, 1974; Margolin and Patterson, 1975). Analyses of sequential interactions conducted by Margolin and Patterson revealed that both parents responded contingently to males more than females; fathers of boys responded contingently and positively more than twice as often as fathers of girls.

Differences in the experience of creating contingencies in the interpersonal realm are augmented by differences in the contingent possibilities afforded by the toys parents provide their boys and their girls. Boys are given a greater variety of toys than girls, and there are important differences in the kinds of toys parents provide for boys and girls (Rheingold and Cook, 1975; Yarrow and others, 1972). The pervasiveness of this differential offering of toys is well illustrated by the "baby X" studies, wherein adults (often themselves parents) reacted to unknown infants of unidentifiable gender who were arbitrarily labeled by the experimenter as boys or girls. In such studies, with few exceptions, adults of both sexes tended to offer girls' sex-typed toys (for example, dolls) more often to children presumed to be girls than to children presumed to be boys. Conversely, male sex-typed toys (for example, a hammer) tended to be offered more frequently to children believed to be boys than to children believed to be girls (Bell and Carver, 1980; Frisch, 1977; Seavey, Katz, and Zalk, 1975; Sidorowicz and Lunney, 1980; Smith and Lloyd, 1978; Will, Self, and Datan, 1976).

Boys' toys, more than girls' toys, afford inventive possibilities (Rosenfeld, 1975), encourage manipulation, and provide more explicit feedback from the physical world. Girls' toys, in contrast, tend to encourage imitation, are more often used in proximity to the caretaker, and provide less opportunity for variation and innovation. Differences in the toy preferences of boys and girls have been documented in numerous studies (for example, Fagot, 1978a; Goldberg and Lewis, 1969; Fein and others, 1975). The developmental implications of these differences in toy preference and availability only recently have been explored (Block, 1981; Hoffman, 1977a). Differentiated exposure to toys with dissimilar characteristics predisposes toward different play and problem-solving experiences for boys and for girls, experiences that may have implications for later cognitive development.

In addition to being more contingently responsive to actions initiated by males than by females, parents have been observed also to provide more physical stimulation for boys than
for girls. Male infants are held and aroused more and are given
more stimulation for gross motor activity (for example, Moss,
1967, 1974; Lewis, 1972a; Parke and O'Leary, 1976; Parke and
Sawin, 1976; Yarrow, 1975). In Yarrow's study of mother/
infant interactions, mothers of males were observed to interact
more frequently with their male infants, at higher intensity levels, and with richer, more varied behaviors. These observational
studies, demonstrating that infant boys are given more stimulation than girls, are consistent with the sex-related socialization
differences in the encouragement of exploratory behaviors
found in later childhood.

Studies of sex-differentiated parental socialization behaviors generally report that boys are given more freedom to explore than girls. Girls have been observed to play more proximally to their mothers (Lewis and Weintraub, 1974; Messer and
Lewis, 1972), to be allowed fewer independent excursions from
home (Callard, 1964; Saegert and Hart, 1976), to be encouraged
by their mothers to follow them about the house (Fagot,
1978b), and to be more closely supervised in their activities
(Newson and Newson, 1968). The differential assignment of
household chores to boys and to girls also reflects proximity
differences, since boys more often are given chores taking them
out of the house and/or farther away from home, while girls are
assigned homebound chores of cleaning, "helping," babysitting
—chores increasing the salience of the family milieu (Duncan,
Schuman, and Duncan, 1973; Whiting and Edwards, 1975).
Chodorow (1974) and Hoffman (1972, 1977a) argue that the
different social contexts experienced by boys and by girls over
the childhood years account for the development of many psychological sex differences, particularly those reflecting the greater
embeddedness of women in social networks in contrast to the
more individualistic, mastery-emphasizing activities of men.

Turning to systematic studies of parent/child interactions
observed in standard settings, we find further evidence for sex-
differentiated parental behaviors. In one study (Block, Block,

and Harrington, 1975), the separate teaching behaviors of fathers and of mothers were videotaped, observed, and independently rated. Greater sex differentiation in the teaching behaviors of fathers than of mothers was found, a finding consistent with other observations showing that fathers exert greater pressure than mothers for sex-appropriate behaviors (Maccoby, 1980). With their sons, fathers set higher standards, attended to the cognitive elements of the tasks, and placed greater emphasis on achievement in the teaching/learning situation. With their daughters, fathers focused more on the interpersonal aspects of the teaching situation—encouraging, supporting, joking and playing, and protecting. Day (1975) found a similar sex-differentiated pattern in adults' teaching behaviors in an experiment where the investigator manipulated the presumption of the sex of her two-year-old subjects. Adults, particularly males, provided more goal-directed reinforcements to presumed boys and expected them to do significantly better on the tasks than presumed girls. Presumed girls were given more compliments and encouragement. Additional studies using the "baby X" experimental paradigm also found that presumed girls received more interpersonal stimulation (for example, smiling) and encouragement in "nurturance play" (Frisch, 1977; Will, Self, and Datan, 1976) and quicker female reactions to crying than did presumed boys (Condry, Condry, and Pogatshnik, 1980). Together, these results indicate that adults, particularly fathers, act in more instrumental, task-oriented, mastery-emphasizing ways with their sons and in more expressive, less achievement-oriented, dependency-reinforcing ways with their daughters (see also Cantor, Wood, and Gelfand, 1977; Hoffman, 1975; Langlois and Downs, 1980; Radin, 1976; Stein and Bailey, 1973).

The lesser paternal emphasis on achievement and mastery in girls is reflected also in maternal behaviors. Mothers of girls have been observed to provide help in problem-solving situations more than mothers of boys, even when their help is not required (Gunnar-vonGnechten, 1977, 1978; Rothbart, 1971; Rothbart and Rothbart, 1976). This kind of "anxious intrusion" also has been observed by Vaughn, Weickgerant, and Kopp (1981). Mothers respond with positive affect to bids for help from girls and are likely to react negatively when boys ask for help (Fagot, 1978b). They also provide girls more immediate physical comfort after a frustrating experience (Lewis, 1972b). Not only do parents appear to deemphasize independent achievement with their daughters, but the results of a recent study by Greif (1979) suggest that parents may devalue their daughters' efforts as well. Studying communication patterns within families, Greif found that parents interrupt their daughters more often than their sons and that mothers are interrupted more frequently than fathers, a finding reported also by Steinberg and Hill (1978). Interruptions may convey a metamessage suggesting that the ideas of females are considered less important, less worthy of respect. Such metamessages may well have a detrimental influence on the development of confidence and self-esteem in women.

As the preceding studies indicate, evidence has been accruing suggesting that parents do treat their sons differently than their daughters in some areas important for later development. Because fathers have been included more often in recent investigations, sex-differentiated socialization emphases not identified in earlier studies have been revealed. Although the researches cited indicate differences in parent behaviors in a number of domains as a function of the sex of the child, more empirical efforts are required to evaluate the robustness of these effects, to define the limits of generalization, to identify factors influencing sex-differentiated parental behaviors, and to evaluate stringently the specific impact, over time, of these sex-differentiated parenting emphases on the personality and cognitive development of sons and of daughters.

Studies of Sex-Differentiated Teacher Behaviors. To the extent that sex-related differences in family socialization patterns are echoed in the behaviors of teachers, the sex-typed behaviors of males and females are given more extensive reinforcement. Considerable evidence for such reinforcement in the classroom exists. Observations of nursery school teachers' behaviors demonstrate in several studies that boys are given more attention, both positive and negative, than girls (Felsenthal, 1970; Meyer and Thompson, 1956; Serbin and others, 1973). This last study also found differences in the responses given to boys and to girls in reaction to solicitation behaviors: Teachers were not only more likely to respond to boys, but they responded in more solution-advancing ways, providing more specific information. Other researches report similar findings (for example, Cherry, 1975; Golden and Birns, 1975). A recent study of teaching behavior with fifth-grade children in the solving of concept evaluation problems is distressing in its implications for intellectually advantaged girls (Frey, 1979). In this investigation, teaching behaviors of men and women tutors were recorded as they taught boys and girls assigned to one of two ability levels (high and moderate achievement). Of the four groups of pupils, *girls in the high-achievement condition received the lowest levels of supportive, ego-enhancing feedback*; they also received significantly fewer laudatory attributional statements and significantly more disparaging attributional statements. The findings from this study cohere with those from other researches of sex-differentiated teacher behavior where teachers have been observed to interact more with boys, to give boys more positive feedback, and to direct more criticism toward girls (Cherry, 1975; Sears and Feldman, 1966; Serbin and others, 1973). Even at the university level, lesser reinforcement of the cognitive achievements of female students is reported. Survey studies of student and faculty attitudes reveal that the intellectual aspirations of female students are taken less seriously by professors (Carnegie Commission, 1973b; Feldman, 1974; Heyman, 1977; Hochschild, 1975). The greater attrition of women in higher education may reflect, among other factors, the pernicious effects of this pattern of discouragement and negative reinforcement of females' intellectual activities, a pattern identified at all educational levels—from nursery school through college. These results from the home, laboratory, and classroom settings suggest that girls, even high-achieving girls, are given less encouragement for their efforts than are their male peers. Gender differences in confidence, self-concept, and problem-solving behaviors noted by Hoffman (1977a), Tyler (1965), and others may well derive from these home and classroom experiences, which often discourage and denigrate the efforts of females.

In addition to specific teacher behaviors, the larger school context reinforces gender differences and traditional sex role behaviors as well. Males hold the more prestigious positions in the school system; female teachers are less professionally identified and committed; schoolyards tend to be sex-segregated as a function of the different activity preferences of boys and girls; and classroom chores tend to be allocated in a sex-differentiated way (Guttentag and Bray, 1977). Further, on the playground, the games in which boys and girls spontaneously participate are sex-differentiated and diverge in their formal characteristics. Lever (1976) analyzed the formal characteristics of games played on the playground by boys and girls and found that girls participated in highly structured, turn-taking games, which are regulated by invariable procedural rules, include fewer players, and less often require contingent strategies. Boys' games, though rule-governed, reward initiative, improvisation, and extemporaneity, involve teams made up of a number of peers, and encourage both within-team cooperation and between-team competition. These sex-differentiated experiences with games also may be expected to influence importantly both social development and approaches to problem solving.

These differences in teacher behaviors, institutional arrangements, and peer activities accentuate differences between males and females and reinforce the sex-differentiating socialization behaviors of parents by extending the network of sex-differentiating socializing agents beyond the family, thus providing continuity in the experiences of the child from the home to the larger world.

In summary, there appears to be appreciable sex-differentiated socialization at home and at school, allowing boys greater freedom to explore and encouraging curiosity, independence, and the testing of oneself in achievement and other competitive settings. This socialization pattern tends to extend the experiences of males. For females, the socialization process discourages exploration, circumscribes spheres of activity, stresses proprieties, and emphasizes close supervision, thus restricting the experiences of females. Access to experience and the opportunity to actively engage the world have been shown by numerous investigators to influence cognitive development (Piaget, 1930, 1952; Hunt, 1961, 1964, 1976; Dennis, 1973; Sigel and Cocking, 1976). It would be expected, therefore, that the sex-differentiated socialization practices described would influence the cognitive and personality development of males and females. In the next section, some conceptual implications of the diverging experiences of boys and girls will be considered from a developmental perspective.

Implications of Sex-Differentiated Socialization

In Chapter One, attention was directed to the implications of different conceptions of gender roles for personality development. In that chapter, ways in which the socialization of traditional gender roles affects the development of ego structures in males and in females were considered. In the present chapter, building on the evidence cited in earlier sections, the focus shifts to the implications of sex-related differences in socialization for the development of cognitive structures.

Applying a developmental perspective to the gender differences observed, the sex-differentiated socialization and parental "shaping" behaviors may be seen as affecting boys and girls in ways importantly influencing the deep structure of their cognitive development. Three fundamental, early bases for later cognitive development can be identified and related to the socialization patterns noted as differentially characterizing the sexes. The three orientations on which so much of subsequent cognitive development depends are (1) *the child's premises* about the responsivity of the world to his or her actions, (2) *the child's opportunities* to "experiment with nature," and (3) *the child's strategies* for responding to discrepant, disconfirming experiences.

Premises About the Responsivity of the World to One's Actions. Experience with self-initiated and self-created contingency relations has been shown to have important cognitive consequences. Yarrow and others (1972) found contingency understandings to be related to general developmental level, goal direction, and exploratory behaviors of infants. To the extent that modes of processing information and the enduring cognitive structures resulting therefrom derive from the child's early and active promotion of contingency relations, parent/child interactions and "shaping" behaviors that are sex-differentiating with respect to such mastery-seeking contingency experience can assume appreciable significance.

Earlier, in summarizing the literature on sex-differentiated socialization, it was noted that boys, more than girls, are directed toward and reinforced for an active orientation toward understanding contingencies in the physical and logical world. Girls, more than boys, seem to be directed toward and reinforced for their engagement in the interpersonal, or social, world. For both sexes, the attention, responsivity, encouragement, and criticism received from parents, teachers, and the larger cultural surround tend to accentuate this difference in orientation.

The physical world available to the child is impressively orderly and permits inference of its underlying rules. In the physical domain, toward which boys tend to be oriented, experience with contingencies permits active problem surmounting. In contrast the social world, toward which girls tend to be oriented, "is complex and . . . fractious, behaving in ways only fuzzily comprehensible. Efforts . . . to test the nature of the interpersonal reality by acting upon it have erratic or dim results" (Block and Block, 1980b, p. 96). In this social domain, contingent relations may be observed but not manipulated; the use of such recognitions, therefore, tends to be problem-escaping in nature (for example, asking for help may get the child past the immediately confronting problem but does not surmount it).

Boys are given toys with more feedback potential and participate in games requiring sequential, manipulative use of contingent strategies. These early and frequent experiences of boys with the possibility of and successful utilization of contingency relations may be expected to benefit their motivation, goal orientation, and development of awareness of the evocative role they themselves play in eliciting effects from the environment. Girls, however, tend to be withheld or discouraged from such day-after-day opportunities to learn to know that they can learn. Consequently, they do not have those early experiences of efficacy (and the consequently developed *sense of efficacy*) that can help build the personality and cognitive foundations on which later instrumental competence and an orientation toward competence depend. I posit, therefore, that boys, more than girls, as presently socialized in this culture, are helped to develop a premise system about the self that presumes or anticipates having consequence, instrumental competence, and mastery.

Opportunities to "Experiment with Nature." With characteristic insight, Piaget (1970, p. 715) has reminded us that "each time one prematurely teaches a child something he could have discovered for himself, the child is kept from inventing it and consequently from understanding it completely." In this connection, Sigel and Cocking (1976) have drawn attention to the effects of insufficient parental "distancing" on the development of children's representational thought. They propose that adult distancing behaviors promote the child's active engagement in problem solving and increase the likelihood that the child will encounter discrepancies between experience and expectation that cannot be assimilated readily. Such discrepancies place demands on the child to alter approach, reexamine earlier understandings, modify premises—that is, to develop new cognitive structures. Data from several sources converge in suggesting that socialization practices fostering proximity, discouraging independent problem solving by premature or excessive intervention, restricting exploration, and discouraging active play may impede the child's achievement of the cognitive recognitions and fluencies that represent the essence of cognitive development.

I have earlier noted that boys, more than girls, are reared in ways encouraging curiosity, independence, and exploration of the environment—behaviors requisite for the kind of experimentation deemed critical by Piaget and others for the development of cognitive structures. In contrast, the more restrictive childrearing practices characterizing parents of girls (emphasis on physical proximity, expectations of "ladylike" behaviors, close supervision, and provision of help in problem-solving situations) lessen the opportunity for girls to engage in active experimentation with the environment, to encounter discrepancies, and to engage in solution efforts. I posit, therefore, that boys, more than girls, as presently socialized in this culture, are afforded greater opportunities for "discovering," "examining," and "understanding" the world in which they must live (Hoffman, 1972).

   Cognitive Strategies for Responding to Discrepant Experiences. The notions of cognitive assimilation and cognitive accommodation, owing largely to Piaget (1954), are widely known in developmental psychology. The concepts are variously understood, not least because Piaget was never entirely clear or consistent in defining and using them. Indeed, in one of his last works (Piaget, 1977), he appears to have fundamentally changed from his earlier characterizations of these concepts.

   As I shall use the terms here, the process of assimilation involves the fitting of new information or experience into preexisting cognitive schemata, while the process of accommodation involves the modification and the formation of cognitive schemata capable of encompassing new information or experience at variance with prior understandings. Although adaptation to new experience, according to Piaget (1954, 1970), always and simultaneously requires both assimilation and accommodation as two sides of (or perspectives on) one coin, the use of the concepts here departs from Piaget in separating these two cognitive strategies (Block, 1982). Of course, all individuals use both modes of processing experience at different times in rapid succession and under different circumstances. Nevertheless, it is useful to consider the relatively *preferred* mode—assimilation or accommodation—characterizing a person. Further, if normatively the assimilative mode has a built-in priority over the accommodative mode, as several considerations suggest (Block, 1982), it becomes of interest to ascertain the personal point at which an individual abandons continuing efforts at assimilation to begin the task of creating a new and integrative accommodation. In reacting to new experiences failing to conform to the expectations generated from existing schemata, some persons have an ability (and even an insistence) to see whether they can encompass the new information in ways that require little or no modification of previously established premises. Other persons encountering new experiential inputs have a greater readiness (and even preference) to leave cognitive schemata that do not mesh readily with the new information and to move on to the formulation of new and sufficient meaning-making structures.

Both assimilation and accommodation, as defined above, may be seen as serving an adaptive evolutionary function. Assimilation conserves existing structures, sometimes in creative ways, providing continuity with the past and perpetuating cultural and familial traditions and historical values. Accommodation results in the creation, sometimes unnecessarily, of new adaptive modes, thus fostering social innovation and cultural change. When both modes of processing experience are available to the individual and when they can be invoked in context-responsive ways, problem-solving effectiveness is broadened. Overreliance on either strategy for processing disconfirming information will prove dysfunctional. The use of procrustean and perseverative methods to fit, shape, or mold new perceptions into preexisting schemata can result in a projective, distorted, perseverative, oversimplified, rigid approach to the world (Perry, 1968), while premature jettisoning of established schemata and zealously sought or passively accepted redefinitions of premises may result in an ahistorical, compartmentalized, overly situational, standardless, transient, seemingly impulsive approach to the world.

The literature reviewed earlier suggests that females grow up in a more structured and directive world than males. Parental supervision, restrictions on exploration, household chore assignments, proximity emphases, and the more frequent—sometimes unnecessary—help provided girls in problem-solving situations combine to create a more canalized and more predictable environment for girls than for boys. Encounters with the world outside the home are both less extensive and more controlled than with boys. Contributing also to the more structured world of girls is the greater structure of their preferred play activities, which, more than the play of boys, involve model availability, instruction, and rule governance (Carpenter, 1979; Fagot, 1973; Lever, 1976). At older ages, the games preferred by girls also are more structured and make fewer demands for improvisation than the games of boys, which often reward extemporaneity and the ability to take advantage of a momentarily advantageous situation. Relatively structured environments, in contrast to those less structured, have been found to elicit less creativity and more compliance in children (Carpenter and Huston-Stein, 1980), to be associated with less task engagement (Fagot, 1973), and to be related to intolerance of ambiguity (Harrington, Block, and Block, 1978). These differences in the learning environments experienced by girls and by boys can be expected to have powerful and general effects on the cognitive strategies invoked at times when expectations fail.

I posit, therefore, that girls, more than boys, are socialized in ways encouraging the use of assimilative strategies for processing new information, while boys, more than girls, are socialized in ways that encourage the use of accommodative strategies when confronted with informational inputs discrepant with prior understandings. Further, I suggest that girls, more than boys, are slower to leave efforts to cognitively assimilate for efforts to cognitively accommodate. Socialization practices creating relatively structured environments, more common in the case of females, emphasize the adaptive rewards of efforts to be assimilative and discourage the anxiety-inducing efforts of innovative accommodation. Boys, experiencing a less predictable world where ad hoc strategies are frequently demanded, are pressed more often—sometimes uncomfortably—to reexamine and even to abandon structures that are proving ineffective. Success in inventive ad hoc solutions, over time, would be expected to benefit boys' self-confidence and their freedom to assume the risk of seeking to restructure.

Admittedly, empirical evidence to support the proposition that males and females differ in their preferred modes for dealing with new informational inputs is sparse. This formulation, however, is consonant in interesting ways with Lynn's (1962) characterization of the differences in both the *nature* and the *process* of identification for males and for females.

Lynn postulated that the task of achieving identification for each sex requires separate methods of learning, methods paralleling the two kinds of learning tasks—problem mastery and lesson learning—differentiated almost thirty years ago by Woodworth and Schlosberg (1954, p. 529): "With a problem to master the learner must explore the situation and find the goal before his task is fully presented. In the case of a lesson, the problem-solving phase is omitted or at least minimized, as we see when the human subject is instructed to memorize this poem or that list of nonsense syllables."

Lynn suggests that the availability of the mother and the visibility of her daily activities provide the daughter with an opportunity to observe, to imitate, and to identify with specific aspects of the mother's role. Therefore, the young daughter's task of achieving identification with the mother and developing a feminine gender role orientation can be viewed as a profound instance of lesson learning. The young son's task of achieving identification with the father, however, is complicated by two factors: the necessity of shifting from an initial identification with the mother to one with the father (a task requiring early accommodation) and the lesser visibility of the father's day-to-day activities outside the home. The opportunity for imitative or template or lesson learning is less available to the young son, and therefore the task of achieving identification with the father and developing a masculine gender role orientation requires extrapolation and can be considered an instance of problem learning. The conceptualization being offered here is consistent with Lynn's formulation in that the relations between assimilation and lesson learning and between accommodation and problem learning are apparent.

In addition to the support for the present argument afforded by Lynn's discussion of the identification process and its sex-differential implications for learning, some—albeit limited—empirical justification can be cited as well. Research findings demonstrating the greater cognitive conservatism of females in problem-solving situations are pertinent. A set of findings surrounding categorization behavior demonstrates that females have narrower category boundaries than males (Block and others, 1981; Crandall, 1965; Pettigrew, 1958; Sherman and Smith, 1967; Wallach and Caron, 1959; Wallach and Kogan, 1959). In summarizing the results of several categorization studies, Silverman (1970, p. 84) notes, "Females are more disposed than males *to accept the basic structure of a stimulus configuration* and to elaborate it only minimally" (italics added). With regard to cognitive problems requiring restructuring, or breaking set, data are quite clear in showing females scoring lower (for a review of these findings, see Block, 1976a, 1976b). Assessments of cognitive risk taking have found females to be more conservative in their judgments than males (for example, Wallach and Kogan, 1959). A study by Duck (1975), seeking to identify factors associated with friendship patterns, demonstrates that the basis for friendships in girls, but not in boys, is similarity in psychological constructs as these are assessed using the Kelly grid technique. The importance of familiar, well-tried pathways for females is to be seen also in the finding by Harter (1975) that girls spent more time than boys on a task after reaching a learning criterion, particularly under the condition of social reinforcement. Boys, in contrast, spent more time on unsolvable problems, seeking to find the key to solution. It is suggested that these results demonstrating females' greater adherence to the midrange in categorization studies, lesser inclination to restructure in set-breaking problems, greater conservatism in judgments involving risk taking, preference for friends sharing similar psychological characteristics, and preference for staying with mastered tasks are consistent with the assimilative mode of dealing with new experience. As such, they offer support for the proposition that females, to a greater extent than males, rely on and invoke assimilative strategies, while males tend more often to manifest or turn to accommodative strategies in problem-solving situations.

Although there has not yet been research directly evaluating preferences for assimilative as compared with accommodative strategies, results of the foregoing studies are suggestive. A necessary next step is to test the tenability of the conjectures offered here. Until targeted research begins to be available and can be brought to bear on the proposition, the heuristic conjecture that boys, more than girls, as presently socialized in this culture, invoke the process of cognitive accommodation would appear to assimilate many of the data and other more informal observations on the different ways the sexes tend to resolve disconfirming experiences.

In coda, I believe that sex-differentiated socialization practices influence the cognitive development of males and females in deeply implicative ways that separately and in summation provide more opportunity for independent problem solving in a variety of contexts for males than for females. The differential provisions for the two sexes to actively engage the larger world outside the familiar and protected home environment can create different premises about the world, develop different competencies, and reinforce the use of different cognitive-adaptational heuristics for dealing with new experience. My conjectures regarding the different self- and world views our current culture may be creating and fostering in males and in females are not offered as complete or as operating in a vacuum. The potential, and even likely, influence of biological factors conjoined with the spiraling, reciprocating, bidirectional effects of child and parent interaction, I recognize as confounded with an interpretation in terms of differential socialization. But also, it should be remembered that the role of biological and bidirectional factors cannot be assessed until the effects of differential socialization are specifically evaluated by cultural, subcultural, or individual family changes.

References

Ainsworth, M., and Bell, S. "Some Contemporary Patterns of Mother-Infant Interaction in the Feeding Situation." In A. Ambrose (Ed.), *Stimulation in Early Infancy.* New York: Academic Press, 1969.

Ashear, V., and Snortum, J. R. "Eye Contact in Children as a Function of Age, Sex, Social, and Intellective Variables." *Developmental Psychology,* 1971, *4,* 479.

Astin, A. W. "Undergraduate Institutions and the Production of Scientists." *Science,* 1963, *141,* 334–338.

Astin, A. W. *The College Environment.* Washington, D.C.: American Council of Education, 1968a.

Astin, A. W. "Undergraduate Achievement and Institutional 'Excellence.' " *Science,* 1968b, *161,* 661–668.

Astin, A. W. "Measuring the Outcomes of Higher Education." In H. R. Bowen (Ed.), *New Directions for Institutional Research: Evaluating Institutions for Accountability,* no. 1. San Francisco: Jossey-Bass, 1974.

Astin, A. W. *Four Critical Years: Effects of College on Beliefs, Attitudes, and Knowledge.* San Francisco: Jossey-Bass, 1977.

283

Astin, A. W., King, M. R., and Richardson, G. T. *The American Freshman: National Norms for Fall, 1975.* Los Angeles: Cooperative Institutional Research Program, University of California at Los Angeles, 1975.

Astin, A. W., and Panos, R. J. *The Educational and Vocational Development of College Students.* Washington, D.C.: *American Council on Education,* 1969.

Atherton, B. F. "Coeducational and Single Sex Schooling and Happiness in Marriage." *Education Research,* 1973, *15,* 221–226.

Bakan, D. *The Duality of Human Existence.* Chicago: Rand McNally, 1966.

Bakan, D. *On Method: Toward a Reconstruction of Psychological Investigation.* San Francisco: Jossey-Bass, 1967.

Baltes, P. B., and Nesselroade, J. R. "Cultural Change and Adolescent Personality Development." *Developmental Psychology,* 1972, *7,* 244-256.

Bandura, A., and Walters, R. H. *Social Learning and Personality Development.* New York: Holt, Rinehart and Winston, 1963.

Bandura, A., Ross, D., and Ross, S. A. "Imitation of Film-Mediated Aggressive Models." *Journal of Abnormal and Social Psychology,* 1963, *66,* 3-11.

Barber, E. G. "Some Perspectives on Sex Differences in Education." Unpublished paper, 1977.

Barlow, G. W. "Modal Action Patterns." In T. A. Sebeok (Ed.), *How Animals Communicate.* Bloomington: University of Indiana Press, 1977.

Barry, H., Bacon, M. K., and Child, I. L. "A Cross Cultural Survey of Some Sex Differences in Socialization." *Journal of Abnormal and Social Psychology,* 1957, *55,* 327-332.

Bateson, G. "Social Planning and the Concept of Deutero-Learning." In L. Bryson and L. Finklestein (Eds.), *Science, Philosophy, and Religion: Second Symposium.* New York: Harper & Row, 1942.

Bateson, G. *Steps to an Ecology of Mind: Collected Essays in Anthropology, Psychiatry, Evolution, and Epistemology.* New York: Ballantine, 1972.

Battle, E. S., and Lacey, B. "A Context for Hyperactivity in Children, over Time." *Child Development*, 1972, *43*, 757-773.

Baumrind, D. "Current Patterns of Parental Authority." *Developmental Psychology Monographs*, 1971, *4*, Pt. 2, 1-103.

Bayer, A. E. "Marriage Plans and Educational Aspirations." *American Journal of Sociology*, 1969, *75*, 239-244.

Bayer, A. E. "College Impact on Marriage." *Journal of Marriage and the Family*, 1972, *34*, 600-609.

Beach, F. A. "Hormonal Modification of Sexually Dimorphic Behavior." *Psychoendocrinology*, 1975, *1*, 3-23.

Beach, F. A. "The Ontogeny of Sex Differences." Paper presented at meeting of the American Psychological Association, Montreal, September 1980.

Becker, W. "Consequences of Different Kinds of Parental Discipline." In M. Hoffman and L. Hoffman (Eds.), *Review of Child Development Research*. Vol. 1. New York: Russell Sage Foundation, 1964.

Bell, N. J., and Carver, W. "A Reevaluation of Gender Label Effects: Expectant Mothers' Responses to Infants." *Child Development*, 1980, *51*, 925-927.

Bell, R. Q., Weller, G. M., and Waldrop, M. F. "New Born and Preschooler: Organization of Behavior and Relations Between Periods." *Monographs of the Society for Research in Child Development*, 1971, *36*, Whole No. 142.

Beller, E. K., and Neubauer, P. B. "Sex Differences and Symptom Patterns in Early Childhood." *Journal of Child Psychiatry*, 1963, *2*, 417-433.

Bem, S. L. "The Measurement of Psychological Androgyny." *Journal of Consulting and Clinical Psychology*, 1974, *42*, 155-162.

Berk, L. E. "Effects of Variations in the Nursery School Setting on Environmental Constraints and Children's Modes of Adaptation." *Child Development*, 1971, *42*, 839-869.

Biller, H. B. *Father, Child, and Sex Roles: Paternal Determinants of Personality Development*. Lexington, Mass.: Heath/Lexington Books, 1971.

Bing, E. "Effect of Childrearing Practices on Development of Differential Cognitive Abilities." *Child Development,* 1963, *34,* 631-648.

Bird, C. "Women's Lib and Women's College." *Change,* April 1972, pp. 60-65.

Blakemore, J. E. O. "Age and Sex Differences in Interaction with a Human Infant." Paper presented at meeting of the Society for Research in Child Development, San Francisco, March 1979.

Block, J. *The Q-Sort Method in Personality Assessment and Psychiatric Research.* Springfield, Ill.: Thomas, 1961.

Block, J. *Lives Through Time.* Berkeley, Calif.: Bancroft Books, 1971.

Block, J. "Assimilation, Accommodation, and the Dynamics of Personality Development." *Child Development,* 1982, *53,* 281-295.

Block, J., and Block, J. H. *The Environmental Q-Set.* (Rev. ed.) Berkeley: Department of Psychology, University of California, 1967.

Block, J., and Block, J. H. "Ego Development and the Provenance of Thought: A Longitudinal Study of Ego and Cognitive Development in Young Children." Unpublished progress report for the National Institute of Mental Health, 1973.

Block, J., and Block, J. H. "A Longitudinal Study of Personality and Cognitive Development." In S. Mednick and M. Harway (Eds.), *Longitudinal Research in the United States.* New York: Praeger, in press.

Block, J., and others. "The Cognitive Style of Breadth of Categorization: Longitudinal Consistency of Personality Correlates." *Journal of Personality and Social Psychology,* 1981, *40,* 770-779.

Block, J., von der Lippe, A., and Block, J. H. "Sex-Role and Socialization Patterns: Some Personality Concomitants and Environmental Antecedents." *Journal of Consulting and Clinical Psychology,* 1973, *41,* 321-341.

Block, J. H. "The Child-Rearing Practices Report." Berkeley: Institute of Human Development, University of California, 1965. (Mimeographed.)

Block, J. H. "Generational Continuity and Discontinuity in the Understanding of Societal Rejection." *Journal of Personality and Social Psychology*, 1972, *22*, 333-345.

Block, J. H. "Conceptions of Sex Role: Some Cross-Cultural and Longitudinal Perspectives." *American Psychologist*, 1973, *28*, 512-526.

Block, J. H. "Debatable Conclusions About Sex Differences." *Contemporary Psychology*, 1976a, *21*, 517-522.

Block, J. H. "Issues, Problems, and Pitfalls in Assessing Sex Differences: A Critical Review of *The Psychology of Sex Differences.*" *Merrill-Palmer Quarterly*, 1976b, *22*, 283-308.

Block, J. H. "Another Look at Sex Differentiation in the Socialization Behavior of Mothers and Fathers." In J. A. Sherman and F. L. Denmark (Eds.), *The Psychology of Women: Future Directions in Research*. New York: Psychological Dimensions, 1979a.

Block, J. H. *Socialization Influences on Personality Development in Males and Females*. Audiotape No. 15/11. Washington, D.C.: American Psychological Association, 1979b.

Block, J. H. "Gender Differences in the Nature of Premises Developed About the World." In E. K. Shapiro and E. Weber (Eds.), *Cognitive and Affective Growth: Developmental Interaction*. Hillsdale, N.J.: Erlbaum, 1981.

Block, J. H., and Block, J. *The California Child Q-Set*. Palo Alto, Calif.: Consulting Psychologists Press, 1980a.

Block, J. H., and Block, J. "The Role of Ego-Control and Ego-Resiliency in the Organization of Behavior." In W. A. Collins (Ed.), *Minnesota Symposia on Child Psychology*. Vol. 13. Hillsdale, N.J.: Erlbaum; New York: Wiley, 1980b.

Block, J. H., Block, J., and Harrington, D. M. "The Relationship of Parental Teaching Strategies to Ego-Resiliency in Preschool Children." Paper presented at meeting of the Western Psychological Association, San Francisco, April 1974.

Block, J. H., Block, J., and Harrington, D. M. "Sex Role Typing and Instrumental Behavior: A Developmental Study." Paper presented at annual meeting of the Society for Research in Child Development, Denver, Colo., 1975.

Block, J. H., and Christiansen, B. "A Test of Hendin's Hypothe-

sis Relating Suicide in Scandinavia to Child-Rearing Orientations." *Scandinavian Journal of Psychology,* 1966, *7,* 267–
288.

Brehm, S. S., and Weinraub, M. "Physical Barriers and Psychological Reactance: 2-Year-Olds' Responses to Threats to Freedom." *Journal of Personality and Social Psychology,* 1977,
35, 830–836.

Bridgeland, M. "Mixed or Single Sex Schools." *London Times
Educational Supplement* 2937, Sept. 3, 1971, p. 4.

Bronfenbrenner, U. "Freudian Theories of Identification and
Their Derivatives." *Child Development,* 1960, *31,* 15–40.

Bronson, W. C. "Dimensions of Ego and Infantile Identification." *Journal of Personality,* 1959, *27,* 532–545.

Bronson, W. C. "Exploratory Behavior of 15-Month-Old Infants
in a Novel Situation." Paper presented at annual meeting of
the Society for Research in Child Development, Minneapolis,
March 1971.

Brown, D. G. "Masculinity-Femininity Development in Children." *Journal of Consulting Psychology,* 1957, *21,* 197–202.

Brown, J. P. "Occupational Development During Adolescence:
The Influence of Interpersonal Communication and Sex
Roles." Unpublished doctoral dissertation, Department of
Psychology, University of Wisconsin, Madison, 1977.

Brun-Gulbrandsen, S. "Sex Role and Youth Delinquency." Institute of Social Research, Oslo, 1958. (Mimeographed.)

Burger, G. K., Lamp, R. E., and Rogers, D. "Developmental
Trends in Children's Perceptions of Parental Child-Rearing
Behavior." *Developmental Psychology,* 1975, *11,* 391.

Burrows, P. B. "Parent-Child Behavior in a Sample of Mexican
Families." Unpublished doctoral dissertation, Department of
Psychology, Harvard University, 1979.

Buss, A. "Instrumentality of Aggression, Feedback, and Frustration as Determinants of Physical Aggression." *Journal of Personality and Social Psychology,* 1966, *3,* 153–162.

Buss, D. M., Block, J. H., and Block, J. "Preschool Activity
Level: Personality Correlates and Developmental Implications." *Child Development,* 1980, *51,* 401–408.

Caldwell, M. A., and Pelau, L. A. "Sex Differences in Same-
Sex Friendship." *Sex Roles,* 1982, *8,* 721–732.

Callard, E. D. "Achievement Motive in the Four-Year-Old Child and Its Relationship to Achievement Expectancies of the Mother." Unpublished doctoral dissertation, Department of Psychology, University of Michigan, 1964.

Cantor, N. L., Wood, D., and Gelfand, D. "Effects of Responsiveness and Sex of Children on Adult Males' Behavior." *Child Development,* 1977, *48,* 1426-1430.

Caplan, P. "Beyond the Box Score: A Boundary Condition for Sex Differences in Aggression and Achievement Striving." In B. Maher (Ed.), *Progress in Experimental Personality Research.* Vol. 9. New York: Academic Press, 1979.

Carlson, R. "Sex Differences in Ego Functioning: Exploratory Studies in Agency and Communion." *Journal of Consulting and Clinical Psychology,* 1971a, *37,* 267-277.

Carlson, R. "Where Is the Person in Personality Research?" *Psychological Bulletin,* 1971b, *75,* 203-219.

Carnegie Commission on Higher Education. "Coeducation and Women's Colleges." *Intellect,* 1973a, *102,* 1973.

Carnegie Commission on Higher Education. *Opportunities for Women in Higher Education.* New York: McGraw-Hill, 1973b.

Carpenter, C. J. "Relation of Children's Sex-Typed Behavior to Classroom and Activity Structure." Paper presented at annual meeting of the Society for Research in Child Development, San Francisco, March 1979.

Carpenter, C. J. "Activity Structure and Play: Implications for Socialization." In M. Liss (Ed.), *Social and Cognitive Skills: Sex Roles and Children's Play.* New York: Academic Press, 1983.

Carpenter, C. J., and Huston-Stein, A. "Activity Structure and Sex-Typed Behavior in Preschool Children." *Child Development,* 1980, *51,* 862-872.

Cava, E. L., and Raush, H. "Identification and the Adolescent Boy's Perception of His Father." *Journal of Abnormal and Social Psychology,* 1952, *47,* 855-856.

Cherry, L. "The Preschool Teacher-Child Dyad: Sex Differences in Verbal Interaction." *Child Development,* 1975, *46,* 532-535.

Chickering, A. W. "The Impact of Various College Environments on Personality Development." *Journal of the American College Health Association,* 1974, *23,* 82–93.

Chodorow, N. "Family Structure and Feminine Personality." In M. Z. Rosaldo and L. Lampere (Eds.), *Women's Culture and Society.* Stanford, Calif.: Stanford University Press, 1974.

Clarke-Stewart, K. A. "Interactions Between Mothers and Their Young Children: Characteristics and Consequences." *Monographs of the Society for Research in Child Development,* 1973, *38,* Whole No. 153.

"Coeducation and Women's Colleges." *Intellect,* 1973, *102* (2351), 9.

Cohen, J. *Statistical Power Analysis for the Behavioral Sciences.* New York: Academic Press, 1969.

Condry, J., and Dyer, S. "Fear of Success: Attribution of Cause to the Victim." *Journal of Social Issues,* 1976, *32,* 63–83.

Condry, S. M., Condry, J. C., and Pogatshnik, L. W. "Sex Differences: A Study of the Ear of the Beholder." Paper presented at meeting of the American Psychological Association, Toronto, August 1980.

Conway, J. "Are Women's Colleges Necessary Today? Yes: They Teach Self-Confidence." *New York Times,* November 13, 1977, sec. 12, p. 13.

Cooper, H. M. "Statistically Combining Independent Studies: A Meta-Analysis of Sex Differences in Conformity Research." *Journal of Personality and Social Psychology,* 1979, *37,* 131–146.

Crandall, J. E. "Some Relationships Among Sex, Anxiety, and Conservatism of Judgment." *Journal of Personality,* 1965, *33,* 99–107.

Crandall, V. C. "Achievement Behavior in Young Children." In W. W. Hartup and N. L. Smothergill (Eds.), *The Young Child: Reviews of Research.* Washington, D.C.: National Association for the Education of the Young, 1967.

Crandall, V. C. "Sex Differences in Expectancy of Intellectual and Academic Reinforcement." In C. P. Smith (Ed.), *Achievement Related Motives in Children.* New York: Russell Sage Foundation, 1969.

Cronbach, L. J. "Beyond the Two Disciplines of Scientific Psychology." *American Psychologist,* 1975, *30,* 116–127.

Cruse, D. B. "Socially Desirable Responses at Ages 3 Through 6." *Child Development,* 1966, *37,* 909-916.

Daehler, M. W. "Children's Manipulation of Illusory and Ambiguous Stimuli, Discriminative Performance, and Implications for Conceptual Development." *Child Development,* 1970, *41,* 225-241.

Dahlstrom, W. G., and Welsh, G. S. *An MMPI Handbook: A Guide to Use in Clinical Practice and Research.* Minneapolis: University of Minnesota Press, 1960.

Dale, R. R. *Mixed or Single Sex School.* Vol. 1. London: Routledge & Kegan Paul, 1969.

Day, K. "Differences in Teaching Behavior in Adults as a Function of Sex Related Variables." Unpublished doctoral dissertation, Department of Psychology, University of Washington, 1975.

Dennis, W. *Children of the Creche.* New York: Appleton-Century-Crofts, 1973.

Di Pietro, J. "Rough and Tumble Play: A Function of Gender." Paper presented at annual meeting of the Society for Research in Child Development, San Francisco, March 1979.

Doob, A., and Gross, A. "Status of Frustrator as an Inhibitor of Horn Honking Responses." *Journal of Social Psychology,* 1968, *76,* 213-218.

Duck, S. W. "Personality Similarity and Friendship Choices by Adolescents." *European Journal of Social Psychology,* 1975, *5,* 351-365.

Duncan, D., Schuman, H., and Duncan, B. *Social Change in a Metropolitan Community.* New York: Russell Sage Foundation, 1973.

Dweck, C. S., and others. "Sex Differences in Learned Helplessness: II. The Contingencies of Evaluation Feedback in the Classroom. III. An Experimental Analysis." *Developmental Psychology,* 1978, *14,* 268-276.

Eagly, A. H. "Sex Differences in Influenceability." *Psychological Bulletin,* 1978, *85,* 85-116.

Eaton, W. O., and Keats, J. G. "Peer Presence, Stress, and Sex Differences in the Motor Activity Levels of Preschoolers." *Developmental Psychology,* 1982, *18,* 534-540.

Ebbesen, E. B., and Haney, M. "Flirting with Death: Variables

Affecting Risk-Taking at Intersections." *Journal of Applied Social Psychology,* 1973, *3,* 303–324.

Eme, R. F. "Sex Differences in Childhood Psychopathology: A Review." *Psychological Bulletin,* 1979, *86,* 574–595.

Emmerich, W. "Structure and Development of Personal-Social Behaviors in Preschool Settings." Educational Testing Service —Head Start Longitudinal Study, November 1971. (ED 063 971)

Emmerich, W. "Socialization and Sex-Role Development." In P. B. Baltes and K. W. Schaie (Eds.), *Life-Span Developmental Psychology.* New York: Academic Press, 1973.

Emmerich, W. "Complexities of Human Development (Review of *The Psychology of Sex Differences* by E. E. Maccoby and C. N. Jacklin)." *Science,* 1975, *190,* 140–141.

Erikson, E. H. *Childhood and Society.* New York: Norton, 1950.

Erikson, E. H. *Identity: Youth and Crisis.* New York: Norton, 1968.

Ernest, J. "Mathematics and Sex." *American Mathematical Monthly,* 1976, *83,* 595–614.

Etaugh, C., Collins, G., and Gerson, A. "Reinforcement of Sex-Typed Behaviors of Two-Year-Old Children in a Nursery School Setting." *Developmental Psychology,* 1975, *11,* 255.

Fagot, B. I. "Influence of Teacher Behavior in the Preschool." *Developmental Psychology,* 1973, *9,* 198–206.

Fagot, B. I. "Sex Differences in Toddlers' Behavior and Parental Reaction." *Developmental Psychology,* 1974, *10,* 554–558.

Fagot, B. I. "Sex Determined Parental Reinforcing Contingencies in Toddler Children." Paper presented at annual meeting of the Society for Research in Child Development, New Orleans, March 1977.

Fagot, B. I. "Sex Determined Consequences of Different Play Styles in Early Childhood." Paper presented at annual meeting of the American Psychological Association, Toronto, August, 1978a.

Fagot, B. I. "The Influence of Sex of Child on Parental Reactions to Toddler Children." *Child Development,* 1978b, *49,* 459–465.

Fagot, B. I., and Littman, I. "Stability of Sex-Role and Play Interests from Preschool to Elementary School." *Journal of Psychology,* 1975, *89,* 285-292.

Fairweather, H. "Sex Differences in Cognition." *Cognition,* 1976, *4,* 231-280.

Fein, G., and others. "Sex Stereotypes and Preferences in the Toy Choices of 20-Month-Old Boys and Girls." *Developmental Psychology,* 1975, *11,* 527-528.

Feldman, K. A., and Newcomb, T. M. *The Impact of College on Students.* Vol. 1: *An Analysis of Four Decades of Research.* San Francisco: Jossey-Bass, 1969.

Feldman, S. *Escape from the Doll's House: Women in Graduate and Professional School Education.* New York: McGraw-Hill, 1974.

Feldman, S., and Nash, S. C. "The Influence of Age and Sex on Responsiveness to Babies." *Developmental Psychology,* 1977, *13,* 675-676.

Felsenthal, H. "Sex Differences in Teacher-Pupil Interaction in First Grade Reading Instruction." *Proceedings of the American Education Research Association,* 1970, *7,* 69.

Fenichel, O. *The Psychoanalytic Theory of Neurosis.* New York: Norton, 1945.

Fox, L. H., Tobin, D., and Brody, L. "Sex Role Socialization and Achievement in Mathematics." In M. A. Wittig and A. C. Petersen (Eds.), *Sex-Related Differences in Cognitive Functioning.* New York: Academic Press, 1979.

Freud, S. *A General Introduction to Psychoanalysis.* Garden City, N.Y.: Garden City Publishing Co., 1943.

Frey, K. S. "Differential Teaching Methods Used with Girls and Boys of Moderate and High Achievement Levels." Paper presented at annual meeting of the Society for Research in Child Development, San Francisco, March 1979.

Frieze, I. "Sex Differences in Perceiving the Causes of Success and Failure." Unpublished manuscript, University of Pittsburgh, 1973.

Frisch, H. L. "Sex Stereotypes in Adult-Infant Play." *Child Development,* 1977, *48,* 1671-1675.

Frodi, A. M., and Lamb, M. E. "Sex Differences in Responsiveness to Infants: A Developmental Study of Psychological and Behavioral Responses." *Child Development,* 1978, *49,* 1182-1188.

Ginsburg, H. J., and Miller, S. M. "Sex Differences in Children's Risk-Taking Behavior." *Child Development,* 1982, *53,* 426-428.

Goldberg, S., Blumberg, S. L., and Kriger, A. "Menarche and Interest in Infants: Biological and Social Influences." *Child Development,* 1982, *53,* 1544-1550.

Goldberg, S., and Lewis, M. "Play Behavior in the Year-Old Infant: Early Sex Differences." *Child Development,* 1969, *40,* 21-31.

Golden, M., and Birns, B. "Social Class and Infant Intelligence." In M. Lewis (Ed.), *Origins of Intelligence: Infancy and Early Childhood.* New York: Plenum, 1975.

Golightly, C., Nelson, D., and Johnson, J. "Children's Dependency Scale." *Developmental Psychology,* 1970, *3,* 114-118.

Gough, H. G. "Identifying Psychological Femininity." *Educational and Psychological Measurement,* 1952, *12,* 427-439.

Gough, H. G. "Theory and Measurement of Socialization." *Journal of Consulting Psychology,* 1960, *24,* 23-30.

Gough, H. G. *Manual for the California Psychological Inventory.* (Rev. ed.) Palo Alto, Calif.: Consulting Psychologists Press, 1964.

Gough, H. G. "Cross-Cultural Validation of a Measure of Asocial Behavior." *Psychological Reports,* 1965, *17,* 379-387.

Gough, H. G. "A Cross-Cultural Analysis of the CPI Femininity Scale." *Journal of Consulting Psychology,* 1966, *30,* 136-141.

Gough, H. G. "An Interpreter's Syllabus for the California Psychological Inventory." In P. McReynolds (Ed.), *Advances in Psychological Assessment.* Palo Alto, Calif.: Science and Behavior Books, 1968a.

Gough, H. G. "College Attendance Among High Aptitude Students as Predicted from the California Psychological Inventory." *Journal of Counseling Psychology,* 1968b, *15,* 269-278.

Gough, H. G. *Manual for the California Psychological Inventory.* Palo Alto, Calif.: Consulting Psychologists Press, 1969.

Goy, R. W., and Resko, J. A. "Gonadal Hormones and Behavior of Normal and Pseudohermaphroditic Nonhuman Female Primates." In E. Astwood (Ed.), *Recent Progress in Hormone Research*. New York: Academic Press, 1972.

Graham, M. F. "Sex Differences in Science Attrition." Unpublished doctoral dissertation, Department of Social Psychology, State University of New York at Stony Brook, 1978.

Graham, M. F., and Birns, B. "Where Are the Women Geniuses? Up the Down Escalator." In C. Kopp and M. Kirkpatrick (Eds.), *Becoming Female: Perspectives on Development*. New York: Plenum, 1979.

Greenglass, E. R. "A Cross-Cultural Study of the Child's Communication with His Mother." *Developmental Psychology*, 1971, *5*, 494-499.

Greever, K. B., Tseng, M. S., and Friedland, B. U. "Development of the Social Interest Index." *Journal of Consulting and Clinical Psychology*, 1973, *41*, 454-458.

Greif, E. "Sex Differences in Parent-Child Conversations: Who Interrupts Whom?" Paper presented at annual meeting of the Society for Research in Child Development, San Francisco, March 1979.

Group for the Advancement of Psychiatry. "The Educated Women: Prospects and Problems." Report No. 92. New York: Group for the Advancement of Psychiatry, 1975.

Gunnar-vonGnechten, M. R. "Control, Predictability, and Fear in Infancy: Differential Effects as a Function of Infant Sex." Mimeo, Stanford University, 1977.

Gunnar-vonGnechten, M. R. "Changing a Frightening Toy into a Pleasant Toy by Allowing the Infant to Control Its Actions." *Developmental Psychology*, 1978, *14*, 157-162.

Gutmann, D. "Women and the Conception of Ego Strength." *Merrill-Palmer Quarterly*, 1965, *11*, 229-240.

Guttentag, M., and Bray, H. "Teachers as Mediators of Sex-Role Standards." In A. Sargent (Ed.), *Beyond Sex Roles*. St. Paul, Minn.: West, 1977.

Haan, N., Smith, M. B., and Block, J. H. "Moral Reasoning of Young Adults: Political-Social Behavior, Family Background, and Personality Correlates." *Journal of Personality and Social Psychology*, 1968, *10*, 183-201.

Hagen, R. E. "Sex Differences in Driving Performance." *Human Factors,* 1975, *17,* 165-171.

Hall, J. A. "Gender Effects in Decoding Nonverbal Cues." *Psychological Bulletin,* 1978, *85,* 845-857.

Halverson, C. F. Personal communication to E. E. Maccoby and C. N. Jacklin, 1971.

Halverson, C. F., and Waldrop, M. F. "The Relations of Mechanically Recorded Activity Level to Varieties of Preschool Play Behavior." *Child Development,* 1973, *44,* 678-681.

Harper, L. V., and Sanders, K. M. "Preschool Children's Use of Space: Sex Differences in Outdoor Play." *Developmental Psychology,* 1975, *11,* 119.

Harrington, D. M., Block, J. H., and Block, J. "Intolerance of Ambiguity in Preschool Children: Psychometric Considerations, Behavioral Manifestations, and Parental Correlates." *Developmental Psychology,* 1978, *14,* 242-256.

Harter, S. "Developmental Differences in the Manifestation of Mastery Motivation on Problem-Solving Tasks." *Child Development,* 1975, *46,* 370-378.

Hartley, R. E. "Sex Role Pressures and the Socialization of the Male Child." *Psychological Reports,* 1959a, *5,* 457-468.

Hartley, R. E. "Some Implications of Current Changes in the Sex Role Patterns." *Merrill-Palmer Quarterly,* 1959b, *6,* 153-160.

Hartley, R. E. "A Developmental View of Female Sex-Role Definition and Identification." *Merrill-Palmer Quarterly,* 1964, *10,* 3-16.

Healey, A. K. "Lady, and One-Third Scholar." *Education Forum,* 1963, *27,* 313-318.

Heilbrun, A. B. "Sex Differences in Identification Learning." *Journal of Genetic Psychology,* 1965, *106,* 185-193.

Heilbrun, A. B., Harrel, S., and Gillard, B. "Perceived Child-Rearing Attitudes of Fathers and Cognitive Control of Daughters." *Journal of Genetic Psychology,* 1967, *111,* 29-40.

Helson, R. "Generality of Sex Differences in Creative Style." *Journal of Personality,* 1968, *36,* 33-48.

Hendin, H. *Suicide and Scandinavia.* Garden City, N.Y.: Doubleday, 1965.

Hermans, H. J., ter Laak, J. J., and Maes, P. C. "Achievement Motivation and Fear of Failure in Family and School." *Developmental Psychology*, 1972, *6*, 520-528.

Hetherington, E. M. "A Developmental Study of the Effects of Sex of the Dominant Parent on Sex-Role Preference, Identification, and Imitation in Children." *Journal of Personality and Social Psychology*, 1965, *2*, 188-194.

Hetherington, E. M. "Effects of Paternal Absence on Sex-Typed Behaviors in Negro and White Preadolescent Males." *Journal of Personality and Social Psychology*, 1966, *4*, 87-91.

Hetherington, E. M. "The Effects of Familial Variables on Sex Typing, on Parent-Child Similarity, and on Imitation in Children." In J. P. Hill (Ed.), *Minnesota Symposia on Child Psychology*. Minneapolis: Lund Press, 1967.

Hetherington, E. M. "Effects of Father Absence on Personality Development in Adolescent Daughters." *Developmental Psychology*, 1972, *7*, 313-326.

Hetherington, E. M., and Deu, J. "The Effects of Father Absence on Child Development." *Young Children*, 1971, *26*, 233-248.

Hetherington, E. M., and Frankie, G. "Effects of Parental Dominance, Warmth, and Conflict on Imitation in Children." *Journal of Personality and Social Psychology*, 1967, *6*, 119-125.

Hetherington, E. M., and McIntyre, C. W. "Developmental Psychology." *Annual Review of Psychology*, 1975, *26*, 97-136.

Heyman, I. M. "Women Students at Berkeley: Views and Data on Possible Sex Discrimination in Academic Programs." Unpublished report, University of California, Berkeley, 1977.

Hilton, I. "Differences in the Behavior of Mothers Toward First- and Later-Born Children." *Journal of Personality and Social Psychology*, 1967, *7*, 282-290.

Hochschild, A. "Inside the Clockwork of Male Careers." In F. Howe (Ed.), *Women and the Power of Change*. New York: McGraw-Hill, 1975.

Hoffman, L. W. "Early Childhood Experiences and Women's Achievement Motive." *Journal of Social Issues*, 1972, *28*, 129-155.

Hoffman, L. W. "Fear of Success in Males and Females: 1965

and 1971." *Journal of Consulting and Clinical Psychology,* 1974, *42,* 353-358.

Hoffman, L. W. "The Value of Children to Parents and the Decrease in Family Size." *Proceedings of the American Philosophical Society,* 1975, *119,* 430-438.

Hoffman, L. W. "Changes in Family Roles, Socialization, and Sex Differences." *American Psychologist,* 1977a, *32,* 644-657.

Hoffman, L. W. "Fear of Success in 1965 and 1974: A Follow-Up Study." *Journal of Consulting and Clinical Psychology,* 1977b, *45,* 310-321.

Hoffman, M. L. "Sex Differences in Empathy and Related Behaviors." *Psychological Bulletin,* 1977, *84,* 712-722.

Holter, H. *Sex Roles and Social Structure.* Oslo: Universitetsforlaget, 1970.

Horner, M. S. "Sex Differences in Achievement Motivation and Performance in Competitive and Non-Competitive Situations." Unpublished doctoral dissertation, Department of Psychology, University of Michigan, 1968.

Horner, M. S. "Femininity and Successful Achievement: A Basic Inconsistency." In J. Bardwick and others (Eds.), *Feminine Personality and Conflict.* Monterey, Calif.: Brooks/Cole, 1970.

Horner, M. S. "Toward an Understanding of Achievement-Related Conflicts in Women." *Journal of Social Issues,* 1972, *28,* 157-175.

Hunt, J. McV. *Intelligence and Experience.* New York: Ronald Press, 1961.

Hunt, J. McV. "The Psychological Basis for Using Pre-School Enrichment as an Antidote for Cultural Deprivation." *Merrill-Palmer Quarterly,* 1964, *10,* 209-248.

Hunt, J. McV. "Intrinsic Motivation and Its Role in Psychological Development." In D. Levine (Ed.), *Nebraska Symposium on Motivation.* Vol. 13. Lincoln: University of Nebraska Press, 1965.

Hunt, J. McV. "The Psychological Development of Orphange-Reared Infants: Interventions with Outcomes (Tehran)." *Genetic Psychology Monographs,* 1976, *94,* 177-226.

Hutt, C. "Curiosity in Young Children." *Science Journal,* 1970, *6,* 68–71.

Jacob, T., and others. "Social Class, Child Age, and Parental Socialization Values." *Developmental Psychology,* 1975, *11,* 393.

Jay, P. "Mother-Infant Relations in Langurs." In H. L. Rheingold (Ed.), *Maternal Behavior in Mammals.* New York: Wiley, 1963.

Jones, H. E. "The California Adolescent Growth Study." *Journal of Educational Research,* 1938, *31,* 561–567.

Jones, H. E. "The Adolescent Growth Study: I. Principles and Methods." *Journal of Consulting Psychology,* 1939a, *3,* 157–159.

Jones, H. E. "The Adolescent Growth Study: II. Procedures." *Journal of Consulting Psychology,* 1939b, *3,* 177–180.

Jones, J. C., Shallcrass, J., and Dennis, C. C. "Coeducation and Adolescent Values." *Journal of Educational Research,* 1972, *63,* 334–341.

Jourard, S. M. "Identification, Parent-Cathexis, and Self-Esteem." *Journal of Consulting Psychology,* 1957, *21,* 375–380.

Kagan, J., and Moss, H. A. *Birth to Maturity.* New York: Wiley, 1962.

Kagan, S., and Madsen, M. C. "Rivalry in Anglo-American and Mexican Children of Two Ages." *Journal of Personality and Social Psychology,* 1972, *24,* 214–220.

Kaminski, L. R. "Looming Effects on Stranger Anxiety and Toy Preferences in One-Year-Old Infants." Unpublished master's thesis, Department of Psychology, Stanford University, 1973.

Katz, J., and Associates. *No Time for Youth: Growth and Constraint in College Students.* San Francisco: Jossey-Bass, 1968.

Keniston, K. "Themes and Conflicts of 'Liberated' Young Women." Nineteenth Annual Karen Horney Lecture, presented at annual meeting of the Association for the Advancement of Psychoanalysis, New York, March 1971.

Kenney, J. B., and White, W. F. "Sex Characteristics in Personality Patterns of Elementary School Teachers." *Perceptual and Motor Skills,* 1966, *23,* 17–18.

Kogan, N. "Masculine and Feminine Modes of Functioning." In S. Messick and Associates, *Individuality in Learning: Implications of Cognitive Styles and Creativity for Human Development.* San Francisco: Jossey-Bass, 1976.

Kohlberg, L. "Development of Moral Character and Moral Ideology." In M. Hoffman and L. Hoffman (Eds.), *Review of Child Development Research.* Vol. 1. New York: Russell Sage Foundation, 1964.

Kohlberg, L. "A Cognitive-Developmental Analysis of Children's Sex-Role Concepts and Attitudes." In E. E. Maccoby (Ed.), *The Development of Sex Differences.* Stanford, Calif.: Stanford University Press, 1966.

Komarovsky, M. "Functional Analysis of Sex Roles." *American Sociological Review,* 1959, *15,* 508–516.

Kurtz, R. M. "Body Attitude and Self-Esteem." *Proceedings of the 79th Annual Convention of the APA,* 1971, *8,* 467–468.

Lamb, M. E. "The Role of the Father: An Overview." In M. E. Lamb (Ed.), *The Role of the Father in Child Development.* New York: Wiley, 1976.

Lamb, M. E. "The Development of Mother-Infant and Father-Infant Attachments in the Second Year of Life." *Developmental Psychology,* 1977, *13,* 637–648.

Lamb, M. E., Owen, M. T., and Chase-Lansdale, L. "The Father-Daughter Relationship: Past, Present, and Future." In C. B. Kopp and M. Kirkpatrick (Eds.), *Becoming Female: Perspectives on Development.* New York: Plenum, 1979.

Langlois, J. H., and Downs, A. C. "Mothers, Fathers, and Peers as Socialization Agents of Sex-Typed Play Behaviors in Young Children." *Child Development,* 1980, *51,* 1237–1247.

Lansky, L. M. "The Family Structure Also Affects the Model: Sex Role Attitudes in Parents of Preschool Children." *Merrill-Palmer Quarterly,* 1967, *13,* 139–150.

Lansky, L. M., and others. "Sex Differences in Aggression and Its Correlates in Middle-Class Adolescents." *Child Development,* 1961, *32,* 45–58.

Lazowik, L. M. "On the Nature of Identification." *Journal of Abnormal and Social Psychology,* 1955, *51,* 75-183.

Leff, J., and Gunn, J. "The Interaction of Male and Female Drivers at Roundabouts." *Accident Analysis and Prevention,* 1973, *5,* 253-259.

Lever, J. "Sex Differences in Games Children Play." *Social Problems,* 1976, *23,* 478-487.

Levine, M. H., and Sutton-Smith, B. "Effects of Age, Sex, and Task on Visual Behavior During Dyadic Interaction." *Developmental Psychology,* 1973, *9,* 400-405.

Lewis, M. "Parents and Children: Sex Role Development." *School Review,* 1972a, *80,* 229-240.

Lewis, M. "State as an Infant-Environment Interaction: An Analysis of Mother-Infant Interaction as a Function of Sex." *Merrill-Palmer Quarterly,* 1972b, *18,* 95-121.

Lewis, M., and Freedle, R. "Mother-Infant Dyad: The Cradle of Meaning." In P. Pliner, L. Krames, and T. Alloway (Eds.), *Communication and Affect: Language and Thought.* New York: Academic Press, 1973.

Lewis, M., and Goldberg, S. "Perceptual-Cognitive Development in Infancy: A Generalized Expectancy Model as a Function of the Mother-Infant Interaction." *Merrill-Palmer Quarterly,* 1969, *15,* 81-100.

Lewis, M., and Weintraub, M. "Sex of Parent, Sex of Child: Socioemotional Development." In R. C. Friedman, R. M. Richard, and R. L. Van de Wiele (Eds.), *Sex Differences in Behavior.* New York: Wiley, 1974.

Lockheed, M. E. "The Modification of Female Leadership Behavior in the Presence of Males." Final report. Educational Testing Service, 1976.

Loevinger, J. "The Meaning and Measurement of Ego Development." *American Psychologist,* 1966, *21,* 195-206.

Loevinger, J. *Ego Development: Conceptions and Theories.* San Francisco: Jossey-Bass, 1976.

Loevinger, J., Wessler, R., and Redmore, C. *Measuring Ego Development 1: Construction and Use of a Sentence Completion Test.* San Francisco: Jossey-Bass, 1970.

Longstreth, L. E. "Birth Order and Avoidance of Dangerous Activities." *Developmental Psychology*, 1970, *2*, 154.

Loo, C., and Wenar, C. "Activity Level and Motor Inhibition: Their Relationship to Intelligence-Test Performance in Normal Children." *Child Development*, 1971, *42*, 967–971.

Lucas, C. J., Kelvin, R. P., and Ohja, A. B. "The Psychological Health of the Pre-Clinical Medical Student." *British Journal of Psychiatry*, 1965, *3*, 473–478.

Lynn, D. B. "Sex Role and Parental Identification." *Child Development*, 1962, *33*, 555–564.

Lynn, D. B. "Curvilinear Relation Between Cognitive Functioning and Distance of Child from Parent of the Same Sex." *Psychological Review*, 1969, *76*, 236–240.

Lynn, D. B. *The Father: His Role in Child Development.* Monterey, Calif.: Brooks/Cole, 1974.

Lynn, D. B. "A Note on Sex Differences in the Development of Masculine and Feminine Identification." In R. K. Unger and F. L. Denmark (Eds.), *Women: Dependent or Independent Variable.* New York: Psychological Dimensions, 1975.

Lynn, D. B., and Sawrey, W. L. "The Effects of Father-Absence on Norwegian Boys and Girls." *Journal of Abnormal and Social Psychology*, 1959, *59*, 258–262.

McCandless, B. R. "Childhood Socialization." In D. A. Goslin (Ed.), *Handbook of Socialization Theory and Research.* Chicago: Rand McNally, 1969.

McClintock, C. G., and Moskowitz, J. M. "Children's Preferences for Individualistic, Cooperative, and Competitive Outcomes." *Journal of Personality and Social Psychology*, 1976, *34*, 543–555.

Maccoby, E. E. (Ed.). *The Development of Sex Differences.* Stanford, Calif.: Stanford University Press, 1966a.

Maccoby, E. E. "Sex Differences in Intellectual Functioning." In E. E. Maccoby (Ed.), *The Development of Sex Differences.* Stanford, Calif.: Stanford University Press, 1966b.

Maccoby, E. E. Personal communication, August 4, 1975.

Maccoby, E. E. *Social Development: Psychological Growth and the Parent-Child Relationship.* New York: Harcourt Brace Jovanovich, 1980.

Maccoby, E. E., and Jacklin, C. N. *The Psychology of Sex Differences.* Stanford, Calif.: Stanford University Press, 1974.

Maccoby, E. E., and Jacklin, C. N. "Sex Differences in Aggression: A Rejoinder and Reprise." *Child Development,* 1980, *51,* 964-980.

McCord, J., McCord, W., and Thurber, E. "Some Effects of Paternal Absence on Male Children." *Journal of Abnormal and Social Psychology,* 1962, *64,* 361-369.

Macfarlane, J. W. "The Berkeley Studies: Problems and Merits of the Longitudinal Approach." In M. C. Jones and others (Eds.), *The Course of Human Development.* Waltham, Mass.: Xerox College Publishing, 1971a.

Macfarlane, J. W. "Objectives, Samples, and Procedures." In M. C. Jones and others (Eds.), *The Course of Human Development.* Waltham, Mass.: Xerox College Publishing, 1971b.

Macfarlane, J. W., Allen, L., and Honzik, M. P. *University of California Publications in Child Development.* Vol. 2: *A Developmental Study of the Behavior Problems of Normal Children Between Twenty-One Months and Fourteen Years.* Berkeley: University of California Press, 1954.

McLeod, J. M., Atkin, C. K., and Chaffee, S. II. "Adolescents, Parents, and Television Use: Self-Report Measures from Maryland and Wisconsin Samples." In G. A. Comstock and E. Rubinstein (Eds.), *Television and Social Behavior.* Washington, D.C.: Government Printing Office, 1972.

McManis, D. L. "Marble-Sorting Rate of Elementary School Children as a Function of Incentive and Performance-Level Pairings." *Perceptual and Motor Skills,* 1966, *23,* 499-507.

Magnusson, D., Duner, A., and Zetterblom, G. *Adjustment: A Longitudinal Study.* New York: Wiley, 1975.

Manheimer, D. I., and Mellinger, G. D. "Personality Characteristics of the Child Accident Repeater." *Child Development,* 1967, *38,* 491-513.

Manheimer, D. I., and others. "50,000 Child-Years of Accident Injuries." *Pacific Health Reports, Public Health Service* (U.S. Department of Health, Education and Welfare), 1966, *81,* 519-533.

Margolin, G., and Patterson, G. R. "Differential Consequences

Provided by Mothers and Fathers for Their Sons and Daughters." *Developmental Psychology,* 1975, *11,* 537-538.

Martin, B. "Parent-Child Relations." In F. D. Horowitz (Ed.), *Review of Child Development Research.* Chicago: University of Chicago Press, 1975.

Martin, J. A., Maccoby, E. E., and Jacklin, C. N. "Mothers' Responsiveness to Interactive Bidding and Nonbidding in Boys and Girls." *Child Development,* 1981, *52,* 1064-1067.

Martin, J. C. "Competitive and Non-Competitive Behavior of Children in a Beanbag Toss Game." University of California, 1973. (Mimeographed.)

Mattfeld, J. "The Impact of the Feminist Movement on Women in Higher Education: Women's Colleges Versus Coeducational Institutions." Unpublished paper. University of California at Berkeley, January 1980.

Mead, G. H. *Mind, Self, and Society.* Chicago: University of Chicago Press, 1934.

Mednick, M. S., Tangri, S. S., and Hoffman, L. W. (Eds.). *Women and Achievement: Social and Motivational Analyses.* Washington, D.C.: Hemisphere, 1975.

Mehrabian, A. "Verbal and Nonverbal Interaction of Strangers in a Waiting Situation." *Journal of Experimental Research and Personality,* 1971, *5,* 127-138.

Messer, S. B., and Lewis, M. "Social Class and Sex Differences in the Attachment and Play Behavior of the Year-Old Infant." *Merrill-Palmer Quarterly,* 1972, *18,* 295-306.

Meyer, J. W., and Sobieszek, B. I. "Effect of a Child's Sex on Adult Interpretations of Its Behavior." *Developmental Psychology,* 1972, *6,* 42-48.

Meyer, W., and Thompson, G. "Sex Differences in the Distribution of Teacher Approval and Disapproval Among Sixth Grade Children." *Journal of Educational Psychology,* 1956, *47,* 385-396.

Miller, D. R., and Swanson, G. E. *The Changing American Parent.* New York: Wiley, 1958.

Miller, D. R., and Swanson, G. E. *Inner Conflict and Defense.* New York: Holt, Rinehart and Winston, 1960.

Minton, C., Kagan, J., and Levine, J. A. "Maternal Control and

Obedience in the Two-Year-Old." *Child Development,* 1971, *42,* 1873-1894.

Mischel, W. A. "A Social-Learning View of Sex Differences in Behavior." In E. E. Maccoby (Ed.), *The Development of Sex Differences.* Stanford, Calif.: Stanford University Press, 1966.

Mischel, W. A., and Moore, B. "Effects of Attention to Symbolically-Presented Rewards on Self-Control." *Journal of Personality and Social Psychology,* 1973, *28,* 172-179.

Mischel, W. A., and Underwood, B. "Instrumental Ideation in Delay of Gratification." Unpublished manuscript, Department of Psychology, Stanford University, 1973.

Mitchell, G. *Sex Differences in Non-Human Primates.* New York: Van Nostrand Reinhold, 1979.

Money, J., and Ehrhardt, A. *Man & Woman, Boy & Girl.* Baltimore: Johns Hopkins University Press, 1972.

Moss, H. A. "Sex, Age, and State as Determinants of Mother-Infant Interaction." *Merrill-Palmer Quarterly,* 1967, *13,* 19-36.

Moss, H. A. "Early Sex Differences and Mother-Infant Interaction." In R. C. Friedman, R. M. Richard, and R. L. Van de Wiele (Eds.), *Sex Differences in Behavior.* New York: Wiley, 1974.

Moulton, R. W., and others. "Patterning of Parental Affection and Disciplinary Dominance as a Determinant of Guilt and Sex Typing." *Journal of Personality and Social Psychology,* 1966, *4,* 356-363.

Mowrer, O. H. "Identification: A Link Between Learning Theory and Psychotherapy." In *Learning Theory and Personality Dynamics.* New York: Ronald Press, 1950.

Moyer, K. E. "Sex Differences in Aggression." In R. C. Friedman, R. M. Richard, and R. L. Van de Wiele (Eds.), *Sex Differences in Behavior.* New York: Wiley, 1974.

Munroe, R. L., and Munroe, R. H. "Effect of Environmental Experience on Spatial Ability in an East African Society." *Journal of Social Psychology,* 1971, *83,* 15-22.

Murphy, L. B., and Moriarty, A. E. *Vulnerability, Coping, and Growth.* New Haven, Conn.: Yale University Press, 1976.

Murray, J. B. "The MF Scale of the MMPI for College Students." *Journal of Clinical Psychology*, 1963, *19*, 113–115.

Mussen, P. H. "Early Sex-Role Development." In D. A. Goslin (Ed.), *Handbook of Socialization Theory and Research*. Chicago: Rand McNally, 1969.

Mussen, P. H., and Distler, L. "Masculinity, Identification, and Father-Son Relationships." *Journal of Abnormal and Social Psychology*, 1959, *59*, 350–356.

Nash, J. "The Father in Contemporary Culture and Current Psychological Literature." *Child Development*, 1965, *36*, 261–297.

Nash, L., and Ransom, T. "Socialization in Baboons at the Gombi Stream National Park, Tanzania." Paper presented at meeting of the American Anthropological Association, New York, September 1971.

Nawas, M. M. "Change in Efficiency of Ego Functioning and Complexity from Adolescence to Young Adulthood." *Developmental Psychology*, 1971, *4*, 412–415.

Newcomer, M. *A Century of Higher Education for American Women*. New York: Harper & Row, 1959.

Newson, J., and Newson, E. *Four Years Old in an Urban Community*. Harmondsworth, England: Pelican Books, 1968.

Oates, M. J., and Williamson, S. "Women's Colleges and Achievers." *Signs*, 1978, *3*, 795–806.

Olweus, D., and others. "Testosterone, Aggression, Physical, and Personality Dimensions in Normal Adolescent Males." *Psychosomatic Medicine*, 1980, *42*, 253–269.

Omark, D. R., and Edelman, M. "Peer Group Social Interactions from an Evolutionary Perspective." Paper presented at annual meeting of the Society for Research in Child Development, Philadelphia, 1973.

Omark, D. R., Omark, M., and Edelman, M. "Dominance Hierarchies in Young Children." Paper presented at the International Congress of Anthropological and Ethnological Sciences, Chicago, September 1973.

Osofsky, J. D., and O'Connell, E. J. "Parent-Child Interaction: Daughters' Effects upon Mothers' and Fathers' Behaviors." *Developmental Psychology*, 1972, *7*, 157–168.

Parke, R. D. "Perspectives on Father-Infant Interaction." In J. D. Osofsky (Ed.), *Handbook of Infancy*. New York: Wiley, 1978.

Parke, R. D., and O'Leary, S. E. "Father-Mother-Infant Interaction in the New Born Period: Some Findings, Some Observations, and Some Unresolved Issues." In K. Riegel and J. Meacham (Eds.), *The Developing Individual in a Changing World: Social and Environmental Issues*. Vol. 2. The Hague: Mouton, 1976.

Parke, R. D., and Sawin, D. B. "The Father's Role in Infancy." *Family Coordinator*, 1976, *25*, 365-371.

Parsons, T., and Bales, R. F. *Family Socialization and Interaction Process*. New York: Free Press, 1955.

Payne, D. E. "Parent-Child Relations and Father Identification Among Adolescent Boys." *Journal of Abnormal and Social Psychology*, 1956, *52*, 358-362.

Payne, D. E., and Mussen, P. H. "Parent Child Relations and Father Identification Among Adolescent Boys." *Journal of Abnormal and Social Psychology*, 1956, *52*, 358-362.

Pedersen, F. A., and Bell, R. Q. "Sex Differences in Preschool Children Without Histories of Complications of Pregnancy and Delivery." *Developmental Psychology*, 1970, *3*, 10-15.

Perry, W. G. *Forms of Intellectual and Ethical Development in the College Years: A Scheme*. Cambridge, Mass.: Harvard University Bureau of Study Counsel, 1968a.

Perry, W. G. "Patterns of Development in Thought and Values of Students in a Liberal Arts College." Final Report, Project No. 5-0825, Office of Education, 1968b.

Pettigrew, T. F. "The Measurement and Correlates of Category Width as a Cognitive Variable." *Journal of Personality*, 1958, *26*, 532-544.

Piaget, J. *The Child's Conception of Physical Causality*. New York: Harcourt Brace Jovanovich, 1930.

Piaget, J. *The Origins of Intelligence in Children*. (2nd ed.) New York: International Universities Press, 1952.

Piaget, J. *The Construction of Reality in the Child*. New York: Basic Books, 1954.

Piaget, J. "Piaget's Theory." In P. H. Mussen (Ed.), *Carmichael's Manual of Child Psychology.* New York: Wiley, 1970.

Piaget, J. *The Development of Thought: Equilibrium of Cognitive Structures.* New York: Viking, 1977.

Portuges, S. H., and Feshbach, N. D. "The Influence of Sex and Socioethnic Factors upon Imitation of Teachers by Elementary Schoolchildren." *Child Development,* 1972, *43,* 981-989.

Radin, N. "The Father and Academic, Cognitive, and Intellectual Development." In M. E. Lamb (Ed.), *The Role of the Father in Child Development.* New York: Wiley, 1976.

Reichenbach, H. *The Rise of Scientific Philosophy.* Berkeley: University of California Press, 1951.

Rheingold, H. L., and Cook, K. V. "The Contents of Boys' and Girls' Rooms as an Index of Parents' Behavior." *Child Development,* 1975, *46,* 459-463.

Richman, N., Stevenson, J. E., and Graham, P. J. "Prevalence of Behaviour Problems in 3-Year-Old Children: An Epidemiological Study in a London Borough." *Journal of Child Psychology and Psychiatry,* 1975, *16,* 277-287.

Riegel, K. F. "The Dialectics of Human Development." *American Psychologist,* 1976, *31,* 689-700.

Rose, R. M., Gordon, T. P., and Bernstein, I. S. "Plasma Testosterone Levels in the Male Rhesus: Influences of Sexual and Social Stimuli." *Science,* 1972, *178,* 643-645.

Rosenfeld, E. F. "The Relationship of Sex-Typed Toys to the Development of Competency and Sex-Role Identification in Children." Paper presented at annual meeting of the Society for Research in Child Development, Denver, Colo., March 1975.

Rosenthal, R. "Combining Results of Independent Studies." *Psychological Bulletin,* 1978, *85,* 185-193.

Rossi, A. S. "Equality Between the Sexes." In R. J. Lifton (Ed.), *The Woman in America.* Boston: Houghton Mifflin, 1964.

Rossi, A. S. "A Biosocial Perspective on Parenting." Paper presented at *Daedalus* conference on the family. American Academy of Arts and Science, Brookline, Mass., May 1976.

Rothbart, M. K. "Birth Order and Mother-Child Interaction in an Achievement Situation." *Journal of Personality and Social Psychology*, 1971, *17*, 113-120.

Rothbart, M. K., and Rothbart, M. "Birth-Order, Sex of Child, and Maternal Help Giving." *Sex Roles*, 1976, *2*, 39-46.

Rozeboom, W. W. "The Fallacy of the Null-Hypothesis Significance Test." *Psychological Bulletin*, 1960, *57*, 416-428.

Rubin, Z. *Children's Friendships*. Cambridge, Mass.: Harvard University Press, 1980.

Russo, N. F. "Eye Contact, Interpersonal Distance, and the Equilibrium Theory." *Journal of Personality and Social Psychology*, 1975, *31*, 497-502.

Rychlak, J., and Legerski, A. "A Sociocultural Theory of Appropriate Sexual Role Identification and Level of Personality Adjustment." *Journal of Personality*, 1967, *35*, 31-49.

Saegert, S., and Hart, R. "The Development of Sex Differences in the Environmental Competence of Children." In P. Burnett (Ed.), *Women in Society*. Chicago: Maaroufa Press, 1976.

Sander, L. W. "Issues in Early Mother-Child Interaction." In N. S. Endler, L. R. Boulter, and H. Osser (Eds.), *Contemporary Issues in Developmental Psychology*. New York: Holt, Rinehart and Winston, 1976.

Sanford, N. "The Dynamics of Identification." *Psychological Review*, 1955, *62*, 106-118.

Sanford, N. "Personality Development in the College Years." *Journal of Social Issues*, 1956, *12*(4).

Santrock, J. W. "Paternal Absence, Sex Typing, and Identification." *Developmental Psychology*, 1970, *2*, 264-272.

Schaeffer, E. S. "Children's Reports of Parental Behavior: An Inventory." *Child Development*, 1965, *36*, 413-424.

Schwenn, M. "Arousal of the Motive to Avoid Success." Unpublished honors thesis, Department of Psychology, Harvard University, 1971.

Sears, P., and Feldman, D. H. "Teachers' Interactions with Boys and Girls." *National Elementary Principal*, 1966, *46*, 30-35.

Sears, R. R. "Identification as a Form of Behavior Development." In D. B. Harris (Ed.), *The Concept of Development*. Minneapolis: University of Minnesota Press, 1957.

Sears, R. R., Maccoby, E. E., and Levin, H. *Patterns of Child Rearing.* New York: Harper & Row, 1957.

Seavey, C. A., Katz, P. A., and Zalk, S. R. "Baby X: The Effect of Gender Labels on Adult Responses to Infants." *Sex Roles,* 1975, *1,* 103-109.

Seligman, M. E. P. *Helplessness: On Depression, Development, and Death.* San Francisco: W. H. Freeman, 1975.

Serbin, L. A., and others. "A Comparison of Teacher Response to the Preacademic and Problem Behavior of Boys and Girls." *Child Development,* 1973, *44,* 796-804.

Sherman, R. C., and Smith, F. "Sex Differences in Cue Dependency as a Function of Socialization Environment." *Perceptual and Motor Skills,* 1967, *24,* 599-602.

Shipman, V. C. "Disadvantaged Children and Their First School Experiences." Educational Testing Service—Head Start Longitudinal Study, 1971. (ED 084 040)

Sidorowicz, L. S., and Lunney, G. S. "Baby X Revisited." *Sex Roles,* 1980, *6,* 67-73.

Sigel, I. E., and Cocking, R. R. "Cognition and Communication: A Dialectic Paradigm for Development." In M. E. Lewis and L. Rosenblum (Eds.), *Communication and Language: The Origins of Behavior.* Vol. 5. New York: Wiley, 1976.

Silverman, J. "Attentional Styles and the Study of Sex Differences." In D. I. Mostofsky (Ed.), *Attention: Contemporary Theory and Analysis.* New York: Appleton-Century-Crofts, 1970.

Singer, J. E., Westphal, M., and Niswander, K. P. "Sex Differences in the Incidence of Neonatal Abnormalities and Abnormal Performance in Early Childhood." *Child Development,* 1968, *39,* 103-112.

Smith, C., and Lloyd, B. "Maternal Behavior and Perceived Sex of Infant: Revisited." *Child Development,* 1978, *49,* 1263-1265.

Smith, M. B., Haan, N., and Block, J. H. "Social-Psychological Aspects of Student Activism." *Youth and Society,* 1970, *1,* 262-288.

Smith, P. K., and Daglish, L. "Sex Differences in Parent and Infant Behavior in the Home." *Child Development,* 1977, *48,* 1250-1254.

References   311

Smock, C. D., and Holt, B. G. "Children's Reactions to Novelty: An Experimental Study of 'Curiosity Motivation.'" *Child Development*, 1962, *33*, 631-642.

Speer, D. C., Briggs, P. F., and Gavalas, R. "Concurrent Schedules of Social Reinforcement and Dependency Behavior Among Four-Year-Old Children." *Journal of Experimental Child Psychology*, 1969, *8*, 356-365.

Spence, J. T. "Achievement and Achievement Motives." Paper presented at meeting of the American Psychological Association, New York, 1979.

Spence, J. T., and Helmreich, R. L. *Masculinity & Femininity: Their Psychological Dimensions, Correlates, & Antecedents.* Austin: University of Texas Press, 1978.

Spence, J. T., Helmreich, R. L., and Stapp, J. "Ratings of Self and Peers on Sex-Role Attributes and Their Relation to Self-Esteem and Conceptions of Masculinity and Femininity." *Journal of Personality and Social Psychology*, 1975, *32*, 29-39.

Stake, J. E., and Stake, M. N. "Performance-Self-Esteem and Dominance Behavior in Mixed-Sex Dyads." *Journal of Personality*, 1979, *47*, 71-84.

Starr, R. H. "Nurturance, Dependence, and Exploratory Behavior in Prekindergarteners." *Proceedings of the 77th Annual Convention of the American Psychological Association*, August 1969.

Staub, E. "A Child in Distress: The Influence of Nurturance and Modeling on Children's Attempts to Help." *Developmental Psychology*, 1971, *5*, 124-132.

Stein, A. H., and Bailey, M. M. "The Socialization of Achievement Orientation in Females." *Psychological Bulletin*, 1973, *80*, 345-366.

Stein, K. B., and Lenrow, P. "Expressive Styles and Their Measurement." *Journal of Personality and Social Psychology*, 1970, *16*, 656-664.

Steinberg, L. D., and Hill, J. B. "Patterns of Family Interaction as a Function of Age, the Onset of Puberty, and Formal Thinking." *Developmental Psychology*, 1978, *14*, 683-684.

Stouwie, R. J. "Inconsistent Verbal Instructions and Children's

Resistance-to-Temptation Behavior." *Child Development*, 1971, *42*, 1517-1531.

Stouwie, R. J. "An Experimental Study of Adult Dominance and Warmth, Conflicting Verbal Instructions, and Children's Moral Behavior." *Child Development*, 1972, *43*, 959-971.

Svare, B., and Gandelman, R. "Aggressive Behavior of Juvenile Mice: Influence of Androgen and Olfactory Stimuli." *Developmental Psychobiology*, 1975, *8*, 405-415.

Tangri, S. "Role-Innovation in Occupational Choice Among College Women." Unpublished doctoral dissertation, Department of Social Psychology, University of Michigan, 1969.

Tauber, M. A. "Sex Differences in Parent-Child Interaction Styles During a Free-Play Session." *Child Development*, 1979, *50*, 981-988.

Tennis, G. H., and Dabbs, J. M. "Sex, Setting, and Personal Space: First Grade Through College." *Sociometry*, 1975, *38*, 385-394.

Terman, L. M., and Tyler, L. E. "Psychological Sex Differences." In L. Carmichael (Ed.), *Manual of Child Psychology*. (2nd ed.) New York: Wiley, 1954.

Terman, L. M., and Tyler, L. E. "The Educated Woman: Prospects and Problems." *Group for the Advancement of Psychiatry*, 1975, *9*, Whole Report, No. 92.

Tidball, M. E. "Perspective on Academic Women and Affirmative Action." *Educational Record*, 1973, *54*, 130-135.

Tidball, M. E., and Kistiakowsky, V. "Baccalaureate Origins of American Scientists and Scholars." *Science*, 1976, *193*, 646-652.

Tieger, T. "On the Biological Basis of Sex Differences in Aggression." *Child Development*, 1980, *51*, 943-963.

Tiller, P. O. "Father Absence and Personality Development in Sailor Families: A Preliminary Research Report." *Nordisk Psykologi*, 1958, Monograph No. 9.

Torrance, E. P. *Rewarding Creative Behavior*. Englewood Cliffs, N.J.: Prentice-Hall, 1965.

Tuddenham, R. D. "A Study of Reputation: Children's Evaluations of Their Peers." In G. G. Thompson, F. J. DiVesta, and J. Horrocks (Eds.), *Social Development and Personality*. New York: Wiley, 1971.

Tudiver, J. "Parental Influences on the Sex Role Development of the Preschool Child." Unpublished manuscript, University of Western Ontario, London, Ontario, 1979.

Tyler, L. E. *The Psychology of Human Differences*. (3rd ed.) New York: Appleton-Century-Crofts, 1965.

Vaughn, B. E., Weickgerant, A., and Kopp, C. B. "Socialization Supporting Mastery and Achievement: Evidence for Gender-Related Differences in Behavior of Mothers Toward Their Very Young Children." Unpublished manuscript, Department of Psychology, University of California at Los Angeles, 1981.

Vinacke, W. E., and others. "Accommodative Strategy and Communication in a Three-Person Matrix Game." *Journal of Personality and Social Psychology*, 1974, *29*, 509-525.

Vogel, S. R., and others. "Maternal Employment and Perception of Sex Roles Among College Students." *Developmental Psychology*, 1970, *3*, 384-391.

von der Lippe, A. "Marital Partner Choice and Parental Identification." Unpublished doctoral dissertation, Department of Psychology, University of California at Berkeley, 1965.

Wadsworth, M. *Roots of Delinquency: Infancy, Adolescence, and Crime*. New York: Barnes & Noble, 1979.

Waldrop, M. F., and Halverson, C. F. "Intensive and Extensive Peer Behavior: Longitudinal and Cross-Sectional Analyses." *Child Development*, 1975, *46*, 19-26.

Wallach, M. A., and Caron, A. J. "Attribute Criteriality and Sex-Linked Conservatism as Determinants of Psychological Similarity." *Journal of Abnormal and Social Psychology*, 1959, *59*, 43-50.

Wallach, M. A., and Kogan, N. "Sex Differences and Judgment Processes." *Journal of Personality*, 1959, *27*, 555-564.

Walraven, M. "Mother and Infant Cardiac Responses During Breast and Bottle Feeding." Unpublished dissertation, Department of Psychology, Michigan State University, 1974.

Watson, J. S. "The Development and Generalization of 'Contingency Awareness' in Early Infancy: Some Hypotheses." *Merrill-Palmer Quarterly*, 1966, *12*, 123-135.

Watson, J. S., and Ramey, C. T. "Reactions to Response-Contingent Stimulation in Early Infancy." *Merrill-Palmer Quarterly*, 1972, *18*, 219-227.

Weller, L., Shlomi, A., and Zimot, G. "Birth Order, Sex, and Occupational Interest." *Journal of Vocational Behavior,* 1976, *8,* 45-50.

Werry, J. S., and Quay, H. C. "The Prevalence of Behavior Symptoms in Younger Elementary School Children." *American Journal of Orthopsychiatry,* 1971, *41,* 136-143.

Wheeler, L., and Nezlek, J. "Sex Differences in Social Participation." *Journal of Personality and Social Psychology,* 1977, *35,* 742-754.

White, M. S. "Psychological and Social Barriers to Women in Science." *Science,* 1970, *170,* 413-416.

White, R. W. "Motivation Reconsidered: The Concept of Competence." *Psychological Review,* 1959, *66,* 297-333.

Whiting, B. B., and Edwards, C. P. "A Cross-Cultural Analysis of Sex Differences in the Behavior of Children Age Three Through 11." In S. Chess and A. Thomas (Eds.), *Annual Progress in Child Psychiatry and Child Development, 1974.* New York: Brunner/Mazel, 1975.

Whiting, B. B., and Pope, C. "A Cross-Cultural Analysis of Sex Differences in the Behavior of Children Aged Three through 11." *Journal of Social Psychology,* 1973, *91,* 171-188.

Whiting, B. B., and Whiting, J. W. M. *Children of Six Cultures.* Cambridge, Mass.: Harvard University Press, 1975.

Whiting, J. W. M. "Sorcery, Sin, and the Superego: A Cross-Cultural Study of Some Mechanisms of Social Control." In M. R. Jones (Ed.), *Nebraska Symposium on Motivation.* Vol. 7. Lincoln: University of Nebraska Press, 1959.

Will, J. A., Self, P. A., and Datan, N. "Maternal Behavior and Perceived Sex of Infant." *American Journal of Orthopsychiatry,* 1976, *46,* 135-139.

Willerman, L. *The Psychology of Individual and Group Differences.* San Francisco: W. H. Freeman, 1979.

Winchel, R., Fenner, D., and Shaver, P. "Impact of Coeducation on 'Fear of Success' Imagery Expressed by Male and Female High School Students." *Journal of Educational Psychology,* 1974, *66,* 726-730.

Winer, B. J. *Statistical Principles in Experimental Design.* New York: McGraw-Hill, 1971.

Witkin, H. A., and others. *Psychological Differentiation.* New York: Wiley, 1962.

Wolfensberger, W. P., and others. "Rorschach Correlates of Activity Level in High School Children." *Journal of Consulting Psychology,* 1962, *26,* 269-272.

Wood, R., and Ferguson, C. "Unproved Case for Coeducation." *London Times Educational Supplement* 3097, Oct. 4, 1974, p. 22.

Woodworth, R. S., and Schlosberg, H. *Experimental Psychology.* New York: Holt, Rinehart and Winston, 1954.

Yarrow, L. J. *Infant and Environment: Early Cognitive and Motivational Development.* New York: Halstead Press, 1975.

Yarrow, L. J., and others. "Dimensions of Early Stimulation and Their Differential Effects on Infant Development." *Merrill-Palmer Quarterly,* 1972, *18,* 205-218.

Yarrow, M. R. "Problems of Methods in Parent-Child Research." *Child Development,* 1963, *34,* 215-226.

Name Index

Subject Index

323